Creating States: Studies in the Performative Language of
John Milton and William Blake

ANGELA ESTERHAMMER

Creating States: Studies in the Performative Language of John Milton and William Blake

UNIVERSITY OF TORONTO PRESS
Toronto Buffalo London

© University of Toronto Press Incorporated 1994
Toronto Buffalo London
Printed in Canada

ISBN 0-8020-0562-4

Printed on acid-free paper

Canadian Cataloguing in Publication Data

Esterhammer, Angela
   Creating states : studies in the performative
language of John Milton and William Blake

   Includes bibliographical references and index.
   ISBN 0-8020-0562-4

   1. Milton, John, 1608–1674 – Language. 2. Blake,
William, 1757–1827 – Language. 3. Milton, John,
1608–1674 – Style. 4. Blake, William, 1757–1827 –
Style. I. Title.

PR3594.E78 1994   821'.4   C94-930169-8

'This Is Just to Say' is from William Carlos Williams, *Collected Poems 1909–1939*,
vol. 1. Copyright 1938 by New Directions Publishing Corporation. Reprinted by
permission of New Directions.

The sketch on p. 108 is reprinted from *Course in General Linguistics* by Ferdinand
de Saussure, edited by Charles Bally and Albert Sechehaye, translated by Roy Harris, by permission of Open Court Publishing Company. (©1972 main text by
Editions Payot, Paris. ©1983 English translation and editorial matter by Roy Harris.
Published 1986 by Open Court Publishing Company, La Salle, Illinois 61301.)

This book has been published with the help of a grant from the Canadian
Federation for the Humanities, using funds provided by the Social Sciences and
Humanities Research Council of Canada.

optimo magistro
Northrop Frye

Contents

viii Contents

References and Abbreviations

All quotations from Milton's poetry are cited from *Complete Poems and Major Prose*, edited by Merritt Y. Hughes (New York: Macmillan, 1957), and quotations from Milton's prose are cited from *Complete Prose Works of John Milton*, general editor Don M. Wolfe (New Haven: Yale UP, 1953–82). All quotations from Blake's work are cited from *The Complete Poetry and Prose of William Blake*, revised edition, edited by David V. Erdman, with commentary by Harold Bloom (Berkeley: U of California P, 1982). References are given by plate (or manuscript page) and line number as assigned by Erdman, followed by page numbers in the Erdman edition (designated as 'E'). All quotations from the Bible are cited from the Authorized (King James) Version.

The following abbreviations are used in references to works of Milton and Blake:

CP	Milton, *Complete Poems and Major Prose*
CPW	*Complete Prose Works of John Milton*
PL	*Paradise Lost*
SA	*Samson Agonistes*
Ann.	Annotations
BU	*The Book of Urizen*
DLJ	*The Design of The Last Judgment*
Eur.	*Europe*
FZ	*The Four Zoas*
J	*Jerusalem*
M	*Milton*
MHH	*The Marriage of Heaven and Hell*
VLJ	*A Vision of The Last Judgment*

Words, Worlds, Acts, and Visions

This is an essay exploring the way certain writers do things with words. The writers are, primarily, John Milton and William Blake, and what they do is put into words a consciousness of divine inspiration or an experience of expanded perception, asking the reader to accept their utterance as emanating from a transcendent authority either external or internal to the self. Their language, in presenting itself as inspired or visionary, posits two related moments of effectual discourse: the poets themselves have heard a voice that alters their perception of the world, and they set out to communicate this verbal experience in a way that will leave their audience with a changed vision. They face the challenge of discovering or inventing a language and a scene of discourse within which the experience of vision might be communicated, and through which its impact on them might be transformed into a creative effect in the external world.

Thus far, the performative power of visionary language would seem to depend on the poet's more or less conscious imitation of a model of language central to Western religious tradition, a tradition in which the term *Logos* names in a unique way the performative dimension of its central text. In the Bible, Logos is the divine force which creates the world, the incarnate force which fulfils the role of hero in that world, the inspirational force which guides the writers of the text, and the kerygmatic or declarative force which moves its readers. Yet literary criticism of the past three decades has attacked Logos as a limited concept, challenging the notion of a transcendent Word by demonstrating that words derive meaning only from their place in a differential structure of signifiers, or that signifiers have no determinate meaning but are irredeemably alienated from signifieds, or that structures of words have meaning only insofar as they reflect and construct the operations of history. The notion of a Word that performs independently of signifying structures or historical circumstances – and, for that matter, the notion of capitalizing the word 'Word' – has been condemned as a mystification perpetuated by those who refuse to take account of cultural specificity and materialist concerns.

I began this investigation with the conviction that, with due respect to post-structuralist and new historicist insights, a writer's consciousness of operating within a theological and literary tradition that privileges certain models of utterance as uniquely creative or effectual must manifest itself in some identifiable way in the order and orientation of words which that writer produces. I still maintain that the writing of visionary poetry is a distinctive activity, and this book is in part a study of what distinguishes visionary language on the level of authorial presence, voice, address, and reference. But as I worked through this study, it became apparent that the claims of certain post-structuralist and historicist approaches also had their place in it. Not only is it impossible for the texts of Milton and Blake to escape their different historical contexts, but many of the texts of both poets are specifically oriented toward the historical moment as the arena in which their utterances are to have an effect. Milton's prose is shaped by the ecclesiastical, legal, and economic discourse of his contemporaries, and even in *Paradise Lost* his concept of inspiration is modified by the linguistic structures characteristic of secular texts. Blake's shorter prophetic books belong to the 1790s genre of radical tractate literature; the influence of popular rhetorical forms and the language sanctioned by societal institutions makes itself felt throughout his work. Milton and Blake go through a parallel evolution from writers of political and anti-prelatical tracts to poets who, having failed in their attempts to alter historical circumstances through a direct address to their contemporaries, reaffirm their faith in individual visionary consciousness – *while continuing to use the forms of a socially or politically performative language.* As these writers are doing things with the Logos, they are also doing things with the political, social, and institutional discourses of their respective societies.

I believe that contemporary theories of performative language address these historical concerns in a way that allows for compromise, or at least beneficial coexistence, with Miltonic inspiration and Blakean creativity. Speech-act theory maintains that words do things, but makes this effectiveness contingent on a complex of factors including the conventions accepted by the relevant sociopolitical community, the circumstances in which words are uttered, the identity of the speaker and the relationship between speaker and hearer, and the grammatical form of the utterance. These criteria are by no means consistent, even in the major formulations of speech-act theory by J.L. Austin and John Searle, and scholars who have adapted Austin's and Searle's principles to linguistics, literary criticism, political science, and other fields have multiplied definitions and examples of when and how speech can be an act.

In what follows, I attempt to develop a speech-act approach which addresses the distinctiveness of visionary language, and which can therefore make possible a more rigorous study of the often vague or naïve concept of visionary poetry. My first chapter sets out the theoretical background, surveying existing forms of speech-act criticism in order to draw out their underlying assumptions about utterances and their contexts. I argue that theories of performative language have gone in two basic directions: toward a focus on societal discourse and power structures as the factors which define verbal performativity, on the one hand, and toward an emphasis on the power of language to posit or create autonomously, on the other. Different as they seem, the two approaches, which I term 'sociopolitical' and 'phenomenological,' are at times compatible. When they are not, it is precisely the distinction between them that can help to uncover the functioning of language in the visionary text. The chapter concludes by outlining a number of philosophical and linguistic models which allow for the intersection of the sociopolitical with the phenomenological performative, focusing, in particular, on the creation of subjectivity in language. In the second chapter, I approach this theoretical discussion from a different direction, by arguing that *both* types of performative language are already implicit in the opening chapters of the Book of Genesis, a text that has even more relevance than has been supposed for the development of a visionary tradition in Western literature.

The remainder of the book seeks to illustrate the significance of the sociopolitical and phenomenological performative, of the scene of discourse and subjectivity in language, through readings of two central poets in the visionary tradition in English literature. In chapters 3 and 4, I address what I take to be two cruxes in Milton's concept of visionary language: first, his self-presentation as an inspired writer in the prose works, which ironically employ the discourse of law and economics; secondly, the model of divinely creative language in the invocations and the account of creation in *Paradise Lost*, a model which is more limiting and hierarchizing, thus more *political*, than Milton may intend. The remaining chapters are devoted to Blake and concentrate on the paradigm of performative language he inherits from Milton and the Bible, a paradigm which, as he is aware, conflicts with the operation of language in his social and political environment. Chapter 5 traces the move from inspired and ideally communicative language to institutional and repressive language in *Songs of Innocence and of Experience*, and chapter 6 examines an analogous conflict between poetic utterance and the restrictiveness of the sociopolitical performative in *The Book of Urizen* and *The Marriage of Heaven and Hell*. The final chapter brings together visions of divine creation and verbal performance from Blake's major epics, culminating in an analysis of the compromise between sociopolitical and phenomenological utterance in establishing the authority of speakers in Blake's *Jerusalem*.

While working on this book, I have received generous financial, collegial, and personal support from many directions. I respectfully acknowledge the assistance of the Social Sciences and Humanities Research Council of Canada, which provided funding for research and travel, and the Canadian Federation for the Humanities, which provided a grant in aid of publication. The staff of the Princeton University Library, the Bodleian Library, the Fitzwilliam Museum, the Tate Gallery, and the Department of Prints and Drawings at the British Museum were most helpful in allowing me to consult their Blake collections. The Departments of English and Modern Languages and Literatures at the University of Western Ontario have provided many kinds of support, particularly some excellent secretarial assistance, and Thomas M. Lennon, as Dean of Arts, has been unfailingly encouraging and helped me cope with the concurrent demands of research and teaching.

I have benefited from the skills of several research assistants at various stages during the writing of this book, and I thank Peter Georgelos, Marcela Moc, and Brian Patton for their hard work. Julia M. Wright provided timely and incredibly efficient research assistance during the final preparation of the manuscript.

A few sections of this book have appeared in the form of articles: part of chapter 2 as 'Speech Acts and World-Creation: The Dual Function of the Performative' in the *Canadian Review of Comparative Literature / Revue Canadienne de Littérature Comparée* 20 (1993); part of chapter 3 as 'Meddling with Authority: Inspiration and Speech Acts in Milton's Prose,' in *Spokesperson Milton: Voices in Contemporary Criticism*, edited by Charles W. Durham and Kristin P. McColgan (Susquehanna UP, 1994); and part of chapter 4 as 'Creation, Subjectivity, and Linguistic Structure in *Paradise Lost*: Milton with Saussure and Benveniste' in *English Studies in Canada* 20 (1994). I am grateful for permission to reprint material from these sources.

I could not wish for more congenial colleagues than those I have at the University of Western Ontario, and I would particularly like to thank Richard F. Green, J. Douglas Kneale, Martin Kreiswirth, John Leonard, Balachandra Rajan, and Tilottama Rajan for their suggestions and constructive criticism. My colleagues have shown great tolerance in listening and responding to a number of work-in-progress excerpts from this project which I presented as internal papers, and I have also learned a great deal from audiences of papers I presented at the Fourth International Milton Symposium, the First Southeastern Conference on John Milton, the 1992 History of European Ideas Conference, and the inaugural conference of the North American Society for the Study of Romanticism.

Finally, John Kozub's inestimable contribution begins with his suggestion for the title, and it goes on from there.

CREATING STATES

1

Performative Language and Visionary Poetry

While speech-act theory *per se* is relatively uncommon as a primary approach to the interpretation of literature, its terms have been so widely disseminated in literary and cultural study that 'performative' can now be used loosely to describe discourse which is operative in society and establishes a social construct, or even, following Paul de Man, to denote the rhetorical dimension of language in general. For both these reasons, this chapter and the following one will work toward a somewhat more technical definition of 'performative' which is specifically relevant to the reading of visionary texts. This will not be an exclusive definition which recognizes only utterances that have an immediate, clearly definable effect in the world (such as 'I call this meeting to order'); even the founders of speech-act theory were ultimately unsatisfied with this limited range of meaning. Rather, the exploration of speech-act theory in this chapter will trace through its various manifestations a few focal points which the theorization of performative language shares with the language of visionary poetry. These are, primarily, the specific utterance (*parole*) and its discursive context, the authority of the speaker, and the role of language in the creation of subjectivity.

Parole and Its Contexts

Most literary scholars are by now acquainted with the basic principles of J.L. Austin's theory of performative language, presented by the philosopher in the 1955 William James lectures at Harvard University and published after his death as *How to Do Things with Words*. Austin tried to account for philosophers' difficulties in analysing certain kinds of sentences according to the logic of true-false propositions by isolating a category he called the performative. Rather than describing reality in a way that might be judged true or false, a performative utterance brings about an action or alters the condition of the speaker, the addressee, or the environment, so that the appropriate criterion for evaluating the relation of the utterance to the world is its 'felicity' or success in achieving an effect. The power of the utterance to perform an act depends on its being spoken by a qualified individual in appropriate circumstances, so as to conform to the conventions accepted by the relevant social group for the successful performance of the act. Thus the utterances 'I will' and 'I now pronounce you husband and wife' have, in North American and British society, the effect of enacting a marriage when, among other things, the former is spoken by a man and a woman in turn, neither of whom is presently married, and the latter by a properly ordained minister or justice of the peace. Austin's preliminary examples of the performative, chosen because the ability of words to affect rather than merely describe the world is clearest in these cases, are instances in which the speaker's qualifications are established by a political or social institution: performing a marriage, baptizing a ship, making a legal will.

Following the preliminary isolation of the performative, *How to Do Things with Words* pursues a series of avenues by which this type of utterance might be defined and distinguished from constative uses of language, or true-false statements about the world. Austin first identifies the types of conventions necessary in order for speech acts to operate, but when his constitutive rules fail to provide a rigorous definition of the performative he attempts to isolate grammatical criteria by which it may be recognized, and finally proposes lists of individual verbs which have various types of performative force. But his most successful and influential analysis of the performative derives from the identification of three perspectives from which any utterance may be considered: *locution*, or the phonetic act of uttering words in accordance with a certain vocabulary and grammar; *illocution*, or the force with which the words are uttered, which determines the type of act (promising, warning, asking, announcing) performed in saying something; and *perlocution*, or the effect that the utterance has on the addressee. This very analysis, however, leads Austin to the conclusion that all utterances, including the most classic examples of true-false propositions, manifest illocutionary or performative force. Saying 'The meeting was at ten this morning' is to perform the illocutionary act of stating, just as much as saying 'I call this meeting to order' is to perform the illocutionary act of declaring the meeting open. Austin's attempt to distinguish between constative and performative breaks down, famously, into an admission of the indivisibility and interdependence of the two categories.

Nevertheless, the concept of performative language has introduced a number of important qualifications into both analytic philosophy and Saussurian linguistics, making it possible to investigate aspects of linguistic usage that pre-Austinian philosophy and linguistics, with their concentration on the locutionary dimension, had trouble explaining. One conclusion Austin is led to is that even descriptive statements – his classic example is 'France is hexagonal' – cannot be judged true or false without reference to circumstances (was the statement made by a top-ranking general or by a geographer?), and that the better category of judgment may be the appropriateness of the utterance in the particular circumstances, for the constative as much as for the performative. Just as Wittgenstein, in his later work, shifts his focus from the meaning to the use of words, Austin finally insists that 'what we have to study is *not* the sentence but the issuing of an utterance in a speech situation' (*How to Do Things* 139).

The notion of illocutionary and perlocutionary force provides a framework for analysing the meaning of an utterance that every speaker of a language understands, even though the meaning is not 'contained' in any component of that utterance. John Searle has elaborated on Austin's principles so as to specify the rules which govern various types of illocutions, rules which form part of the competence of those who use the language and which help to explain why it is possible to say one thing and mean another. The work of Austin and Searle allows us to recognize a distinction between the locutionary or grammatical dimension of an utterance and its illocutionary role within a scene of discourse. Thus the assertion 'I wish you wouldn't leave' can, in appropriate circumstances, function not as a description of a state of mind but as a request or an imperative: 'Don't leave!' Similarly, someone who says to a dinner-table companion, 'Can you reach the salt?' does not expect a yes-or-no answer, but expects the addressee to understand 'Pass me the salt,' and to respond accordingly. The locutionary act of saying 'Can you reach the salt' may also constitute the illocutionary act of asking the addressee to pass the salt, and it may achieve the perlocutionary effect of having the salt passed (or, depending on circumstances, of pleasing, annoying, or interrupting the addressee). Searle is among those who have recognized the opportunities afforded by these categories for a new understanding of figurative language, and linguists have found wide-ranging applications for them in the study of verbal phenomena such as irony, hyperbole, and taboos.

The common element in all these approaches is a focus on the *context* of the utterance. The attention to context, and thus to the uniqueness of the individual utterance, may be identified as one of the major qualifications that speech-act theory introduces to Saussurian linguistics and to the philosophy of language. Whereas Saussure privileged *langue*, the abstract structure which makes possible the use of a language by individual speakers, over *parole*, the concrete and unique utterance, and whereas analytic philosophy tends to study propositions independently of their discursive context, speech-act theory demonstrates that the circumstances surrounding actual utterances play a crucial role in the functioning of a linguistic system. A competent speaker has internalized not only a system of grammar and vocabulary, but also a system of conventions whereby certain words or phrases used in certain situations or by certain speakers have a determinable significance, which may be quite different from that dictated by grammar and vocabulary alone. We recognize the difference in the meaning and force of 'OUT,' for instance, when it is shouted by an umpire standing behind home plate, when it is written on one of two swinging doors, and when it is addressed to a dog by a woman with arm and index finger extended.

Austin (and, even more self-consciously, Searle) begins with the apparent desire to develop universally valid systems for identifying performatives and their effects. But every definition they attempt must rely so heavily on the context of individual utterances that it becomes, ironically, a 'system' of the unique and contingent. While Austin's insights have been interpreted by many of his followers as a rule-governed system that allows individual utterances to function as illocutions, it is significant that Austin himself was never able to develop a full-fledged theory of speech acts. Rather, the arrangement of *How to Do Things with Words* as a succession of red herrings, or blind alleys through which the performative-constative opposition is followed, and the repeated failure to discover a stable standard by which this opposition can be measured, highlights the importance of the unreliable and ultimately indeterminable facet of utterances: the speech situation. Because the significance of circumstances and context is built into the definition of the speech act, it has been virtually impossible for either philosophers or linguists to develop a comprehensive and reliable theory of performative language.[1]

---

1 The work of John Searle is the most ambitious attempt to construct a universal theory, and it is an enterprise which Searle aligns, somewhat defensively, with the Saussurian study of *langue*: 'It still might seem that my approach is simply, in Saussurian terms, a study of "parole" rather than "langue." I am arguing, however, that an adequate study of speech acts is a study of *langue*' (*Speech Acts* 17). Several scholars, however, have expressed their uneasiness with Searle's theory, particularly as it applies to speech acts in literature and fiction; my own reservations will appear over the course of this book. Moreover, in shifting

The Speaker as Performer

Given the importance of the speech situation in Austin's philosophy of speech acts, it is perhaps not surprising that the central problem of his theory, from the point of view of literary critics, is also a problem of context. This is Austin's famous, or infamous, exclusion of non-serious speech, and of utterances in plays or poems, from the province of speech-act theory:

... a performative utterance will, for example, be *in a peculiar way* hollow or void if said by an actor on the stage, or if introduced in a poem, or spoken in soliloquy ... Language in such circumstances is in special ways – intelligibly – used not seriously, but in ways *parasitic* upon its normal use – ways which fall under the doctrine of the *etiolations* of language. All this we are *excluding* from consideration. Our performative utterances, felicitous or not, are to be understood as issued in ordinary circumstances. (*How to Do Things* 22)

The limitation imposed by Austin has functioned as a challenge rather than a deterrent to literary critics; in fact, it has been the starting point for almost all of the most significant critical essays on the speech-act hypothesis. In 'Signature Event Context,' Jacques Derrida bases his deconstruction of Austin on the charge that the 'ordinary language' which Austin analyses is marked by the deliberate exclusion of utterances perceived as marginal, parasitic, or non-serious. By disallowing the citation of performative utterances in non-standard circumstances, Austin is banishing to a '*ditch* or external place of perdition' a dimension of iterability which must be recognized as intrinsic to the performativity of language (*Limited Inc* 17). Defensively, John Searle responds that Austin was not making a metaphysical exclusion but rather suggesting that non-serious speech acts were not the best choices to begin with when developing a theory of standard cases ('Reiterating the Differences' 203–5); but the accuracy of this claim hardly dispels the objections of deconstructionist critics since Searle only sustains the hierarchical logic of normal and supplementary cases. Jonathan Culler supports Derrida's contention that 'the iterability manifested in the inauthentic, the derivative, the imitative, the parodic, is what makes possible the original and the authentic' (Culler 120), adding that Austin's insistence

the focus from *parole* to *langue*, and in attempting to formulate a general theory of speech acts which will address fundamental problems in the philosophy of language, Searle has had to introduce concepts which are so general that they are of limited usefulness in analysing individual utterances in specific contexts. The best example may be his universal concept of intentionality, according to which an illocutionary act is defined in part by the speaker's intention to perform that illocutionary act.

on seriousness seems to contradict his preliminary claim that performative utterances do not require a serious intention on the part of the speaker. Culler is led to the conclusion that he claims Austin tried to avoid: that illocutionary force is determined by the ungraspable totality of context affecting a particular utterance, including those elements which render the context non-serious or non-standard. Far from an explanatory system, this view of performative utterances would end in a proclamation of the indeterminacy of meaning, since 'meaning is context-bound, but context is boundless' (Culler 123).

Other critics who comment on Austin's rejection of the non-serious, or the controversy between Derrida and Searle which developed out of it, virtually all rely on some version of the same argument: that the context which defines an actor's or poet's role is analogous to that which defines the role of any speaker whom Austin would recognize as a serious agent in the real world. Mary Louise Pratt and Barbara Johnson both respond in a way which seems entirely consistent with Austin's priorities. They maintain that all speakers in the everyday world are to some extent acting a part, a situation that becomes most explicit when someone speaks '*as* Prime Minister' or '*as* a trained professional.' Johnson points out the irony of excluding explicitly dramatic situations from a theory that undertakes to explore 'speech acts' and the 'performative' aspect of language (65–6). She brings the question of seriousness to bear on the interpretation of all performative utterances, and gestures toward the enormous implications of such an inclusive concept of performativity for our understanding of societal organization:

The performative utterance thus automatically fictionalizes its utterer when it makes him the mouthpiece of a conventionalized authority ... Behind the fiction of the subject stands the fiction of society, for if one states that society began with a prohibition (of incest) or a (social) contract, one is simply stating that the origin of the authority behind a performative utterance is derived from a previous performative utterance whose ultimate origin is undeterminable. (60)

Mary Louise Pratt's argument is more relevant to the speech-act theory of H.P. Grice than to Austin, but she also emphasizes the extent to which speech-act philosophers assume that speakers are 'authentic, self-consistent, essential' subjects, while in reality 'people always speak from and in a socially constituted position,' a position that is constantly shifting ('Ideology' 62–3). Stanley Fish, finally, stresses the significance but also the indeterminateness of context, arguing that we have to infer intentions and meanings no matter whether the speaker is on a stage or face to face with us: 'If by "stage utterances" one understands utterances whose illocutionary force must be inferred or constructed, then all utterances are stage utterances, and one cannot mark them off from utterances that are "serious" ' ('With the Compliments' 705).

Fish's assumption that Austin excludes fictional and dramatic speech because it does not allow for full presence, and thus seems more difficult to connect with an originating intention, deviates somewhat from Austin's original statement. It is not at all clear that by 'stage utterances' Austin *did* understand utterances whose illocutionary force must be inferred across a distance; rather, what disturbs Austin about words spoken in a play is that they do not have the same performative force as words spoken outside the drama, and that the actor is not committed to or by the words he or she utters. Austin's non-seriousness is not Fish's non-presence, and yet Fish's response to Austin is analogous to those of the other critics cited above. All of them attempt to out-Austin Austin; if he focused on *parole* by calling attention to the societal conventions that allow utterances to function in particular circumstances, they argue that the serious/non-serious distinction highlights precisely the significance of *parole*, because it demands that contexts be investigated even further. Situating an utterance in a non-standard context reveals the assumptions we make about the authority, agency, and intentions of the speaker in understanding any speech act. Conceding, with Austin, that context is the determining element of illocutionary force, these critics defend drama and play-acting as one type of context that can offer especially valuable insights into the workings of performativity.

The analysis of fiction, or what to do with structures of words in which reference to external reality is suspended and which do not perform the illocutionary acts that the same words would in a real-world situation, is a further ramification of the problem of context. 'Walt Whitman does not seriously incite the eagle of liberty to soar,' Austin writes, content to dismiss poetic uses of language from his theory for the time being (*How to Do Things* 104). Yet the apparent anomalies caused by performatives in fictional contexts are unavoidable for critics whose particular concern is imaginative literature, and whose struggles with referentiality may cause them to sympathize with the note of frustration in R.A. York's statement that 'poetry ... often seems to represent a type of conspicuous futility in language' (21). The question of performatives in fiction has been taken up in very different ways by Barbara Herrnstein Smith, who proposes that imaginative literature is the fictive representation or imitation of real-world discourse; by John Searle, who believes that fictional writing invokes a set of 'horizontal conventions' which suspend the 'vertical conventions' normally governing the relation between language and the world; and by Wolfgang Iser, who concludes from a similar analysis of horizontal and vertical conventions that fiction reorders the real-world functions of language and uses them to create a context for its own interpretation. The linguistic and philosophical problem of reference adjoins speech-act theory at this point, along with the question of world-making as it has been formulated by both philosophers and narratologists.[2]

Utterance and Context: Two Directions for Analysis

Given a focus on the individual utterance and its unique context, it is possible to formulate two types of interpretive approaches to the literary text based on speech-act principles. One approach privileges the audience and context of the literary utterance, while the other privileges the speaker and the act of utterance itself. The audience-centred approach, first of all, concerns itself with those elements of context that determine the performative force of an utterance at a particular place and time, where 'utterance' may refer either to words spoken by characters within the text or to the text itself as illocutionary act. In either case, this approach is likely to bring the historical context of the work to bear on interpretation. To the extent that performative force depends on the conventions and institutions of the society within which an utterance operates, speech-act theory legitimizes the study of social discourses contemporary with a given text.[3]

But the uniqueness of *parole* also has an ahistorical, phenomenological dimension. Considered as the utterance of an individual poet, the literary text constitutes a postulate which may elicit belief, willing suspension of disbelief, or some other commitment, depending on a set of variables which include the generic and grammatical structure of the utterance and the status of the speaking voice. This second type of speech-act reading analyses the way the literary utterance both depends on, and constructs, the authority of the speaker or poet.

2 See, for example, recent work by Henry Staten, who builds on the philosophy of Hilary Putnam and Saul Kripke; Thomas G. Pavel, who provides connections between speech-act theory, world-making, and fictionality; and Mario J. Valdés, who explores the application of the philosophy of world-making to the reading of literature, though without explicit reference to performative language.
3 An essay like Sandy Petrey's 'The Reality of Representation: Between Marx and Balzac,' which analyses the performative nature of social representation in fictional and non-fictional texts of the nineteenth century, makes the affinities of this approach with new historicism and cultural materialism particularly clear.

As a preliminary way of isolating the issues involved in establishing the poet's authority to make a performative utterance, we might compare the case of real-world performatives that derive their effectiveness from the unique identity of the speaker (or writer), such as the signing of a cheque or the giving of consent during a wedding ceremony. As Derrida has demonstrated, these acts are less straightforward than they seem. The effectiveness of the signature depends on both uniqueness *and* iterability; the signature on a cheque is valid because it was performed by a specific individual, but it is verifiable precisely because it can be reproduced, or checked against any number of identical signatures by that individual. It is, Derrida argues, a fundamentally paradoxical gesture, insofar as it registers the absence of the subject but also holds fast to the subject's having-been-present at a specific time in the past (*Limited Inc* 19–20). What is more, Derrida's meditation on the American Declaration of Independence reveals that the authorizing signature must be regarded as an event which at once depends on *and* brings into being the identity of the signatory. The Declaration guarantees the freedom of 'the people,' while 'the people' simultaneously guarantees the Declaration by signing it as a free agent: 'The signature invents the signer' ('Declarations' 10). Analogously, the authority of the poet and the speech act of uttering a poem must be regarded as interdependent. The visionary poet, in particular, stakes the effectiveness of his or her utterance on a claim to divine inspiration, or an event which confers special powers of perception and understanding, but this claim only has meaning insofar as the audience believes, and thus ratifies the effectiveness of, the poetic text. Credibility, moreover, is likely to depend on the author's ability to echo or iterate conventions of invocation and prophetic speech that have been used by other poets in the tradition. The poet's authority, even his or her subjectivity, is as much a function of the utterance as a guarantor of it.

These two approaches to the literary text are roughly parallel to two types of speech-act theories which some critics have identified, distinguishing between those which define illocution in terms of external or pragmatic circumstances, and those which seek formal or intrinsic criteria for defining illocutionary force.[4] Austin set the pattern for both these projects by attempting to pin down the performative first in terms of external societal conventions (such as the existence of an accepted procedure for the performance of the speech act), then in terms of internal grammatical criteria

4 Stanley Fish makes this distinction at the end of 'With the Compliments of the Author' (720–1); see also chapter 3 of *Speech Acts and Literary Theory*, where Sandy Petrey outlines and distinguishes some important speech-act theories using similar criteria.

(such as the ability to make the performative quality of any utterance explicit by rephrasing it to include a verb in the first-person present). More importantly, for the purposes of this book, the two speech-act approaches tend to generate two substantially different forms of speech-act criticism. Critics who concentrate on context or sociohistorical environment usually focus their attention on speech acts *in* the literary text, while those who study poetic authority and the phenomenological status of utterance usually regard the text itself *as* a speech act. In the first type of theory, the critic analyses speech acts within the world that the text creates or imitates; this may or may not involve comparisons between the things that are done with words by characters in the text and things done with words in an external sociopolitical environment. In the second category, the critic treats the whole of the text as, or at least by analogy with, a speech act, analysing it as the utterance of an individual author, again with or without taking into consideration the author's historical moment. The two approaches lend themselves, furthermore, to the study of different genres. Speech acts in the text become a subject for analysis when the text is expansive enough to create a world of verbal acts in a social context, and especially when the world within the text imitates an actual society, as in the realist novel or neoclassical drama. The text as a whole presents itself most readily as a speech act, on the other hand, when it is the utterance of a single speaker who is trying to effect something through his or her utterance, as in most lyric poetry. While they are related in various important ways, the distinctiveness of these approaches has not been emphasized strongly enough and the resultant confusion has made it difficult to distinguish the projects of critics who have allied speech-act theory with widely divergent critical stances.

In the rest of this chapter and throughout the book, I will be using the terms 'sociopolitical performative' and 'phenomenological performative' to distinguish the two approaches I have outlined. Here, *sociopolitical* refers to an utterance which more or less explicitly derives performative force from the speaker's (and audience's) position within a societal institution (the church, the law, the class system), as well as a mode of interpretation which analyses performative utterances by appeal to historical, political, or institutional circumstances. But literary critics also use the term 'performative' in a different sense, to refer to an author's ability to 'create' reality through poetic or fictional utterance, independently of societal conventions but in accordance with literary conventions that ascribe creative (or visionary, or prophetic) authority to the speaking voice and elicit the reader's or hearer's assent. This type of utterance, and the corresponding interpretive approach, is here called the *phenomenological* performative, since its concern is the positing of phenomena whose existence is determined, not by historical reality, but by some other set of criteria. As I will argue in the following chapter, the recurrent paradigm for the phenomenological performative, in speech-act theory and in visionary poetry, is divine creation by the word. If performative utterances in poetry do not create phenomena of the same order as does the divine word, they may nevertheless lay claim to a similar type of performativity: non-conventional, extra-societal, deriving from the will or intentionality of the speaker alone.

Speech Acts in the Text

Austin's exclusion of utterances spoken by an actor on stage has been undermined to the extent that speech-act theory has made its most considerable and productive impact on literary theory in the study of drama. As a form in which speaking and acting are inseparable, which invokes generic conventions as well as the behavioural conventions of the society it portrays, and which takes place in a public context, drama has proven a valuable illustration of the way social reality is both created and reflected by verbal exchange. Sandy Petrey has observed that there is a direct correlation among a society's dependence on formal or prescribed utterances, the amount of (neo)classical drama it produces, and the openness of the drama (and the society) to speech-act analysis (*Speech Acts* 109). Thus Louis XIV's France, Golden Age Spain, and Elizabethan England have provided the material for both the earliest and the most searching essays in speech-act criticism.[5]

Analysing speech acts performed by characters in a play is conceptually unproblematic. It might even be said to evade Austin's stricture against non-serious utterances by considering the world of the drama as if it were the real world, and giving the characters credit for the seriousness of their utterances under those circumstances. Thus when Lear says to Cordelia, at the beginning of Shakespeare's play,

Here I disclaim all my paternal care

5 Two of the most important critiques of speech-act theory and its relation to literature, Stanley Fish's long essay on *Coriolanus* ('How to Do Things with Austin and Searle: Speech-Act Theory and Literary Criticism,' in *Is There a Text* 197–245) and Shoshana Felman's book on Molière's *Don Juan* (*The Literary Speech Act*), focus on dramatic texts. See also Elias L. Rivers, ed., *Things Done with Words: Speech Acts in Hispanic Drama*, a volume of essays resulting from a seminar held at Stony Brook in 1984 on speech-act theory and Golden Age drama, and the work of Richard Ohmann, especially 'Speech, Literature, and the Space Between.'

Propinquity and property of blood,
And as a stranger to my heart and me
Hold thee, from this, for ever   (1.1.113–16)

the declaration is an explicit and bona fide speech act on the part of King
Lear, even if it is true (as Austin feared) that the *actor* playing Lear has not
disowned the actress playing Cordelia. Studies of speech acts in fiction
encounter a greater number of methodological problems, because the illu-
sion that the text delineates a separate reality is often complicated by the
presence of a narrative voice which reminds the reader that there are at
least two contexts in which the words of the novel can function – as utterances of characters, or utterances of an author in the real world. When we
read the first words of *Moby-Dick*, 'Call me Ishmael,' to whom is that directive addressed and by whom is it spoken? Is the illocution best described as
a conversational self-introduction by a fictional character, a preliminary ori-
enting statement by the author, or the author's act of positing a fictional
character and a fictional world? At what point and on what basis do we
decide among the possibilities? Critics who analyse illocutionary force in
fiction tend to feel the need for a more or less fully developed theoretical
framework to help distinguish the situations of author and narrator, reader
and implied audience, and to help define the mode of reality to which language in fiction refers.[6]

6 The need for these distinctions is evident throughout Mary Louise Pratt's *Toward a Speech
Act Theory of Literary Discourse*, which adapts Searle's notion of rules or appropriateness
conditions governing verbal behaviour and, more specifically, H.P. Grice's theory of the
Co-operative Principle governing ordinary conversation, in order to define the 'literary
speech situation' and propose it as a basis for the interpretation of narrative. Pratt's book
plays a fundamental role in opening up the possibilities that speech-act theory offers for
the reading of narrative. In her view, the literary speech situation encompasses the previously unacknowledged relationship of 'literary' narrative to a wide range of 'non-literary'
genres. Her methodology establishes the relevance of numerous aspects of a narrative's
context, including the implied cooperative relationship between author and audience, the
various kinds of pre-selection that a narrative must go through before it reaches publication, and the fulfilment or violation of generic norms.
   On the other hand, the work of Sandy Petrey represents a solidly Austinian approach to
speech acts in the novel. Petrey's readings of nineteenth-century French realist fiction in its
sociohistorical context focus attention not only on the way a societal context allows
speech acts to function, but also on how speech acts constitute and bring a community
into existence in the first place. Petrey's essays on Balzac ('Castration, Speech Acts, and the
Realist Difference,' 'The Reality of Representation') are an important example of the critical
approach I define in this chapter as the sociopolitical reading of performative language.

Nevertheless, speech acts in fiction, particularly realist fiction, provide important examples of how performative language functions in the context of sociopolitical conventions. To begin to illustrate the significance of performative language in the world of the novel, we might draw an example from nineteenth-century fiction which is more or less contemporary with Blake's very different use of words in *Jerusalem*, the subject of the final chapter of this book. From the opening pages of Jane Austen's *Sense and Sensibility*, the determining factors in plot development and character motivation are marriage and inheritance, aspects of life in society which are regulated by two of J.L. Austin's prime examples of speech acts, the wedding ceremony and the will. The centrality of these and other verbal declarations is attested by the fact that the tensions and conflicts in the novel are driven by discrepancies between private sentiment and public statement. Elinor and Marianne Dashwood both risk the tragic consequences of an emotional attachment which is not ratified by a formal engagement. Throughout the novel Austen plays on the ambiguity of the term 'engagement,' which refers to involvement in social, business, or financial activity, but also to a state specifically defined by a man's spoken proposal and a woman's spoken acceptance. Marianne's suffering is a direct consequence of Willoughby's failure to say the words which would alter her status from private sweetheart to acknowledged fiancée. The significance of such a declaration as a publicly sanctioned speech act is tellingly summed up in the nineteenth-century euphemism 'to speak' for a man's formal declaration of love and proposal of marriage.

The performative power of declarations in a society where the power structure is so extensively determined by marital alliances and lines of inheritance is reflected by Austen's satirical account of the way Mrs Ferrars, disapproving of her son Edward's engagement to Elinor Dashwood, first declares him no longer her child, then reinstates him to the status of son, but not to that of elder son, even though he is her first-born and even though she has meanwhile disavowed her younger child, Robert:

After a proper resistance on the part of Mrs Ferrars ... Edward was admitted to her presence, and pronounced to be again her son ... [H]ere it plainly appeared, that though Edward was now her only son, he was by no means her eldest; for while Robert was inevitably endowed with a thousand pounds a-year, not the smallest objection was made against Edward's taking orders for the sake of two hundred and fifty at the utmost; nor was anything promised either for the present or in future ... (Austen 362–3)

Carried away by the socially constitutive power of speech acts, Mrs Ferrars uses her authority as head of the family and controller of its property to translate her private indignation into public declarations. The humour of the passage relies on the obvious futility, in one sense, of Mrs Ferrars's histrionics; she will have an elder son Edward and a younger son Robert no matter what she says. Yet her declarations do have the effect of altering Edward's and Robert's legal status as heirs, a fact which obviously has real consequences for the condition of their lives. As the object of Austen's satire, Mrs Ferrars's pronouncements expose the ironic discrepancy between physical reality and social reality, or what Searle calls brute facts and institutional facts, even more clearly than do the ordinary societal speech acts (engagements, marriages, wills) that the nineteenth-century novel portrays.

Yet the study of performative language in the novel easily slides over to the subtly different question of the text's status as speech act. In *Speech Acts and Literary Theory*, for instance, Sandy Petrey cites an example from *Jane Eyre* to demonstrate how an utterance can work within the world of the novel analogously to the way it works in ordinary life, but then deduces from this example that 'comparable conventional agreements produce fictional characters and their fictional world' (*Speech Acts* 10). Suddenly, attention shifts from conventions of societal behaviour to conventions of fiction-writing, from relationships between characters in the novel or persons in the real world to relationships which connect the two realms to one another. Petrey's allusion to a contract between author and audience introduces a substantially different approach to speech-act interpretation, one that raises considerably more complex questions concerning the ontological status of literary texts.

The Text as Speech Act

While questions of author-audience relationship have been addressed in terms of the novel by Mary Louise Pratt and others, the concept of the text as authorial utterance has special relevance for lyric poetry. Speech-act studies of poetry are still relatively uncommon, however, and present methodological challenges of their own. It is less obvious than in the case of the drama or novel that speech-act theory is even relevant to the interpretation of poetic texts. When Wordsworth proposes the language really used by men as an alternative to poetic diction, he does not necessarily share the assumptions of twentieth-century philosophers who turned their attention to the operations of ordinary language, and even a fundamentally dialogical genre like the Coleridgean conversation poem is far removed from the one-on-one dialogue that is the explicit or implicit model of most speech-act linguistics. The term 'literature,' which came into vogue in the late eighteenth and early nineteenth century, originally referred mainly to poetry and designated a type of discourse removed from the verbal operations of 'society,' a word which came into its modern use more or less simultaneously. That the twentieth century has in large measure upheld the alienation of poetry from referentiality and societal action is illustrated by the pervasiveness of Archibald MacLeish's dictum 'A poem should not mean / But be' (41).

But if MacLeish's statement denies poetry an empirically referential and active role, it simultaneously affirms the poem's existence in a mode of reality distinct from that of the empirical world. The sense in which a poem can 'be' is not the sense in which, for instance, a tree 'is': one would be tempted to call the poem's mode of existence intransitive, if that term could be meaningfully applied to the copula. Poetic discourse posits reality in a self-reliant and self-reflexive way that does not appeal to either reference or perception, if those are our ordinary ways of establishing existence in language and in the physical world. What Roland Barthes has said of modernist writing could be said of poetry in general: its mode of existence is analogous to that evoked by the middle voice in Greek grammar, in that it exists 'for its own sake,' independently of a subject-object distinction (Barthes 20). Yet to describe poetic discourse as independent of reference and the criterion of truth is to echo Austin's original definition of performative utterance. Performatives may be dependent on societal convention, but they have a referential autonomy that seems tantalizingly similar to the status of poetry in its ability to posit existence.

The popularity of Mallarmé among critics who explore the function of poetry as performative language demonstrates the tendency to associate this type of performativity with a positing which appears to turn away from history and reference.[7] But a few critics have also used Mallarmé's work to demonstrate the interaction between literary positing and social action. In an essay which examines the performative dimension of Mallarmé's poem 'Salut,' Steven Winspur offers more specific terminology than most critics for the study of literary texts as performative utterances, referring to them as 'text acts.' Winspur attempts to establish the centrality of text acts through a move that repeats Derrida's inversion of the hierarchy of speech

---

7 See, in particular, Barbara Johnson's 'Poetry and Performative Language: Mallarmé and Austin' (52–66) and Derrida's 'The Double Session' (*Dissemination* 173–286).

and writing in *Of Grammatology*. He proposes that 'text acts ground their speech-act cousins, and not the other way around':

Our actions are always grounded in preexistent textual models (whether these be poetic, journalistic, filmic, or whatever), and the power of certain literary texts ... resides precisely in their *recasting* the performative force inherent in such models. (Winspur 184)

Winspur's main example of a text which recasts performative force in this way is 'Salut,' one of Mallarmé's many 'circumstantial' poems which translates an actual utterance (the poem was delivered as a toast during a banquet on 15 February 1893) into a text that celebrates the performative force of all poetry, thus demonstrating 'the *continuation of life* ... that comes through our *actions* with words' (Winspur 180). Winspur is primarily interested in showing that both speech-act theory (recast according to Wittgensteinian principles) and poetry (recast according to Mallarméan example) are fundamentally ethical activities. Central to his argument is the demonstration that Mallarmé's poetry moves from historical circumstance (the 1893 toast) to text act (the ahistorical performativity of the lyric poem) while revealing the 'textual' or rule-governed basis of all public action. In the terms I have outlined above, this means that the speech-act dimension of Mallarmé's poetry involves a deliberate synthesis of the sociopolitical performative with the phenomenological performative. The historical circumstances in which 'Salut' is originally uttered are interdependent with the performativity of lyric poetry in general, a performativity which the text both invokes and establishes.

Like Winspur, I find that the attempt to determine what kind of speech act a poem is leads back to Wittgenstein, whose *Philosophical Investigations* raise so many of the central concerns of speech-act philosophy *avant la lettre*. Wittgenstein's analysis of imagining is a kind of synecdoche of his entire project in the *Investigations* of undermining the idea that meanings of words exist as object-like entities in the mind. Wittgenstein brings us to the realization that our ordinary concept of the 'mental image' has a mimetic basis: it depends on an unrecognized analogy with sensory perception of an empirical world. This misconception, in turn, is brought about by the 'grammatical movement' by which we impose a subject-object structure on the experience of imagining:

You have a new conception and interpret it as seeing a new object. You interpret a grammatical movement made by yourself as a quasi-physical phenomenon which you are observing. (§401)

The delusory parallel that we draw between sensory perception, the subject-object structure of language, and the mental image is exposed when we compare the experience of imagining with the experience of pain perception (although the grammatical parallel between *eine Vorstellung haben*, 'having an image,' and *Schmerzen haben*, 'having pains,' does not come through adequately in English translation).

Two further ramifications of the concept of imagining present themselves, which together provide a basis for adapting Wittgenstein's discussion to the context of poetic utterance. First, Wittgenstein redirects his definition of imagining back toward an analogy with perception, but specifies that it is like 'a new way of looking at things' (rather than, as above, 'seeing a new object'). Described in this way, the relationship of the mind to the world has explicit aesthetic overtones:

But there is an objection to my saying that you have made a 'grammatical' movement. What you have primarily discovered is a new way of looking at things. As if you had invented a new way of painting; or, again, a new metre, or a new kind of song. (§401)

Imagining, by this account, is analogous to genre, or to the artist's perspective in a work of art, in that it brings into existence a unique way of seeing but not a visual or actual object which one might speak of owning or exchanging. If I imagine a room, Wittgenstein suggests, I may 'have' a 'visual room,' but the word 'have' can only be understood by analogy with its ordinary use: I do not possess the visual room, nor can I walk around in it or point to it. The image exists in the mind the same way as it exists in a verbal postulate, independently of possession, reference to reality, proof, disproof, or even the propositional form which would make the conditions of truth or falsity meaningful.

Secondly, Wittgenstein proposes that imagining might be characterized as a distinctive way of speaking:

'It's true I say "Now I am having such-and-such an image," but the words "I am having" are merely a sign to someone *else*; the description of the image is a *complete* account of the imagined world.' – You mean: the words 'I am having' are like 'I say!...' You are inclined to say it should really have been expressed differently. Perhaps simply by making a sign with one's hand and then giving a description. (§402)

Our habitual form of expression when we communicate the idea of imagining is 'I am having ... an image' ('Ich habe ... [eine] Vorstellung'), but

Wittgenstein invalidates the literal (or even metaphorical) meaning of the formula and reinterprets it as a conventional discourse marker which has the effect of calling attention to the description that is to be given, as if by a hand signal or an ejaculation like 'I say!' ('Jetzt Achtung!'). The implication is that the description will be understood in a different register from ordinary language. Wittgenstein's way of characterizing what we do when we imagine renders imagining homologous with many kinds of speech acts, in that we recognize certain expressions as performative by the presence of conventional formulas such as 'I promise that' or 'I declare,' expressions which, among other things, give what follows the status of a *dictum* rather than a *factum*. This introductory formula, which includes a verb in the first-person present, alerts us to the subjectivity of the utterance and indicates that it needs to be understood in a different register from constative or referential statements.

The ability of language to posit, and the equivalent status of postulate and image, is most apparent in a poem which maintains an ambiguous relationship to empirical reality, because (like Mallarmé's 'Salut') it simultaneously evokes the moment of its composition *and* emphasizes the gap separating that moment from the present of our reading. By the same token, the text simultaneously highlights and renders ambiguous the distinction between ordinary language and literary language. Take, for example, Keats's final haunting fragment:

> This living hand, now warm and capable
> Of earnest grasping, would, if it were cold
> And in the icy silence of the tomb,
> So haunt thy days and chill thy dreaming nights
> That thou would wish thine own heart dry of blood,
> So in my veins red life might stream again,
> And thou be conscience-calm'd. See, here it is –
> I hold it towards you.   (Keats 503)

Beginning with a deictic 'this,' the text appears to ground itself in present reality, connecting the *manu*script itself (the poet's 'hand' in the sense of 'handwriting') to the body and the consciousness that produces it. As a speech act uttered by a living Keats, the poem would do just that, but as a text act its impact is reversed so that it marks, instead, the temporal gap separating us from Keats, who is dead. The hand was necessarily warm at the time of writing, but it is cold at the time of reading, whether that is 1898 (when the fragment was first published) or the present. From the reader's perspective, the conditional sentence which makes up most of the text ('would, if it were cold ...') has become a constative reality (it *is* cold). The illocutionary force of the lines is that of a threat, or perhaps a perverse promise, that the poet's dead hand will haunt the living reader, but in the act of reading the lines that threat is actualized and the promise fulfilled. A series of insistent monosyllables –'see here it is' – constitutes the moment of most intense reality or of most intense imagination, depending on whether the words refer to the simple gesture of extending a hand, a conventional token of societal bonding, or to the conjuring of a ghostly hand through the language of the poem. The fragment ends with an explicitly dialogical formulation, 'I' and 'you' eerily joined by an 'it' which refers to both the living hand and the dead one. 'It' is also the text itself, handed to us so that it may be actualized – 'brought to life' – during our encounter with it.

Unlike the case of the realist novel, the role of speech-act theory in the reading of 'This Living Hand' is not to implicate the text in historical conventions or discourses, but rather to de-historicize it by strangely superimposing the moment of writing onto the moment of reading. In both these moments the language of the poem is invested with performative force, but its function as the speech act of a living poet is disconcertingly incommensurate with its function as a text act. The constative and performative dimensions of the text seem, in fact, to change places when the lines are read as a specific utterance by a historical Keats and when they are read as a de-historicized lyric. Moreover, the literary genre of the fragment is far from definite; it may be a reproachful lyric addressed by Keats to his lover Fanny Brawne, or the speech of a character in an uncompleted historical drama. The illocutionary force of the lines, particularly the frame of reference for deictics and the performative or constative function of the verb 'is,' varies depending on the generic context in which the lines are placed.

The disjunction between performatives in ordinary language and the phenomenological performative comes into clearer focus still in William Carlos Williams's poem 'This Is Just to Say,' a text which directly invokes the categories of speech-act theory:

This Is Just to Say

I have eaten
the plums
that were in
the icebox

and which
you were probably
saving
for breakfast

Forgive me
they were delicious
so sweet
and so cold

Like 'This Living Hand,' the poem is grounded at the beginning and the
end in lived reality and, through the copula, in the category of being:
'This *Is* Just to Say / I have eaten'; 'they *were* delicious.' The past tense is
significant: the plums being no more, their existence and affects, on
which so much depends, can only be posited and imagined. In prefacing
the utterance with the combined title and first line 'This Is Just to Say,'
Williams makes the performative dimension of his language explicit. As
Austin demonstrates in *How to Do Things with Words*, even a statement
that appears constative ('The cat is on the mat') is revealed to be a
speech act when the implicit first-person subject and verb are explicitly
expressed ('I state that the cat is on the mat'). 'I state that' and 'This Is
Just to Say' lift the utterance out of the realm of true-false propositions by
reminding us that what follows is not a universal truth, but a circumstantial utterance limited by a historical context and a conceptual frame of reference. Elsewhere, Williams reveals that the poem began as an ordinary
(and presumably truthful) note to his wife, and the context-dependence
of performative language is highlighted by the difference in the status
and function of the same utterance when it appears in a note taped to
the refrigerator and in a volume of poetry. In its poetic incarnation, Williams's attempt 'just to say,' or to posit, 'is' all that takes place, and the
poem reveals how much – in everyday life, in poetry – depends on the
act of just saying.

Williams's entire text may be read as an elaboration of the self-referential 'This Is' with which it begins; the poem, in other words, simultaneously
presents and explains what 'this' which we are reading is. 'This Is' serves as
the Wittgensteinian gesture that calls attention to an imaginary conception,
and warns the listener that the language describing that conception must
be understood in a different register from ordinary language. Here, 'This Is'
alerts the reader that the copula is not to be understood as referring to
existence in the real world, but that we must concede to it the power of

establishing an independent reality ('this *is*'). As a deictic, 'this' can only be actualized within a specific scene of discourse – a fact that calls attention to the ephemerality of positing, which occurs only in the instant in which a reader encounters the poem, in the non-existent moment of presence and presentness when 'this' is 'here' with us 'now.' On the other hand, the self-referentiality of 'this' renders the utterance completely irrefutable, since it refuses to rely on non-subjective points of reference. ' "I" is not the name of a person, nor "here" of a place, and "this" is not a name,' Wittgenstein writes; 'it is characteristic of physics not to use these words' (§410). Deictics are only for discourses which can stand the intrusion of subjectivity. Emile Benveniste points out that it is easy to imagine a long linguistic text such as a scientific treatise in which deictics like 'I' and 'you' never occur, essential as they are to virtually all spoken discourse (217–18). They are also essential, I would argue, to poetic texts which attempt to ground the performativity of their language in an authority located in the writer's individual consciousness.

Sociopolitical versus Phenomenological Performatives

In identifying and delineating what I take to be two different speech-act approaches to the literary text, I have implied that they may lead to very different, at times incompatible, conclusions. This divergence may be demonstrated most clearly through a brief comparison of readings of Blake's *Songs of Innocence and of Experience* by two critics who have little in common apart from their mutual reliance on the terms of speech-act theory: Gavin Edwards, whose analysis of performative language in 'London' leads to a characterization of Blake as a politically engaged critic of his society; and Samuel Levin, whose reading of 'Holy Thursday' demonstrates his conviction that poetry is a mimetic speech act in which we can only participate by a complete and willing suspension of disbelief.

For Edwards, first of all, Blake's poem 'London' is 'overwhelmingly concerned' with social and political acts, and (not unlike *Sense and Sensibility* in the reading outlined above) revolves around the institutions of 'Church, Law, property, generational inheritance, and marriage' (Edwards, 'Repeating the Same Dull Round' 28). Edwards notes that the speech acts of chartering, banning, cursing, and marking occur in the poem in forms other than the first-person present, or as 'deactivated' performatives ('charter'd'; 'marks,' 'ban,' and 'curse' as nouns). This suggests that the poem describes a situation in which institutions have already imposed labels on individuals, although those individuals collaborate in their own 'marking' by accepting the conventions which continue to give institutional utterances their performative force. 'London,' in this reading, is concerned with 'the power of discourse to effect (in both senses) the development of physical life and human relationships' (31), and the relevant context for interpretation includes the debate between Burke and Paine on the nature of charters, as well as contemporary market relations and the condition of London's oppressed. Edwards's reading concludes with a focus on the 'complicity of the Observing "I" ' in 'London' (40), which he reads as a manifestation of the crisis of objectivity and identification in eighteenth-century writing and which points to the necessity of regarding literature as social discourse: 'We are beginning to define the historically specific position that literature may have held among other forms of social relationship, specifically its overwhelmingly, and perhaps crucial, ideological function, its role in the forging of manacles' (39).

There is a world of difference between Edwards's conclusions, framed in the vocabulary of new historicism and cultural materialism, and Samuel Levin's interpretation of a Blake poem as speech act. Levin concurs with Richard Ohmann that a poem should be regarded by both poet and reader as an imitation or mimetic representation of a real-world illocutionary act. His own contribution to the analysis of poem as speech act is the identification of a conventional gesture or formula that parallels Austin's 'I state that' or Wittgenstein's 'I say!' The 'higher sentence' that makes the illocutionary force of a poem explicit is, according to Levin, 'I imagine myself in and invite you to conceive a world in which ...,' a formula that we may infer as the preamble to any work of imaginative literature (150). This form of reading (as I have suggested is true in general of readings which treat the entire text as a speech act) is most appropriate to the lyric, 'the type of most personal and private expression' (155). More specifically, Levin implies that a speech-act reading of this sort focuses attention on the vatic element in literature, since the imaginative lyric represents the kind of illocutionary act 'that we associate with the seer, the *vates*, the vessel, the sibyl, the kind of act attributed to someone inspired with unnatural powers' (154).

In order to demonstrate the difference between the illocutionary force of a poetic text and that of ordinary language, Levin employs the same technique used elsewhere by John Searle (*Expression and Meaning* 61–70) and Barbara Herrnstein Smith (272), of placing a literary text – here, Blake's 'Holy Thursday' from *Songs of Innocence* – side by side with a non-fictional passage. His conclusion is that if we as readers are to render the poem a totally successful speech act, we must accede to its intended perlocutionary effect by suspending our disbelief and assenting to the reality created by the poetic utterance. Levin takes this conclusion to an extreme by suggesting that we have not completely suspended disbelief as long as we still read metaphors as metaphors; if we are truly to enter the poet's world, and thus render the poem's implied preamble effective, we must consider figurative language literally true. This is, in effect, to elide the distinction that has just been drawn between poetic discourse and ordinary language, to suggest that a poem's claim goes beyond that of a posited reality to an existent reality, something that can only come about through a kind of transcendent (in Levin's term, 'unnatural') power. The discrepancy with Edwards's speech-act reading of 'London' is glaringly evident. Where Edwards implicates the poem more and more deeply in contemporary political and social discourses, Levin sees the poem as leading out of the everyday world into its own imagined reality; while Edwards's Blake is an observer and social commentator, Levin's Blake is a mystic and magician.

The comparison is skewed by the fact that Edwards's essay represents a much more concentrated study of Blake than does Levin's, but it should at least be clear that a reading of the text as phenomenological speech act does not coexist complacently with an analysis of sociopolitical speech acts in the text. Instead of referring to an existing historical context, performative utterances in literature may seem to create a world in defiance of the existing one, to demonstrate the poet's imaginative independence from the social conditions of his or her utterance. Yet my attempt in this book is to bring the two speech-act approaches together, not by eliding differences, but by demonstrating how the sociopolitical performative and the phenomenological performative interact in specific texts, with or without the author's awareness that this is happening. The two types of performatives may appear in confrontation with one another, the poet trying to oppose or resist the discourse of institutions with a speech act that derives authority from private visionary consciousness. They may also converge within the same utterance, since language, even when used with a conscious appeal to visionary tradition, is necessarily implicated in, perhaps limited by, contemporary social and political discourses. Milton and Blake express their consciousness of inspiration with varying degrees of awareness that they are simultaneously employing verbal formulas and forms of address derived from the rhetoric of law, economics, or politics. The speech-act model focuses attention on the positions from which these poets are speaking and the authority behind their words – and on the way these positions and sources of authority shift over the course of their careers. Milton and Blake have in common the attempt to use language to alter the behaviour of their contemporaries at a critical historical juncture.

When these attempts fail, their response is to retain the rhetoric of declaration and personal and public address and use it to create ideal audiences, like Milton's Adam and Eve in conversation with Raphael or the four groups of readers to whom the four chapters of *Jerusalem* are addressed. This aspect of Milton's and Blake's writing provides a unique insight into the interference between sociopolitical and phenomenological speech acts, as well as the interdependence of language and reality and the way each of those terms performs the other.

The Integration of Sociopolitical and Phenomenological Performatives: Searle and Benveniste

Even outside of a literary context, it is possible to explore the distinction between the sociopolitical and the phenomenological performative by contrasting the speech act which manifestly depends for its effectiveness on the wielding of political or institutional power, on the official status of the speaker, and on the conventions accepted by a societal group, with the speech act which depends instead (in ways which still have to be defined more closely) on the consciousness and unique identity of the speaker and the conventions of language itself. Austin did not distinguish these categories; on the contrary, his identification of illocutionary force draws them together by suggesting that ordinary self-expression functions in the same manner as official declarations. Rather, the distinction has been brought about by Austin's followers in their attempts to establish reliable methods of categorizing the performative. Both John Searle and Emile Benveniste have advanced theories of speech acts which attempt to put sociopolitical performatives in a different category from performatives which rely on the intention or consciousness of the speaker and the rules of language. But, I would argue, the strict categorization breaks down in both cases and serves instead to demonstrate the interaction between the two kinds of speech acts. In the case of Benveniste, the relationship between sociopolitical and phenomenological performatives exposes a crucial connection between authority and subjectivity which is particularly significant for the discourse of the visionary poet.

John Searle has given direction to some literary-critical work on the performative by providing a more fully developed theory of illocutionary acts than Austin was able to, though Searle's theory also introduces terms and assumptions which radically change the emphasis of Austin's philosophy. Searle systematized speech-act theory by developing a taxonomy of illocutionary acts, in which possible illocutions are divided into five classes based on the relationship of speaker to hearer and utterance to external world. For our purposes, the most intriguing of the five categories is the final class of declarations, which 'bring about some alteration in the status or condition of the referred to object or objects solely in virtue of the fact that the declaration has been successfully performed' (*Expression and Meaning* 17). This is the only type of performative in which the 'direction of fit' between word and world goes both ways: the world is immediately made to fit the words, and by virtue of this the words fit, because they now describe, the world. The examples Searle gives of declarations fall into two categories: an utterance may act as a declaration when speaker and hearer hold certain positions within an 'extra-linguistic institution,' or, in special cases, when the speaker is somehow outside the normal order of language altogether, as when God decrees, 'Let there be light.' What these categories have in common is the requirement of some authorizing power as a supplement to the rules of language alone. Leaving aside the very interesting second category of divine utterances until the next chapter, we may note that the first category corresponds to Austin's standard-setting examples of performatives: solemnizing a marriage, baptizing a ship, giving orders to a subordinate. In other words, Searle's standard declaration is a sociopolitical speech act. Yet Searle is uneasy enough about the role of the sociopolitical performative in Austin's theory to criticize Austin for giving too much weight to institutional authority:

Austin sometimes talks as if he thought all illocutionary acts were like this, but plainly they are not. In order to make a statement that it is raining or promise to come and see you, I need only obey the rules of language. (*Expression and Meaning* 7)

For Searle, the sociopolitical performative is a special category of illocutionary act, distinct from acts governed solely by the 'rules of language,' though he suspects Austin of having 'sometimes' conflated these categories. The distinction Searle makes here is in keeping with his habit of locating societal institutions outside the realm of language, referring to them repeatedly as 'extra-linguistic institutions.' These strict inclusions and exclusions suggest that Searle leaves out what is at least implicit in Austin – a recognition that societal institutions only exist insofar as they are created by speech acts (charters, vows, declarations of independence) and kept in existence by the exercise of verbal performativity. Conversely, the conventions or rules of language are inevitably affected by society and its institutions. Austin demonstrates this when he points out that only certain formulas are accepted for the performance of a speech act, even in ordinary language: one can, for instance, perform the illocutionary act of insulting someone, but not by saying, 'I insult you,' since that formula lacks collective acknowledgment (*How to Do Things* 30–1). Or, to use Searle's own example of making a statement, one might say that the rules of language are no longer sufficient to account for the illocutionary force of an ideologically charged utterance such as 'No means no.' Although the utterance does not require any extra-linguistic authority on the part of the speaker, its illocutionary force cannot be accounted for by the rules of language alone (according to which it would be a simple tautology); moreover, the illocutionary force is likely to vary depending on whether the speaker is a man or a woman, a judge or a stand-up comedian.

As Petrey writes, all Austinian performatives *are* of the 'extra-linguistic institution' (or sociopolitical) kind if the term 'institutional' is understood in its broader sense to mean 'all the protocols ... establishing and preserving a social formation' (*Speech Acts* 64). By breaking the bond between language and institutions, and making each responsible for separate categories of speech acts, Searle ironically highlights the fact that discourse and social action are not separated in Austin's theory, but rather placed on a continuum. In its original form, the theory of performative language makes it possible to consider the speech acts of Milton or Blake, like those of ordinary speakers, as *both* discourse in a societal context and manifestations of an intrinsic function of language.

A more specific connection between institutional and non-institutional performatives, but one with equally wide-ranging implications, is afforded by the work of the structuralist linguist Emile Benveniste. Benveniste's work, which finds applications not only in the field of linguistics but in philosophy, psychology, and anthropology, is relevant to speech-act theory because he developed, or at least proposed, his own notion of verbal performativity before coming into contact with the work of Austin and the Oxford school. While Benveniste's concept of the performative has been considered problematic and inconsistent by many scholars, his work also offers a powerful insight which can help consolidate different forms of the performative: that is, the idea of subjectivity in language.

To focus on the intrusion of the subject and the subject's temporal and spatial perspective is really to return to the notion of *parole* as the proper domain of the performative. In *How to Do Things with Words*, Austin suggests only fleetingly that all performatives share a dimension of presence and presentness that is lacking from constative language: in all performatives, he writes, 'there is something which is *at the moment of uttering being done by the person uttering*' (60). In the case of the explicit performative with a verb in the first-person present, this element of subjectivity is manifest ('*I* call this meeting to order'), but apparently constative statements are seen to be performative precisely when the subjective dimension is exposed ('*I* state that the cat is on the mat'). Written performatives such as wills and laws might seem to be exempt from this principle, yet even they manifest illocutionary force only when they are instantiated or applied in particular circumstances. The will requires a subjective 'I give and bequeath' as well as an assumption that a personal consciousness guarantees that 'I,' even though the person is no longer alive. Similarly, 'thou shalt not steal' acquires performative force from the fact that a reader or hearer encountering the utterance will assume the place of 'thou.'

The title and argument of Benveniste's 1958 essay 'Subjectivity in Language' reveal the importance of this concept to his notion of the performative. Like Austin, Benveniste begins by remarking on the asymmetry between some first-person formulations and other forms of the same verb. In beginning a sentence with 'I presume (that) ...' or 'I swear ...,' the speaker converts a proposition into a subjective utterance. The utterance is equivalent to an act as a logical consequence of Benveniste's central tenet concerning the relationship of human beings and language: that linguistic communication is possible only because every speaker is able to actualize the system of language in a unique instance of discourse, an instance in which the subject itself is created:

The utterance is identified with the act itself. But this condition is not given in the meaning of the verb, it is the 'subjectivity' of discourse which makes it possible ... This is a consequence of the fact that the instance of discourse that contains the verb establishes the act at the same time that it sets up the subject. (Benveniste 229–30)

Thus the act of swearing brought about by 'I swear that ...' depends on and participates in a more universal act, by which the subject itself is created through the subjective utterance.

In a later essay on 'Analytic Philosophy and Language,' Benveniste responds to Austin's theory by trying to define his notion of the performative more rigorously, particularly since he felt Austin had erred in watering down his definition of the performative to the extent that it ceased to exist as distinct from the constative. Yet Benveniste's own definition becomes slippery because he wants to make performativity relative to both the linguistic order and the social order but seems unable to reconcile the two.

He first attempts a rigorous linguistic definition, according to which 'performative utterances are those in which a declarative-jussive verb in the first person of the present is constructed with a dictum' (234–5), but later seems to revoke this criterion in favour of a defining concept of authority: 'A performative utterance ... has existence only as an act of authority ... The criterion is here and not in the choice of verbs' (236). Once more, if less explicitly, phenomenological and sociopolitical performatives seem isolated into different categories.

While it would be difficult to eliminate all ambiguity from Benveniste's notion of the performative, which is in any case never developed more fully, some critics have oversimplified the contradiction between the linguistic and the social and missed the major point of Benveniste's definition,[8] which integrates the two types of performatives more closely than might appear at first. His linguistic criterion, to begin with, actually combines a verbal formula with the notion of authority, since it is assumed that a declarative-jussive verb can only be issued (or issued meaningfully) by a speaker with the requisite authority. This is strongly implied by Benveniste's examples of declarative-jussive performatives, all of which are utterances that belong in a political, legal, military, or other institutional context. Ironically, the essential role of authority in bringing about this class of utterance becomes clearest when Benveniste admits an exception: some utterances, such as 'The chair in Botany is declared vacant,' may lack the declarative-jussive verb 'because they are only implicitly attributed to *the authority entitled to produce them*' (235, my italics). Benveniste's first definition actually has as much to do with power as it does with grammar.

When Benveniste proposes a second possible class of performatives, it appears quite different from the first since it involves a type of utterance that 'does not emanate from a recognized power but posits a personal commitment for the one who utters it' (235). Yet the second type of performative turns out to be homologous with the first. What the two groups of utterances have in common is that they are 'authenticated' as acts. A performative always creates a new situation, and it is unique to a definite time and place; by virtue of these two properties, it is self-referential in the sense of 'referring to a reality that it itself constitutes by the fact that it is actually uttered in conditions that make it an act' (236) – an idea which parallels Searle's definition of declarations, in which the 'direction of fit' between words and world goes both ways. A performative, Benveniste reiterates at this point, 'has existence only as an act of authority.' Ben-

8 See, for instance, Petrey's critique of Benveniste (*Speech Acts* 43–7).

veniste's choice of words is misleading (since his *first* class of performatives, and not the present one, contains explicitly authoritative declarations), but he immediately qualifies his notion of 'acts of authority' as 'first and always utterances made by those to whom the right to utter them belongs' (236). Authority, thus defined, is more akin to *authorship*; it includes institutional power, but also the autonomy of the subject. Since I and no one else have the authority to swear, promise, or pledge myself, these 'personal' performatives are on an equal footing with those authorized by societal institutions.

The crux of the whole definition is subjectivity and the actualization of discourse. Benveniste disqualifies formulations that Austin would call performative, such as imperatives and warning signs, on the grounds that they do not invoke subjectivity by employing a first-person verb, and they are not self-referential (that is, they do not denominate the act that is to be performed). He cautions that the status of an utterance itself as act must not be confused with the act that is likely to result from it, nor with the interpretation (as of a warning sign) that is drawn from it by a reader or listener. Benveniste's theory is valuable for the way it focuses attention not on perlocutionary effect, nor on the felicity of a performative utterance, but on the way performance occurs in the actualization of the linguistic system and the creation of subjectivity in a particular instance of language use. His final statement in the essay 'Analytic Philosophy and Language' concerns his understanding of 'the very object of analytic philosophy': namely, 'the specificity of language in the circumstances in which the linguistic forms one chooses to study are valid' (238), where the terms 'specificity' and 'circumstances' reaffirm his commitment to *parole* rather than *langue*.

Authority and Subjectivity: Benveniste and Barthes

Benveniste's diverse linguistic studies all reflect his fascination with the way languages are constructed so as to allow individual speakers to appropriate the entire structure of *langue* to themselves in the here and now of utterance. Accordingly, he emphasizes the asymmetry between the first and second persons ('I/you') and the third ('he,' to which Benveniste refuses to accord the status of 'person' at all), as well as the asymmetry of verb forms, deictics, and concepts of being as they are reflected in the forms of the copula in different language systems. All these elements, which explicitly form the basis of Benveniste's notion of the performative and are implicitly contained in Austin's as well, are valuable in extending the notion of performativity to first-person forms – ranging from invocation to tractate literature – which are favoured by poets like Milton and Blake.

Benveniste's claim is that the possibility of positing a subject linguistically has as its consequences both the ability to communicate in language and the existence of subjectivity itself. 'Language,' he writes, 'is possible only because each speaker sets himself up as a *subject* by referring to himself as *I* in his discourse' (225); conversely, 'it is in and through language that man constitutes himself as a *subject*, because language alone establishes the concept of "ego" in reality, in *its* reality which is that of the being' (224). The pronouns 'I' and 'you' have no meaning or referent except in actual instances of discourse, yet they are central components of all linguistic systems. In 'The Nature of Pronouns,' Benveniste adds to the 'I/you' category such forms as demonstratives ('this') and adverbs of time and place ('here,' 'now,' 'today,' 'tomorrow'), insisting that traditional accounts of deixis are not enough to explain the function of these parts of speech because they neglect the presentness and uniqueness of the instance of discourse, which is to say its dependence on the subject:

It is pointless to define these terms and the demonstratives in general by deixis, as is generally done, unless one adds that the deixis is contemporary with the instance of discourse that carries the indicator of person; it is from this reference that the demonstrative takes its property of being unique and particular each time, which is the uniqueness of the instance of discourse to which it refers. (219)

Wittgenstein, who italicizes the word 'this' with self-conscious frequency in *Philosophical Investigations*, also emphasizes the necessary component of presence in the deictic by asserting that demonstratives can never be without a bearer. It must always be possible to point to the referent of 'this': 'It might be said: "so long as there is a *this*, the word 'this' has a meaning too"' (§45).

The criterion of specificity to the moment of utterance differentiates 'I' and 'you' from 'he'; Benveniste habitually refers to the latter as a 'non-person' to emphasize that it is never dependent on the instance of discourse and can be replaced by other referential formulas ('Los,' 'the Eternal Prophet,' 'the father of Orc').[9] The same asymmetry obtains between 'here' and 'there,' 'tomorrow' and 'the day after.' One of many significant corollaries is that discourse-dependent terms resemble Austinian performatives in that they lack the referentiality and truth-value of constative statements: 'Since they lack material reference, they cannot be misused; since they do

9 In 'Relationships of Person in the Verb,' Benveniste reveals that his thinking about the third person parallels that of the Arab grammarians, whose terms for our first, second, and third persons he translates, respectively, as 'the one who speaks,' 'the one who is addressed,' and 'the one who is absent' (197).

not assert anything, they are not subject to the condition of truth and escape all denial' (220).

Discourse-dependent pronouns and adverbs figure crucially in Milton's and Blake's assertions of authority, and the context of Wittgenstein's philosophy and Benveniste's linguistics makes it possible to identify in these utterances an invocation of presence and an attendant evasion of true-false conditions. Milton's introduction of '*my* advent'rous Song, / That with no middle flight intends to soar,' like the Blakean admonition 'Mark well *my* words,' constitutes both a construction of subjectivity and an assertion of the subject's authority. Keeping in mind Benveniste's notion of authority as the right to make a certain utterance, the claim that these lines contain might be paraphrased: 'The one saying this is I, and I am the one authorized to say it.' Visionary poetry in its entirety may be regarded as performative discourse in that it is a sustained act of asserting authority on the part of the speaker, a condition which is reflected on the level of grammatical structure throughout the text, especially in the case of deictics and the copula. As Benveniste writes,

Any verb of speaking, even the most common of all, the verb *say*, is capable of forming a performative utterance if the formula, *I say that* ..., uttered under the appropriate conditions, creates a new situation. That is the rule of the game. (236)

On the other hand, visionary poets are also victims of the subjectivity of language. An appeal to subjectivity is the only way to convey their sense of authority, yet subjectivity risks being exposed as always and only a function of language. In the same breath with the claim to authority comes an admission of limits: 'This can only be said by saying "I," and "I" only has meaning in terms of what is being said.'

The power and the limitations of the writing 'I' in both literary and historical discourse have been explored by Roland Barthes, who addresses the convergence of literature and linguistics in structuralist criticism in terms heavily influenced by Benveniste's insistence on subjectivity. Since the relations between the *scriptor* and language are actualized only in the moment of writing, the 'generating center of linguistic time is always the present of the speech-act' (Barthes 14), and we cannot assume that the subject actualized as 'I' in the discourse is the same as the person who existed before the instance of writing or the person who survives it (51). Though Barthes is thinking mainly of the modernist text which deliberately sets out to construct the writer, I would maintain that poetry in which the identity and authority of the 'I' is as central as it is in Milton or Blake is necessarily open to the same perils and possibilities, since it must also confront what Barthes calls the 'scandal' of discourse – the integral role of the pronoun, the 'most dizzying of the shifters' (20). Like their common model, biblical proclamation, the texts of Milton and Blake exist in a unique relation to temporality, referring equally to something that happened, something that will happen, and something that happens only and always in the instant of writing.

'It is in language that an expectation and its fulfilment make contact,' Wittgenstein writes (§445), commenting on the fact that the words 'he is coming' seem to mean both the same and different things when used on their own and when used in the sentence 'I expect he is coming.' His observation represents another approach to the difference between linguistic and actual existence: 'language abstracts from this difference, for it speaks of a red patch whether it is there or not' (§446). While Wittgenstein's aim is to liberate us from the idea that a mental image must accompany verbal expression ('as if one were to believe that a written order for a cow ... always had to be accompanied by an image of a cow' [§449]), Benveniste would demonstrate how the subjectivizing 'I expect ...' turns 'he is coming' from *factum* to *dictum*, from a proposition into an instance of discourse. The role of linguistic structure itself in bridging the gap between expectation and existence is also evident in the word-play of Wittgenstein's German sentence: 'In der Sprache berühren sich Erwartung und Erfüllung.' The sentence expresses the philosophical sense in which language does not distinguish between a 'coming' and a 'prospective coming,' but also the phonological sense in which the linguistic vessel 'Er——ung' can be 'filled' by either *warten* or *füllen*, anticipation or completion.

A further perspective on the fluctuations of being in language is afforded by Benveniste's distinction between verbs of existence, such as English 'to be,' and the 'copula function' which, in many languages, can be expressed by nominal sentences and other non-verbal constructions (e.g., Latin *omnis homo mortalis*, 'every man [is] mortal'). Benveniste recognizes the defining elements of the verb as the cohesive function ('to organize the elements of the utterance into a complete structure') and the generally unacknowledged assertive function ('endowing the utterance with a predicate of reality') (133). Verbs forge horizontal relationships between elements in the sentence as well as vertical relationships between the linguistic utterance and the nature of things: 'Added implicitly to the grammatical relationship that unites the members of the utterance is a "this *is!*" that links the linguistic arrangement to the system of reality' (133). This definition allows Benveniste to separate verbal *function* from verbal *forms* and justify the existence of nominal or pronominal constructions which have a copula function, since this function differentiates itself from the verb by the lack of an assertive 'this is.' Thus, a language which has both a verb for 'to be' and an alternative grammatical construction which fulfils the copula function can choose between a form of 'is' which implies existence in reality and one which does not.

These gradations of the postulate of existence form the background for a study of poetic creation and visionary poetry, a form of writing which places heightened demands on the reader to distinguish between different modes of existence: between utterances that purport to describe reality ('Milton is the author of *Paradise Lost*'), utterances which refer to an imaginative order ('Milton is in Beulah'), and utterances which escape referentiality altogether in the manner identified by Bertrand Russell ('Blake's three daughters are the authors of *Paradise Lost*'). These questions are central to the issue of poetic authority as well as to the distinction, and the continuity, between Milton as writer of serious political tracts and sacred history, and Blake as creator of an imaginative universe and writer of ironic and hyperbolic prose. In a more extreme way than historical discourse (a genre with which texts like *The Reason of Church-Government* and *The Marriage of Heaven and Hell* still have clear affinities), visionary poetry employs what Barthes has termed the 'reality effect.' Barthes proposes that 'speech-act signs' – mainly deictics – evoke in all historical discourse a non-chronological, mythic, or cosmogonic time:

... the presence, in historical narration, of explicit speech-act signs tends to 'de-chronologize' the historical 'thread' and to restore, if only as a reminiscence or a nostalgia, a complex, parametric, non-linear time whose deep space recalls the mythic time of the ancient cosmogonies, it too linked by essence to the speech of the poet or the soothsayer ... (130–1)

By the end of his essay 'The Discourse of History,' Barthes has reconceptualized speech-act signs in terms of the 'reality effect,' a concept that (it is not always remembered) relies on speech-act theory and speaks of the displacing of referentiality by authority:

... we can say that historical discourse is a fake performative discourse in which the apparent constative (descriptive) is in fact only the signifier of the speech-act as an act of authority. (139)

The identification of historical discourse as a 'fake performative' can both illuminate and be illuminated by the type of 'history' being written in *Para-*

dise Lost or Jerusalem, where the present of the speech act and the writer's self-presentation as inspired creator act as guarantees of authority. In these narrative forms of visionary poetry, the focus shifts from what happened to the *telling of* what happened, who is telling it and why it is being told. The four passages of first-person address by the narrator of *Paradise Lost*, at the beginning of books 1, 3, 7, and 9, establish the fundamental direction of the narrative by inserting the composition of the poem itself into the structure of expectation and fulfilment that motivates so much in the poem, particularly its faith that a lost paradise may be compensated for by a 'paradise within thee, happier far.' In human life, expectation and fulfilment are separated by a gulf of experience; the expectation created within the poem, that human-kind will live a life of obedience in Paradise, has its fulfilment indefinitely deferred. But the poet avoids the same error, not only because he justifies the ways of God to men where Adam and Eve questioned them, but because it is in his language that expectation and fulfilment make contact. The invoca-tions set up a conditional situation – 'If answerable style I can obtain,' 'I may assert Eternal Providence, / And justify the ways of God to men' – and the nar-rative, by its very existence, enacts the fulfilment of that condition (i.e., in writing the poem Milton *does* obtain answerable style and justify God's ways). Even the most basic elements of linguistic structure contribute to the sense that the poem is the fulfilment of the very expectation that its language creates. Unlike its human protagonists, *Paradise Lost* as a verbal structure does not need to regain paradise, for on the level of language and grammar, by analogy with Wittgenstein's red patch, 'paradise' is present even in 'par-adise lost.'

Blake's prefaces to four groups of readers in *Jerusalem* have a similar effect, setting up a rhetorical structure which ultimately helps make possible the fulfilment of his poetic vision in dialogue and declaration: 'And I heard the Name of their Emanations they are named Jerusalem.' Both the prefaces and the conclusion of the poem raise the issue of Blake's authority to bestow names and make declarations, and since the last word of the text is also its title, *Jerusalem* becomes a large-scale study in the autonomous and self-referential character of performative utterance. The final line of the poem, which reintroduces a personal 'I' but also performs the text's ultimate act of authoritative naming, is an indicator of the complex relationship between authority and subjectivity in the discourse of the visionary poet.

The Deconstructive Turn

As one of the most influential adaptations of speech-act theory to the study of texts, the assimilation of the terms 'performative' and 'constative' by deconstruction generates a final perspective on the relevance of performative language to a study of visionary poetry. The encounter between speech-act theory and deconstruction has important implications for the intersection of the sociopolitical and phenomenological facets of performative language, despite the fact that deconstruction is often accused of turning its back on historical concerns. Sandy Petrey has voiced a particularly strong criticism of Jacques Derrida and Paul de Man for making the performative into a concept which designates 'language that, instead of effecting something within and outside itself at once, refuses all association with the outside to proclaim that its autonomy and self-absorption are inviolable' (*Speech Acts* 148). In its deconstructive incarnation, the tension between performative and constative becomes a malaise of language itself. Derrida's focus, in his celebrated debate with Searle over Austin's theory of language, is the dehiscence within language and consciousness that is revealed when we realize that iterability or *non*-uniqueness is a necessary condition of performative utterance. In the highly adapted form of speech-act theory incorporated in the methodology of de Man in *Allegories of Reading*, the performative and the constative are, again, inherent qualities of language whose irreconcilability makes the functioning of the text impossible and possible at once.[10] Both approaches would seem to ignore the societal orientation crucial to Austin and especially to his more historically and politically minded followers.

De Man's most famous use of speech-act terminology is in a reading of Rousseau's *Confessions*, where he concentrates on the episode in which Rousseau accuses the servant Marion of stealing a ribbon, a crime of which he himself is guilty. For de Man, the incident demonstrates the split between the performative and constative dimensions of language, since Rousseau's utterance of the name 'Marion' effectively fulfils the performative function of excusing Rousseau precisely because 'Marion' lacks any cognitive or constative meaning. But de Man's key point, that 'performative rhetoric and cognitive rhetoric ... fail to converge' (*Allegories* 300), is even more clearly illustrated by his discussion of Rousseau's political writings. The analysis of promising in the *Social Contract*, which sets out de Man's radical interpretation of constative and performative as something like semiology and rhetoric, is an important study of the intersection between the language of sociopolitical institutions and individual self-expression.

---

10 For further adaptations of a de Manian concept of the performative, especially in the context of Romantic literature, see Cynthia Chase and Andrzej Warminski.

For de Man, Austin's distinction between the locutionary and illocution-ary functions exposes the way language promises a cognitive, theoretical, or abstract truth which is always already undone by the actualization of the same language by an individual speaker (or writer) in a concrete speech situation (or text). What a text says must thus be set against what it does in literary history, and what it says about language and figuration set against its own figural structures and effects. The aporia de Man discovers in the language of Rousseau's *Social Contract*, which is equally explicit in any political use of language and is implicit in all language whatsoever, is that the structure or grammar of language itself renders meaning, in a particular referential instance, impossible:

There can be no text without grammar: the logic of grammar generates texts only in the absence of referential meaning, but every text generates a referent that subverts the grammatical principle to which it owed its constitution. (*Allegories* 269)

This is de Man's paraphrase of a passage from the *Social Contract*, which is worth quoting because it reveals still more clearly that the problem lies in the tension between the system of language and the particular instance of discourse – *langue* and *parole*.

Why is the general will always right, and why do all citizens constantly desire the well-being of each, if it were not for the fact that no one exists who does not secretly appropriate the term *each* and think of himself when he votes for all ...? Which proves that the equality of right and the notion of justice that follows from it derive from the preference that each man gives to himself, and therefore from the nature of man. (Quoted in *Allegories* 269)

The aporia of the legal text, which de Man considers a paradigm for the figural dilemma of any text, emerges from the conflict of general and par-ticular will in the social contract and the impossibility of conceiving of the state as a metaphorical totalization of individuals. The expression of each person's individual will (the perspective of 'I') in terms of the collec-tive will (the perspective of 'we') is illegitimate, but it is also, given the structure of the state and especially of language, inevitable. 'The general will is by no means a synthesis of particular volitions,' de Man writes (*Allegories* 261) – a statement reminiscent of Benveniste's frequent con-tention that, on the grammatical level, 'we' is, strictly speaking, *not* a first-person plural because it cannot be conceived of as a plurality of 'I's ('"we" is not a multiplication of identical objects but a *junction* between

"I" and the "non-I," no matter what the content of this "non-I" may be'
[Benveniste 202]).

De Man argues that the identity of the individual and that of the state are
defined by two distinct semiotic models. This is a profoundly political
insight, despite de Man's insistence that he is purely interested in the textual implications ('We are not here concerned with the technically political
significance of this text ... Our reading merely tries to define the rhetorical
patterns that organize the distribution and the movement of the key terms
...' [*Allegories* 258]). But even as a principle of language de Man's insight is
political, at least in the wider sense of politics defined by Petrey as 'the sum
of the conventions that invariably make speech act' (*Speech Acts* 64). This
aspect emerges when the parallel with Benveniste is developed further.
Rousseau's, and de Man's, contention that each person will read or apply
the law in terms of his or her own subjectivity would be for Benveniste a
commonplace that derives from the nature of *langue*. The symmetry
between Rousseau's phrase 'secretly appropriate the term *each*' and Benveniste's claim that 'each speaker ... *appropriate[s] to himself* an entire language by designating himself as *I*' (226) reveals Rousseau's dilemma to be
another version of the scandal by which language constructs subjectivity
and yet pretends, as a system, to override the subjective. It is not surprising,
considering Benveniste's influence on Barthes, that de Man's argument is
also reminiscent of Barthes's reality effect. The instance of (historical) discourse, Barthes claims, inevitably creates a signified, and the temptation is
to elide the real-world referent with the signified so as to ('secretly'?) pretend that the discourse relates to the transcendental referent itself, while in
fact it relates only to the signified (or, in de Man's terms, the referent it has
constructed). In the present case, this means that the 'we' or 'collective "I" '
is a purely fictional signified generated by the social contract, though in
order to act on the contract we must elide the difference between the 'collective "I" ' and the real-world referent, a collection of individual 'I's.

The language that these critics and philosophers have in common
reveals that, whether the subject is real estate or the intellectual property of
visionary poets, the issues involved are ownership and power. The 'appropriation' of a grammatical or legal system by the individual, especially in
the French of Rousseau or Benveniste, indicates a concern with *le propre*,
with property and control. Having dismissed the political from his essay, de
Man finally allows it back in by using the *Social Contract* as a practical (i.e.,
performative) example of law-making in the concluding section of his
essay, ultimately describing it as the kind of textual allegory that 'generate[s] history' (*Allegories* 277). The *Social Contract*, in de Man's reading,

continues to promise political change even after it has deconstructed the validity of promising. The relevance of this example for the study of authority in visionary poetry is cemented by de Man's argument that the *Social Contract*, in making promises which depend on their own fulfilment, postulates a transcendent authority – God – as the metaphor of the law's origin, and thus casts the individual lawgiver as a usurper of divine voice. The writer's simultaneous assertion and usurpation of the divine authority that he postulates as the origin of his text brings about an unexpected resonance between de Man's reading of Rousseau and the readings of Milton and Blake in this book.

For thinkers as diverse as Benveniste and de Man, the performativity of language – the way it instantiates subjectivity, or the way it generates its own referent – disrupts the constative dimension of language as a suprasubjective structure. If this is a valid account of how language operates, what are the implications for poets who rely on subjectivity (both Milton and Blake emphasize the intrusion of 'I' into their discourse) and explicitly undertake the generation of a signified (both are attempting to create a world through language), but who also need to maintain contact between their language and the reader's world, and cannot ignore the stability and conviction that inheres in constative statement? My proposal throughout the readings that follow is that these conflicts come to the fore in the work of Milton and Blake when their inspired utterance, which idealizes truth and the transcendent authority of the divine or the imagination, confronts the discourse of institutions, which depends on the reality effect and derives its authority from societal convention. Different as these discourses appear, both hinge – in ways that may emerge as homologous – on the performative aspect of language. Therefore, the crucial stage of this encounter between theological and political discourses, manifested in the major epics of Milton and Blake, is the forging of a compromise between poetic utterance and societal pronouncement, to produce a visionary poetry which relies, sometimes uneasily, on a transcendent consciousness *and* a rhetoric determined by sociopolitical context. Milton writes with an awareness of the role of language in establishing economic and legal contracts in his increasingly bourgeois environment, while in Blake's work the conflict between inspired voice and the Austinian performative becomes the subject of ironic reflection. From the *Songs of Innocence and of Experience*, which contain a dark suspicion of the insidiousness of institutionally authorized language, to *The Marriage of Heaven and Hell*, which begins to articulate the different ways language can claim authority, to his epic attempts to turn performative utterance to his own advantage and reclaim a voice that will have the authority once granted to inspiration, Blake's work may be read as a struggle to maintain the validity of individual voice in an age when institutions, not individuals, have control over speech acts. Yet the instantiation of subjectivity in language remains a constant challenge, for the poets as well as for their readers. As Milton modifies the biblical narrative of creation by adding deictics and second-person address, Blake punctuates his mythologizing narratives with 'here' and 'now' and 'Mark well my words'; reminding us always of the subjectivity and contemporaneity of verbal utterance, both of them recall to us the ultimate origins of the discourse of history in all our imaginations.

2

Speech Acts and World-Creation

Die Bibel, indem sie sich selbst als Offenbarung betrachtet, muß notwendig die sprachlichen Grundtatsachen entwickeln.

Walter Benjamin

Supernatural Performatives

While taking into account the concern of some speech-act critics with the phenomenological dimension of poetic utterance, or the way poetry seems able to bring a world into being simply by positing it, the previous chapter located this concern within the context of a theory that regards the speech act primarily as a social construct. The present chapter begins at the other extreme, to delineate a model of performative language that may seem to have little in common with the Austinian speech act. This is the ideal performativity of divine language, epitomized in the Judeo-Christian tradition by God's act of speaking the universe into existence in the first chapter of Genesis. If the Bible as a whole is precisely concerned with the Word's entry into, its actions in and on, human society – a process which, I shall argue, begins as early as the *second* chapter of Genesis – it nevertheless opens with a model of performative utterance which pre-exists and transcends convention, operating instead as a pure expression of divine will. This ideal of a language which derives effectiveness from the consciousness of the subject and the intentionality of the utterance holds an irresistible fascination for both visionary poets and philosophers of language, often mastering their awareness that authority in human communication is dependent on power relations and the social contract.

John Searle makes room for the 'supernatural performative' in his taxonomy of illocutionary acts, in the extraordinary passage on declarations already alluded to in the previous chapter. Searle's definition of the declaration, and his normative examples, suggest that this category approximately corresponds to Austin's original intuition about what constitutes a performative. Like Austin's preliminary examples of performing a marriage, baptizing a ship, or making a will, Searle's declarations require 'a special position of the speaker and hearer' within 'such institutions as the church, the law, private property, [and] the state' (Searle, *Expression and Meaning* 18). His normative examples overlap with Austin's and include marrying, firing and resigning, appointing, excommunicating, christening a battleship, and declaring war. The declaration is the only one of Searle's five categories which does not involve a 'sincerity condition'; it contrasts, for instance, with the *assertive*, which expresses a psychological state of 'Belief,' or the *directive*, which expresses 'want (or wish or desire)' on the part of the speaker (*Expression and Meaning* 12–14). Therefore, the declaration is also the only one of Searle's illocutions which fully accords with Austin's original contention that an 'inward and spiritual act' is irrelevant to the existence of the performative, or that an illocutionary act is 'constituted not by intention or by fact, essentially but by *convention*' (*How to Do Things* 9, 128).

Yet the two exceptions with which Searle qualifies his definition fly in the face of Austinian theory. His examples of declarations which require no extra-linguistic institution are 'supernatural declarations,' such as 'Let there be light,' and metalinguistic declarations or 'declarations that concern language itself,' such as the giving of a definition or the bestowing of a name (*Expression and Meaning* 18). Sandy Petrey, for one, takes Searle to task for these exceptions, protesting that there is an unbridgeable dichotomy between Austin's speech acts, which function by virtue of a societal context, and God's speech acts, which function in the absence of society, convention, and even audience: 'divine beings are totally incapable of performative speech' since 'where God is, speech-act theory has nothing to say' (*Speech Acts* 63, 100). Petrey's distinction is valid and important, yet I am less content than he is with the conclusion that Searle's standard declarations and his exceptional cases are two categories of utterances that both do what they say, but 'have nothing else in common' (*Speech Acts* 63). Rather, I would like to pursue the fact that Searle's two exceptions correspond to those uses of language in the opening chapters of Genesis which have had the strongest influence on the history of philological thought: creation by the word, and acts of naming. Why does the Judeo-Christian account of human history begin with Searle's two non-institutional declarations – or, conversely, why does Searle feel the need to accommodate his theory of ordinary language so as to include the extraordinary cases of *fiat* and name-giving? How does this inclusion reflect on the standard declaration and its basis in societal institutions?

Genesis 1–3 in the Philosophy of Language

Searle is hardly alone among philosophers of language in looking to Genesis for instances of language use. Until the nineteenth century, while philology was still largely directed toward a study of the origin of language, the primary source for evidence of linguistic origins was Genesis 2:19–20, where Adam is given authority and ability by God to call each creature by its proper name:

And out of the ground the LORD God formed every beast of the field, and every fowl of the air; and brought them unto Adam to see what he would call them: and whatsoever Adam called every living creature, that was the name thereof.

And Adam gave names to all cattle, and to the fowl of the air, and to every beast of the field ...

The authority of Scripture gave rise to a belief in Adamic language, an original, motivated speech in which words expressed the essence of the things they named, but which was lost or corrupted either at the Fall or at the destruction of the Tower of Babel. In an overview of the history of the Adamic language hypothesis, Robert Essick traces the way serious appeals to the authority of Scripture degenerated, as early as the seventeenth century, into purely conventional citations of Genesis in the context of theories which were essentially secular in their analysis of mentalism, empiricism, and the arbitrary nature of signification (*William Blake* 40). Yet what is less often noted is that the fascination with Genesis survived the nineteenth-century evolution of philology into linguistics. If the biblical myth of creation began as sacred authority and lapsed into conventional allusion, it has become, perhaps involuntarily, a subtext and a well of imagery for modern linguistic and philosophical writing.

Since the nineteenth century, the philosophy of language has allowed the imagery of the Garden of Eden myth to infiltrate its account of language as social contract. In his argument about the contractual nature of language, the scandal of metaphor, and the primacy of lying in 'On Truth and Lying in an Extra-Moral Sense,' Nietzsche juxtaposes the imagery of Genesis with images from the sphere of economics. His characterization of truths as defaced currency, 'coins which have lost their image and now can be used only as metal, and no longer as coins' (*Friedrich Nietzsche* 250), is one of the most famous instances of the common nineteenth-century comparison of linguistic signification to the arbitrary value-system that currency represents. Using a similar metaphor, Coleridge contrasts the everyday use of words as 'the *arbitrary marks* of thought, our smooth market-coin of intercourse with the image and superscription worn out by currency' with the kind of language which expresses the essence of either the subject or the object (*Biographia* 2.122). Like John Searle, Coleridge prefers a language which expresses individual consciousness, rather than one governed purely by societal convention, and he holds fast to a language 'used allegorically to body forth the inward state of the person speaking.' Nevertheless, the prominence of the image of money, an image drawn from the realm of institutional facts rather than the brute facts of physical experience, reflects the nineteenth century's concern with conventional or arbitrary signification. The metaphor of a monetary system also serves Saussure as an illustration of the concept of linguistic value (*Course* 113–14), though his preferred image in the *Course in General Linguistics* is the game of chess, an image which in turn becomes characteristic of twentieth-century language philosophy through Wittgenstein and his account of language games. The paradigm shift from coins to games signals, among other things, a twentieth-century recognition that language does not operate according to a single contract but according to many sets of rules related by family resemblance.

Yet the influence of the philological tradition and its appeal to Genesis makes itself felt even in Nietzsche's revolutionary essay when he addresses the question 'What is a word?' and promptly lights on 'the tree' and 'serpent' as words which illustrate the metaphoricity inherent in the grammatical and semantic structure of language. The biblical allusion is conspicuous in the German text, where Nietzsche chooses the unusual phrase *Genesis der Sprache* to refer to the origin of language, instead of the standard *Ursprung der Sprache*, which appears in the title of Johann Gottfried Herder's essay of 1770, and indeed in Nietzsche's brief essay 'Vom Ursprung der Sprache,' written exactly a century later. Moreover, the repetition of the initial *ge-* in the clause which follows provides a kind of visual echo of Nietzsche's unusual diction:

Wie dürften wir, wenn die Wahrheit bei der *Genesis* der Sprache, der *Ge*sichtspunkt der *Ge*wissheit bei den Bezeichnungen allein entscheidend *ge*wesen wäre, wie dürften wir doch sagen: der Stein ist hart: als ob uns 'hart' noch sonst bekannt wäre und nicht nur als eine ganz subjektive Reizung! (*Werke* 3.2.372; my italics)

(What would allow us, if the truth about the origin of language, the viewpoint of the certainty of terms, were alone decisive, what would allow us to say, 'The stone is hard,' as if 'hard' were known to us otherwise than as a subjective stimulation!) (*Friedrich Nietzsche* 248)

The interference of rhetoric with semiology is complicated further if we admit a play between the German prefix *ge-* and the Greek word for 'earth' (*gē*). Thus, even as the sentence specifically denies the relationship of language to physical experience, the signs of a dead language evoke 'earth' within it, and even as it denies the validity of an essentialist account of naming which would attempt to establish the 'certainty of terms,' the passage is informed by images from the Genesis myth.

To read in this way is, of course, to resuscitate worn-out metaphors and restore the exchange value of the linguistic coin. Nietzsche's writing virtually demands that we do just that; while he attempts to demonstrate the arbitrariness involved in our assignation of gender to common nouns such as the 'masculine' tree (*der Baum*), and the bias inherent in our decision to refer to a winding motion in the name of the serpent (*die Schlange*) but not of the worm, the resonance of his examples tempts us to conclude that they are not arbitrary but deeply motivated. Tilottama Rajan has argued that, rather than dissociating language from truth, Nietzsche is actually acknowledging the effectiveness of metaphorical relations. His essay belongs in a tradition of language theory that 'valorize[s] metaphor as closer to the source(s) of things, because it disseminates and thus perpetually renews meaning' ('Displacing Post-Structuralism' 466). When Nietzsche writes explicitly on language in Genesis, he stresses its relational aspect. In 'On the Origin of Language,' he briefly but significantly comments on the fact that even the Old Testament, 'the only religious document with a myth about the origin of language, or something of the sort,' does not really address itself to linguistic origin (*Friedrich Nietzsche* 210). Rather, the existence of language is presupposed; both God and Adam use language to name things, thereby expressing the *relation* of those things to the human subject. 'Logisch geht es also jedenfalls nicht bei der Entstehung der Sprache zu,' Nietzsche concludes in 'On Truth and Lying' (*Werke* 3.2.373) – roughly translated, but with Nietzschean emphasis, '*logical* it ain't, in any case, the way language originates.' Depending on how much weight we give to the Greek and biblical roots of the word 'logical,' the sentence may disintegrate into either a paradox – the origin of language has nothing to do with *logoi* or words – or an ironic denial that the origin of words has anything to do with the divine Logos invoked by theories of the motivated sign. But if it denies logical connections, perhaps the sentence implicitly affirms metaphorical ones. The logic of Nietzsche's essay demonstrates how language falsifies our physical experience of the world, but its rhetoric reveals the irresistible influence of our mythological and literary experience, as expressed in a metaphorical tradition reaching back to the beginning of the Bible.

Saussure's *Course in General Linguistics* also sets out to demystify the relationship between language and experience, yet it too is strongly influenced by the language of the opening chapters of Genesis. Arguing for the arbitrariness of the linguistic sign, Saussure sets himself against those for whom 'language, reduced to its essentials, is a nomenclature: a list of terms corresponding to a list of things' (*Course* 65). The nomenclature model is the one that derives from the myth of Adamic naming, in which each name properly and adequately designates one created thing. Far from banishing the imagery of Genesis, however, Saussure seems to recall it when he chooses, as his primary examples of the linguistic sign, *equos* and *arbor* – an animal and a tree. As he substitutes for the nomenclature model his own model of the sign as a link between concept and sound-pattern, Saussure retains *arbor* as his main example. In other words, he co-opts the central images of the Garden of Eden myth, once the main evidence for a motivated language, to illustrate the arbitrariness of linguistic relations (e.g., 'Whether we are seeking the meaning of the Latin word *arbor* or the word by which Latin designates the concept "tree," it is clear that only the connexions institutionalised in the language appear to us as relevant' [*Course* 66–7]). In terms of its imagery at least, his theory puts itself forward as a reinterpretation of the linguistic implications of cosmogonic myth.

If the tree in Saussure's *Course* illustrates the distinction between signifier and signified in the linguistic sign, in Kenneth Burke's philosophy of language it functions as a marker of difference on other levels of the linguistic system. In *The Rhetoric of Religion*, the tree is Burke's habitual image when he distinguishes between word and thing ('the word "tree" is *not* a tree' [283]) and between literal and metaphorical levels of meaning (8–9, 254). It provides the focus for his contrast between the world of 'sensory images' and that of 'mythic images,' a distinction which approximately corresponds to Searle's opposition of brute and institutional facts. For transformational grammarians, even the use of 'tree diagrams' – in French simply *arbres* – might be regarded as a subtle instance of the symbol's pervasiveness. In a theological context, finally, Martin Buber makes the tree an image which speaks of the dissociation of subject and object, or the lapse from an 'I-Thou' to an 'I-It' relationship between the human subject and the environment:

But whenever the sentence 'I see the tree' is so uttered that it no longer tells of a relation between the man – *I* – and the tree –*Thou* –, but establishes the perception of the tree as object by the human consciousness, the barrier between subject and object has been set up. The primary word *I-It*, the word of separation, has been spoken. (Buber 23)

The reappearance of the tree as a primary image for the differential functioning of language and consciousness, in writers as diverse as Nietzsche, Saussure, Buber, and Burke, seems to point toward linguistic undercurrents in the second and third chapters of Genesis. The tree is the first example of a marked sign that Judeo-Christian mythology offers, the first object to be set apart from others of the same kind by purely institutional standards. This is a corollary of the fact that the second chapter of Genesis introduces, in the divine prohibition and the consequent curse, the Bible's first examples of the sociopolitical speech act. Thus the speech act which differentiates the tree also marks the site of a significant distinction between the Garden of Eden narrative in Genesis 2–3, which is known to biblical scholars as the Jahwist or 'J' text, and the Priestly or 'P' myth of creation in Genesis 1. While performative speech is a central component of both myths, they illustrate two different kinds of performativity, both of which have important implications for visionary poetry.

Phenomenological Performatives: The 'P' Myth

Without referring specifically to speech-act theory, Kenneth Burke has analysed the significance of Genesis 1 for linguistic philosophy. His work makes explicit what is often implicit in poetic texts which allude to the creation narrative: that the belief that words can be instruments of meaningful action is nowhere more forcefully imaged than in a myth in which a deity creates the world through acts of speech.[1] Philosophically, the 'P' myth also shares some of the central concerns of transcendental phenomenology, in ways that may be illuminated by Derrida's reading of Husserl. In

---

1 My reading of the first three chapters of Genesis is in sympathy with Burke's (in *The Rhetoric of Religion* and part 1, chapter 3 of *A Grammar of Motives*) insofar as we both treat the myth as a logical paradigm, though for Burke it is a paradigm of the Christian schema of sacrifice and redemption and for human action in general, while I address its implications for inspiration and poetic creation. I am also more concerned than Burke with the rhetorical dimension of the text and with distinctions between the diction of the 'P' and 'J' accounts, especially in the Authorized Version, which resonates in English visionary literature from the seventeenth century onward.

Speech and Phenomena, Derrida explores the basis for and the potency of phonocentrism as exemplified in the moment of *s'entendre parler*, the ability to simultaneously utter, hear, and understand one's own speech. 'Hearing-oneself-speak' appears to tether voice to its origin, to make spoken language inseparable from presence, intention, and consciousness. But precisely because this kind of auto-affection seems to transcend the difference between interiority and exteriority, allowing the subject to experience his or her own utterance without passing through the sphere of the other, it also conceptualizes that difference:

... the unity of sound and voice, which allows the voice to be produced in the world as pure auto-affection, is the sole case to escape the distinction between what is worldly and what is transcendental; by the same token, it makes that distinction possible. (Derrida, *Speech and Phenomena* 79)

When we apply Derrida's account of the metaphysics of presence to the domain of cosmogonic myth, as he himself appears on the verge of doing in *Of Grammatology*, spoken language appears as the ideal medium for conceptualizing the idea of world-origin:

The system of 'hearing (understanding)-oneself-speak' through the phonic substance – which *presents itself* as the nonexterior, nonmundane, therefore nonempirical or noncontingent signifier – has necessarily dominated the history of the world during an entire epoch, and has even produced the idea of the world, the idea of world-origin, that arises from the difference between the worldly and the nonworldly, the outside and the inside, ideality and nonideality, universal and nonuniversal, transcendental and empirical, etc. (*Of Grammatology* 7–8)

The privileged status of voice in both the 'P' myth of creation and Husserl's phenomenology suggests a parallel between Husserl's account of speech as the speaker's expression of a meaning-intention, and the concept of God which lies behind the performative utterances of Genesis 1. Derrida's account of the way expression necessarily introduces a distinction between exteriority and interiority corresponds, in turn, to the way divine utterance in 'P' brings about the distinction between an originary consciousness and a material creation.

The undecidability that Derrida describes reappears in the New Testament's counterpart to the opening chapters of Genesis, the beginning of the Gospel of John. Its paradoxical formulation seems to hover between establishing and transcending the opposition of interiority and exteriority, as it affirms that the Word both *is with* God and *is* God. The ambiguity has obvious significance for the theological doctrine of the Trinity, but it may also speak to the phenomenological concern with consciousness and expression:

In the beginning was the Word, and the Word was with God, and the Word was God. The same was in the beginning with God. (John 1:1–2)

As a phenomenon inseparable from the being of God (by analogy with the *s'entendre parler* that characterizes human speech), God's spoken word assures the presence of God as origin. At the same time, the external dimension of speech as sound or material signifier is, in the case of the divine utterance, accorded an ultimate exteriority as world – that which stands over against God, hears him as other, and responds to his words. The cohesion of interiority and exteriority in the concept of creation by the word is constantly threatening to break apart, as illustrated by John 1:1–2 or, even more strikingly, by Faust's infamous translation of the Gospel of John in Goethe's drama:

It says: 'In the beginning was the *Word*.'
Already I am stopped. It seems absurd.
The *Word* does not deserve the highest prize,
I must translate it otherwise
If I am well inspired and not blind.
It says: In the beginning was the *Mind*.
Ponder that first line, wait and see,
Lest you should write too hastily.
Is mind the all-creating source?
It ought to say: In the beginning there was *Force*.
Yet something warns me as I grasp the pen,
That my translation must be changed again.
The spirit helps me. Now it is exact.
I write: In the beginning was the *Act*.

(Goethe 40)

Unwilling to locate originary power in the 'word,' Faust rejects the intrinsic notion of 'mind' (*Sinn*) in favour of increasingly outward-directed faculties and concepts, 'force' (*Kraft*) and 'act' (*Tat*). Fittingly, Faust's soliloquy coincides with the emergence of the principle of negation in an externalized and material form, as Mephistopheles, who first appears to Faust in this scene. In a less diabolical but equally revealing vein, the very term 'utterance,' which we are tempted to use synonymously with 'speech,' privileges and enshrines the metaphor of exteriority or 'outerance' in hearing-oneself-speak.

If we now draw the internal-external opposition into a more strictly rhetorical frame of reference, we may identify two contrasting aspects in the language of the 'P' and 'J' creation myths, which I will call the intransitive and transitive aspects. The *intransitive* aspect manifests itself when language concentrates on and tries to maintain a certain interiority; ignoring external reference, it sets up a self-reliant or self-reflexive standard of truth. This intransitive quality may be a feature of divine utterance, when it derives power from the intrinsic consciousness or intentionality of the speaker and creates things from nothing, or it may appear on the level of the narrative itself, as a proclamatory or kerygmatic mode of expression. If, by analogy with Derrida's deconstruction of Husserl, the acknowledgment of exteriority and difference is inevitable, the intransitive narrative nevertheless maintains an emphasis on the self-sufficiency of the speaking consciousness and of performative language.

On the other hand, language may be oriented toward exteriority and objectivity, and cosmogony may be conceived of as a process of ordering elements which already exist apart from the creator. Cosmogonic narrative may be termed *transitive* when its primary reference is to existing objects which must be named, marked, organized, or differentiated from one another. Because the transitive text refers to an existing world, hearers or readers may test its validity against their own experience; the narrative thus assumes a constative dimension, in that it admits the criterion of truth and falsity. All of these ways in which language can effect or affect empirical phenomena are relevant to the biblical myths of creation, and their relative significance to the two different traditions that make up the creation account in Genesis helps to characterize the conflicted paradigm of performative language that this narrative provides.

In the 'P' account, which appears in Genesis 1:1–2:4a, the intransitive dimension dominates both on the level of God's language and on the level of the narrative itself. Employing speech acts that do not depend on any agent or object apart from the voice and its origin, God speaks entities into being: 'Let there be light' (1:3); 'Let there be a firmament in the midst of the waters' (1:6); 'Let there be lights in the firmament of the heaven' (1:14). The 'P' narrative is characterized by ritualistic language that makes abundant use of numerology, parallelism, and refrains, yet at the core of this cultural and religious formalism lies a vision of language which can create things from nothing so that the resulting world is coexistent and perfectly correspondent with the words. It is a kind of performativity that operates in the utter absence of society or convention, relying solely on the intentionality of the Elohim's utterance.

This intransitive quality is reflected on the level of narration, since 'P' never evades the self-consciousness of being a verbal account of a cosmogony that is effected through the use of words. The narrative presents itself as the absolute emergence of world and text, in a manner that is only approximately conveyed by the opening words of the Authorized Version, 'In the beginning.' The first word of the Hebrew text, $b^e reshith$, cannot be satisfactorily translated in its context, but the likeliest translations yield the sense that origination itself is being defined here.[2] What is being evoked is not 'a' beginning or 'the' beginning, but rather the very activity, 'beginning' (Josipovici 67). There is nothing before the word 'beginning,' but by the end of the account there exists a highly ordered *something* which has been brought into existence by the effect of language on the imagination of the reader or listener. As Gabriel Josipovici puts it, 'the world which those opening words bring into being is not just the world of the book, but (so it is asserted) the very world in which we who are reading the book exist' (61). Instead of concerning itself with empirically verifiable statements, the 'P' narrative declares *how* origins may be conceptualized and commemorated. It belongs to the mode that Jean-François Lyotard identifies as 'narrative knowledge,' a discourse which, unlike modern scientific knowledge, is not subject to argumentation or proof but contains its own legitimation independently of any assertion of authority on the part of either the narrator or the hero of the narrative (*Postmodern Condition* 18–27). Qualities that Lyotard identifies as distinguishing features of narrative knowledge – including a rhythmic, repetitive sense of time which lends itself to ritual

---

2 $B^e reshith$ may either be an absolute form of the noun 'beginning' preceded by a preposition but without a definite article (i.e., 'in beginning'), or a construct form with adverbial function, in which case the definite article would normally be omitted (i.e., 'in-[the]-beginning-of'). The two possible translations, especially when combined with the indicative verb which follows (*bara*, 'created'), yield two equally unsatisfactory versions of the main clause in Genesis 1:1–3: respectively, 'In beginning God created ...' and 'In the beginning of God's creating the heaven and the earth ... God created ...' For detailed discussion of the opening words of the Bible and their significance for the concept of origin, see Eichrodt, Josipovici (53–64), and Andrew Martin (2–4).

The absolute character of this beginning to both world and book is intensified by the fact that $b^e reshith$ is also the title 'Genesis,' the first word of the text having been adopted as the name of the book. It is also worth noting that the opening of the Gospel of John, *en archē*, 'in beginning,' corresponds exactly to the opening of Genesis with regard to the omission of the article (and the resulting difficulty of translation).

performance, and the presence of a variety of speech acts in addition to simple denotation – are especially conspicuous in Genesis 1.

If the bold 'Let there be light; and there was light' is the paradigmatic example of divinely creative language, this paradigm might seem to be watered down in all the subsequent acts of creation. Later in Genesis 1, the immediacy of divine utterance seems compromised by the supplemental statement that 'God made' the firmament, the heavenly bodies, and the rest, after issuing his declarative statements. Yet the text reflects a constant faith in the immediate effectiveness of divine utterance by adding the formula 'and it was so' after the divine *fiat* in all but one of the remaining creative acts:

And God said, Let the earth bring forth the living creature after his kind, cattle, and creeping thing, and beast of the earth after his kind: *and it was so.*

And God made the beast of the earth after his kind ... (Genesis 1:24–5; my italics)[3]

Conversely, not all of God's utterances in Genesis 1 are performatives on the model of 'Let there be light.' His other speech acts, the naming and blessing of created entities, are more transitive or object-directed. By the third day of creation, the divine utterances include imperatives that reorder or realign elements which already exist separately from the Elohim: 'Let the earth bring forth grass' (1:11); 'Let the waters bring forth abundantly the moving creature that hath life' (1:20). This outward-directed utterance, which Searle would call a 'directive,' is most evident at the end of the chapter, where God blesses and instructs the newly-created human beings ('Be fruitful, and multiply' [1:28]). Yet it is significant that the narrative still makes do with the divine utterances themselves. No response on the part of an audience is necessary; indeed, the presence of auditors is never explicitly taken account of. It is assumed that the divine utterances alone are sufficient to consolidate and perpetuate the world-order that is brought into existence by the Elohim's creative acts.

Similarly, God's acts of naming in Genesis 1 are less referential than

3 It has been suggested that the 'And God made' clauses (1:7a, 12a, 16a, 17a, 18a, 21) are vestiges of an earlier myth which portrayed God as a physical creator, or else the later additions of an editor who felt the need for increased anthropomorphism in the account of creation (*Interpreter's Bible* 1:472). Although this atomistic approach to the text, which identifies different strands within the 'P' narrative, is now being questioned, the idea of slippage between creation by the word and physical making provides an interesting parallel to Faust's compulsion to render 'word' as 'act.' The same atomistic approach allows for the hypothesis that 'and it was so' originally followed the *fiat* in the remaining case as well (i.e., the second day, vv. 6–9), as it in fact does in the Septuagint.

they may seem. The verb translated as 'name' in the 'P' text (*kara*) might be more accurately rendered 'call out' or 'proclaim': the narrative portrays God as announcing the names of things, rather than referring to them by their names (Josipovici 64). Moreover, God's naming of the created elements establishes a difference between them which is conceived of in spatial terms – perhaps as an extension of the primary distinction between interiority and exteriority which expression itself creates. When the God of Genesis 1 distinguishes between day and night or land and sea, he establishes a type of difference in which opposites are assigned their proper places *as contraries*, but one is not defined in terms of, or as the *negation* of, the other (i.e., darkness is 'darkness' rather than 'not-light,' and vice versa). It is true that only the light (i.e., only the entity explicitly created by God) is affirmed as good; nevertheless, the Authorized Version overstates the subordination of darkness to light when it speaks of God dividing 'the light from the darkness' and 'the day from the night' as if light and day were privileged terms. The Hebrew has God dividing, in a parallel construction which specifically indicates parity rather than subordination, 'between the light and between the darkness,' 'between the day and between the night' (Genesis 1:4, 14; Greenstein 66). Each member of a pair of terms complements the other, as established in the chapter's ritual refrain, according to which the evening and the morning together make up a unit of time.

Thus, even when the 'P' account admits a more transitive kind of language, it does so in a way that maintains the centrality of an intrinsically authoritative speaking consciousness. Difference is not value-laden in this myth, nor does the effectiveness of performative utterance ever depend on communal acknowledgment of the speaker's authority or the legitimacy of the speech act. The Elohim's utterances are non-Austinian performatives in that their success is a function of the inherent and absolute authority of the speaker, not of societal convention. The distinguishing feature of the 'P' myth of creation is the projection of an ideally effective voice, whose affinities with spirit, will, and consciousness are affirmed again in the cosmogonic Psalm 33: 'By the word of the LORD were the heavens made; and all the host of them by the breath of his mouth ... For he spake, and it was done; he commanded, and it stood fast' (vv. 6, 9).

Sociopolitical Performatives: The 'J' Myth

A duality in the notion of verbal performance emerges when 'P' is contrasted with the 'J' narrative in Genesis 2:4b–3:24. The 'J' myth has a clear orientation toward communal order and concerns itself throughout with the establishment of the first man's relationships to animals, to woman, and to God. Accordingly, 'J' recognizes a second type of performative utterance, one which involves referential and contractual language and institutes a new order among already existing elements. This performative corresponds, moreover, to a second type of difference, the arbitrarily established binary opposition in which two terms, one marked and the other unmarked, inevitably fall into a hierarchical order. In contrast to 'Let there be light,' the prototype of the speech act in 'J' is Yahweh's command to the man in Genesis 2:16–17 not to eat of the tree of the knowledge of good and evil:

And the LORD God commanded the man, saying, Of every tree of the garden thou mayest freely eat: But of the tree of the knowledge of good and evil, thou shalt not eat of it: for in the day that thou eatest thereof thou shalt surely die.

The utterance immediately marks one tree off as different, not in the sense in which the opposed but complementary elements of Genesis 1 are physically distinguished from one another, but as an institutional fact established by Yahweh's utterance. The woman, trying to erase the difference that the divine utterance has made, reveals the tree's empirical likeness to the rest of the garden when she describes it (in Genesis 3:6) as 'good for food' and 'pleasant to the eyes,' just like all the other good and pleasant trees that Yahweh causes to grow in Genesis 2:9. Nevertheless, Yahweh's speech act marks it as a 'Tree, of many, one' – like that tree in the 'Intimations' ode which abruptly recalls to Wordsworth the loss of glory from the earth (187). The effectiveness of the prohibition in distinguishing the tree, linguistically as well as legally, is brought home by the fact that it is virtually always referred to by Yahweh as 'the tree, whereof I commanded thee that thou shouldest not eat' – rather than as 'the tree of the knowledge of good and evil' or 'the tree which is in the midst of the garden,' either of which would serve to identify it as well. If the speech acts of Genesis 1 are analogous to the *s'entendre parler* of pheonomenology, the corresponding twentieth-century parallel for Yahweh's speech act is Saussure's definition of the linguistic sign as determined purely by difference and not by positive terms. The prohibition effectively makes the tree into a sign whose 'most precise characteristic is in being what the others are not' (*Course* 117).

A specific contrast between the characteristic speech acts of the 'J' and 'P' myths emerges when Yahweh's prohibition is compared with the institution of the Sabbath in Genesis 2:2–3. At first glance, both might seem to be utterances which arbitrarily mark one day or one tree as different, solely because an authoritative speaker has declared it to be so. Yet it is significant that the origin of the Sabbath coincides with its formal establishment. Having reached the seventh day in narrative time, the 'P' account relates that God ended his work and that he 'blessed the seventh day, and sanctified it: *because* that in it he had rested from all his work' (Genesis 2:3, my italics). The proclamation and blessing of the Sabbath is an intrinsic aspect of the origin of the day itself, brought about simultaneously through God's action (or rather, his cessation from action). By contrast, the trees in the garden already exist at the point when Yahweh marks one of them as different in its relation to the hearer of his utterance.

Yahweh's speech act functions like a law or a constitution in the way it circumscribes behaviour by means of authoritative language, rendering future conduct (the eating of the tree) unlawful which would otherwise have been harmless.[4] In this regard, it is entirely appropriate that this chapter should refer to the deity by the divine name 'YHWH Elohim.' YHWH, the ritually and phonetically unpronounceable name of God, is replaced in reading or recitation with the euphemism 'Adonai' and translated in the Authorized Version as 'LORD God,' a title which, in both Hebrew and English, carries connotations of social status and political authority. The 'J' account is informed by a consciousness of power relationships on the part of the writer and the characters themselves. The woman is tempted by the idea that she and her husband might be 'as gods,' and it is when Yahweh realizes that 'the man is become as one of us' that he banishes him from the garden and the tree of life lest the threat to the heavenly host become a permanent one. In this context, it is not surprising that language in 'J' reflects a political dimension that is absent from 'P.'

Kenneth Burke derives from the 'J' creation myth another hierarchical opposition which is, for him, one of the defining characteristics of human action. This is the principle of negation, which for Burke takes its definitive form, not as the constative 'is not,' but rather as 'shall not.' In the terms outlined in the previous chapter, 'shall not' is performative because it constitutes an explicit directive and because, as a second-person verb form, it is context-dependent, challenging the hearer or reader to fill the place of the elided 'you.' Burke's principle of negativity becomes the foundation of social organization since it underlies the distinction between 'mine' and 'thine' (i.e., we

---

4 Cf. Westermann: 'There are three basic ways in which man's conduct in community can be limited: by the taboo, the command (or prohibition), and the law. Each of these three is institutionally conditioned: the taboo is pre-personal, the command is personal, the law is post-personal' (*Creation* 91). Westermann's interpretation differs from my own in that he distinguishes between prohibition and law whereas I am concerned to demonstrate how they function analogously as speech acts. Nevertheless, his theological commentary supports my argument about the sociopolitical role of the performative in the 'J' myth.

understand 'mine' to mean 'not thine'). He describes the distinction as one which is discovered by means of language, but also forms the basis for a host of verbal formulations – 'laws, deeds, contracts, precepts, prison sentences, educational policies, businesses, revolutions, religions, etc., etc.' (*Rhetoric of Religion* 285) – all of which Austin would identify as explicit performatives and the societal institutions that public speech acts sustain. The 'mine-thine' distinction, which Burke also translates into the performative 'No trespassing,' is precisely what Yahweh institutes when he distinguishes the one tree which is his from the rest of the trees, which he presents to the man. Interpreting the 'J' myth in terms of the distinction between the deictics 'mine' and 'thine' also reveals a parallel with Benveniste, for whom the instantiation of subjectivity as marked by deictics is fundamental to linguistic performativity, and indeed to every communicative act.

All of this points to the recognition that the 'J' account introduces a type of speech act and a type of difference which are intrinsic to the use of language in ordinary interpersonal relations. The myth focuses on differences which attract cultural bias, differences to which society adds the designations positive and negative, accepted and taboo: such is the difference between male and female, clothed and naked, perhaps even (in a Nietzschean vein) good and evil. 'Good' in 'P' is the unconditioned and unfocused approbation of the refrain, 'and God saw that it was good,' but in 'J,' 'good' has become one half of Milton's 'two twins cleaving together,' a thing that cannot be known without knowing evil (*CPW* 2:514). A host of other speech acts defined by societal convention and power relationships feature prominently in the myth, the most significant being the curse and the bestowing of names. The effect of Yahweh's sentence on those who disobey his command is to separate the serpent out from other beasts ('thou art cursed above all cattle, and above every beast of the field' [Genesis 3:14]) in much the same manner as the tree was separated out from other trees, and to establish domination and subordination as the characteristic terms of relationships between the sexes and between the serpent and humankind. The curse itself is a type of speech act which must be understood in Austinian terms, insofar as a curse cannot exist unless there is a recognized formula for cursing or at least until cursing is acknowledged by a collectivity as a possible act.[5] The conventional quality of this speech act demonstrates in turn the extent to which the myth is directed toward a community of hearers or readers which is, so to speak, in a better

5 Compare Austin's discussion of insulting, which is recognized as a conventional procedure in virtually all societies although the expression 'I insult you,' except in certain very specialized contexts, will not do as a way of invoking the convention (*How to Do Things* 30–1).

position to understand the significance of God's curse than are Adam and Eve. It is this community, rather than the first human beings, which recognizes precedents and established formulas for speech acts like prohibiting, cursing, and naming.

As an etiological myth which accounts for suffering in human existence and inequality in relationships, 'J' is transitive in yet another sense. Regardless of whether a particular audience accepts the myth's explanation, the *logic* of the etiological narrative appeals to the audience's own experience. The narrative asks us to recognize experiential truths (that childbirth is painful or that tilling the soil is hard work) and then to accept the explanation that it offers for them. Without implying that 'J' is in any sense proto-science, we might conclude that the myth approaches Lyotard's definition of 'scientific knowledge' insofar as it appeals to, or at least allows for, empirical verification. A heuristic classification of the different kinds of performative language in the opening chapters of Genesis might then be proposed:

	Intransitive	Transitive
Divine Utterance	'Let there be light'	'Thou shalt not eat of it'
Narrative Language	narrative knowledge, proclamation	scientific knowledge, constation

The ritualistic 'P' myth, lacking an obvious awareness of speaker, addressee, or scene of discourse, contains its legitimation within itself, just as the deity who declares, 'Let there be light,' does so on the basis of an inherent, non-conventional, non-consensual type of authority. By contrast, the 'J' myth is informed by the operation of sociopolitical performative language, which it projects back onto a story about the beginnings of social order. 'J' is transitive insofar as it appeals, ultimately, to the truth of the reader's or hearer's experience, and the divine speech acts in the story are similarly transitive inasmuch as they operate in and on a social context.

Scenes of Creation in Philosophy and Literature

As for Searle's taxonomy of speech acts, it may now be possible to identify the motivation behind his attempt to ally 'Let there be light' with the institutionally authorized declaration. The fusing of the 'P' and 'J' traditions in Genesis constitutes a similar conjunction of societally dependent speech acts with performative utterances that depend on divine will alone. Just as the writer of 'P' needs to posit an originary voice, so Searle's appeal to the creative *fiat* in Genesis may be interpreted as the desire for an effectual language grounded in the will and personal consciousness of the speaker. The dependence of Searle's speech-act theory on the category of intention fits with this desire. His theory of speech acts is, among other things, an attempt to integrate the divergent movements in the philosophy of language which concentrate on the use and the meaning of expressions, and the speaker's intention (meaning) is a major component of Searle's definition of illocutionary force (use):

In the performance of an illocutionary act in the literal utterance of a sentence, the speaker intends to produce a certain effect by means of getting the hearer to recognize his intention to produce that effect; and furthermore, if he is using words literally, he intends this recognition to be achieved in virtue of the fact that the rules for using the expressions he utters associate the expression with the production of that effect. (*Speech Acts* 45)

While he regards conventions or constitutive rules as the basis of illocutionary acts, Searle also restores individual intention to a central place in the definition of the performative – perhaps as a defensive response to the mounting evidence in speech-act linguistics that language is in large measure the reflection and the basis of a communal economy. His attempt to incorporate 'Let there be light,' and to admit the ability of speakers to perform the speech act of naming or designating without the sanction of an extra-linguistic institution, challenges both Austin's reliance on societal convention and Saussure's repeated insistence that no individual can alter the language system, certainly not by private volition. Yet Searle's move is also an attempt to reassert the possibility of meaning, perhaps even the integrity of the self, a move that might be translated into a version of the Cartesian *cogito*: 'I declare, therefore I am.'

The same desire for the expression and effectiveness of the individual will is what I believe motivates the subtext of allusions to biblical creation which often informs visionary poetry. The paradigm of creation by the word frequently surfaces in passages which, on another level, seem to be evoking the societally dependent performative. Thus, scenes of creation in visionary literature often intensify the conflicted nature of the performative which has emerged from the Genesis account.

Coleridge's 'Kubla Khan,' for instance, implies (if it does not develop) a parallel between Kubla Khan's creation of a physical paradise and the poet's spiritual or artistic recreation of that paradise. It is less often noted that Kubla's creative act is also a revision of biblical creation. Gardens, trees, rivers, and sea figure as prominently in the poem as they do in the opening chapters of Genesis, and Kubla's pleasure-dome mimics the dome-shaped firmament of Hebrew cosmology:

> In Xanadu did Kubla Khan
> A stately pleasure-dome decree:
> Where Alph, the sacred river, ran
> Through caverns measureless to man
>   Down to a sunless sea.
> So twice five miles of fertile ground
> With walls and towers were girdled round:
> And there were gardens bright with sinuous rills,
> Where blossomed many an incense-bearing tree;
> And here were forests ancient as the hills,
> Enfolding sunny spots of greenery.   (*Complete Poetical Works* 1:297)

The final strophe of Coleridge's poem imagines an origin for the world-dome which echoes biblical origins, as the unearthly poet, like the Elohim in Genesis 1, builds 'in air' by the power of his voice:

> Could I revive within me
> Her symphony and song,
>   To such a deep delight 'twould win me,
> That with music loud and long,
> I would build that dome in air

But the dome initially owes its existence to Kubla, whose performative utterance is a 'decree' authorized by his position as Khan. If it is possible to hear an ironic echo of 'In the beginning God created' behind 'In Xanadu did Kubla Khan / A stately pleasure-dome decree,' it is also necessary to distinguish the immediate effectiveness of God's utterance from the effectiveness of Kubla's, which the poem represents as equally immediate but which we realize is dependent on the labour of unseen gardeners and stonemasons who are compelled by an imperial proclamation.

'Kubla Khan' celebrates the role of language in creation, but its subtext is an awareness that language creates by circumscribing and delimiting an object, just as Kubla's encompassing walls and towers enclose a measured plot of the measureless landscape. In his description of the pleasure-garden, Coleridge brings out latent connotations of ordering and limitation in the etymology of the word 'paradise,' which derives from a Persian word meaning 'orchard.' Moreover, the space Kubla Khan defines for himself is one from which, amid the sounds of a sublime landscape, he hears a language of political strife: 'Ancestral voices prophesying war.' If the text implies an analogy – or a contest – between Kubla Khan's imperialistic creation and the Poet's expressive re-creation, perhaps it is significant that the politically charged appellation 'Kubla Khan' has imposed itself as the title of the poem. Only the subtitle ('A Vision in a Dream') indicates that the text also constitutes what Coleridge elsewhere described as a repetition of divine creation in the finite mind: an imaginative vision.

The uneasy relationship of poetic expression and political speech act – the dark side, as it were, of Shelley's contention that poets are the unacknowledged legislators of the world – is also a subject of Friedrich Hölderlin's allegorical lyric 'Nature and Art, or Saturn and Jupiter.' Jupiter, the representative of Art, is simultaneously acknowledged and condemned in this poem as the force which gives laws, apportions lots, and exerts verbal authority over the world while his deposed father, who was once greater than Jupiter although he never pronounced commands or required a title ('wenn schon / Er kein Gebot aussprach und ihn der / Sterblichen keiner mit Nahmen nannte' [*Sämtliche Werke* 2:37]), laments inarticulately and unnamed in the abyss:

> down the abyss you hurled
> The holy father once, your own parent, who
> Long now has lain lamenting where the
> Wild ones before you more justly languish,
>
> Quite guiltless he, the god of the golden age:
> Once effortless and greater than you, although
> He uttered no commandment, and no
> Mortal on earth ever named his presence.   (*Poems and Fragments* 165)

The poem ends by expressing an affinity between Jupiter and the human poet, two sons of time whose utterance is both politically charged ('welcher ... Geseze giebt') and supernaturally prophetic ('und, was die / Heilige Dämmerung birgt, verkündet' [*Sämtliche Werke* 2:38]):

> I'll know you then, Kronion, and hear you then,
> The one wise master who, like ourselves, a son
> Of Time, gives laws to us, uncovers

> That which lies hidden in holy twilight.   (*Poems and Fragments* 167)

If the poem is primarily a late contribution to the eighteenth-century art-and-nature debate, its association of Art with a figure of political tyranny also betrays Hölderlin's anxiety over the sources and limits of verbal authority. Like Blake's myth of the degeneration of the creative language of ancient Poets into the pronouncements of Priesthood (to be discussed in a later chapter), 'Nature and Art' requires us to recall the common origin of politically effective language and of artistic expression in an inarticulate natural world.

If the disjunction between the creative word and the political pronouncement is a source of anxiety for the Romantics, it is a still more urgent issue for a twentieth-century writer like Hermann Broch, whose own experience as an exile from Nazi Germany renders him hypersensitive to the political power of utterance. Broch's novelistic epic *The Death of Virgil* is an extreme and magisterial response to the artist's anxiety over the role of performative language in enacting political, or at least societally determined, authority. The novel chronicles the final hours of Virgil's life, which are, for Broch, an allegory of the perils of the *epos* (both word and epic) in the Western history of empire. The dying Virgil must learn to let go of his position as the poet of imperial Rome; most of the novel charts his growing awareness of the way language collaborates with imperialism, both in the declarations of his friend Octavian when he speaks in his official persona as Caesar Augustus, and in Virgil's own literary production inasmuch as it justifies the ways of empire.

For an elucidation of the role of the performative in Genesis, the most significant aspect of *The Death of Virgil* is the novel's climax: a rewriting of the scene of creation in which Broch attempts to transcend the disjunction between the two types of performative language. In the final chapter of the novel, Virgil's death is described from his own perspective as a vision of being borne away across the water. Among the vestiges of his earthly life that he leaves behind are names, particularly names which wield political authority. Caesar Augustus lays aside his power along with his names ('seine Macht entglitt ihm, sie entglitt ihm mit dem Namen, mit all den Namen, die er bisher getragen und die er allesamt ... jetzt abtun mußte' [*Kommentierte Werkausgabe* 4:416]), and the boy Lysanias, before losing his identity altogether, loses the politically charged name of 'Führer' by which Virgil has known him ('kaum mehr ein Führer, nur noch ein Weisender' [*Kommentierte Werkausgabe* 4:425]). The dissolution of socio-political authority is accompanied by the dissolution of the logical foundations of language, including the division between subject and object on which both perception and signification had rested and, significantly, the division between external appearance and internal essence ('die Verwandlung des Außen ins Innen ... die Einswerdung von Außengesicht und Innengesicht' [*Kommentierte Werkausgabe* 4:417]).

The conclusion of *The Death of Virgil* represents Broch's attempt to transcend not only the politicization of language which has marred Virgil's literary efforts and his own, but even the division between interiority and exteriority that seems to mark all utterance. After witnessing the dissolution of the world in the reverse order of its creation, from animals to plants to stars to earth to light itself, Virgil participates in an eternal re-creation which centres on the vision of an ideally performative word:

... hervorbrechend als das reine Wort, das es war, erhaben über alle Verständigung und Bedeutung, endgültig und beginnend, gewaltig und befehlend, furchteinflößend und beschützend, hold und donnernd, das Wort der Unterscheidung, das Wort des Eides, das reine Wort ... (*Kommentierte Werkausgabe* 4:453–4)

(... breaking forth as a communication beyond every understanding, breaking forth as a significance above every comprehension, breaking forth as the pure word which it was, exalted above all understanding and significance whatsoever, consummating and initiating, mighty and commanding, fear-inspiring and protecting, gracious and thundering, the word of discrimination, the word of the pledge, the pure word ...) (*Death of Virgil* 481)

The word which is absolutely pure and unified and yet remains, like the utterance of Yahweh, a 'word of discrimination,' is one that Virgil, and Broch, can only imagine 'jenseits der Sprache,' beyond language; and the unity of interiority and exteriority is purchased at the cost of denying the utterability of the word, at least for the poet: 'unaussprechbar war es für ihn' (*Kommentierte Werkausgabe* 4:454). Even if Broch's mystical vision is successful, it would seem to confirm that the language of creation as we know it is inextricably bound up with difference, delimitation, and power.

The Death of Virgil bears witness to the concern that Broch feels for the potentially destructive force that language can represent in the social order and for the collaboration of art with this force. But the novel also reveals his ultimately Romantic allegiance (shared, perhaps unconsciously, by philosophers of language) to the creative power of cosmogonic myth: 'Aller Mythos gipfelt in Kosmogonie: er ist das Ur-Bild des Aussagbaren, primitiv, dennoch unerreichbar an Einfachheit' ('All myth culminates in cosmogony:

it is the prototype of the expressible, primitive, yet unrivalled in its simplicity') (*Kommentierte Werkausgabe* 9:203). The Romantic desire for expressive creativity motivates recurring allusions to and images of the supernatural performative as manifested in the 'P' myth of creation. Yet the Romantic poets, like Broch, cannot ignore the role that performative language plays in the shaping of a social and political order. The result is a conflicted model of poetic and cosmogonic creation, the roots of which may be traced to the double focus of the biblical account of creation, whose two narrative traditions distinguish between the theological-phenomenological and the sociopolitical performative while also incorporating these speech acts into a single narrative of beginnings.

Some of the most subtle and provocative juxtapositions of the two paradigms of performative language occur in the work of Milton and Blake, poets whose claim to authority often rests simultaneously on the concept and imagery of God's creative utterance and on socially constituted speech acts. Moreover, the relation between the two types of performative speech and the poet's awareness of this relation differ in the texts of these two writers in ways which open up a new perspective on the influence of Milton on Blake, and the influence on both of the discourse of their contemporaries. Milton insists on the presence of a creative Logos as both the subject of his writing and the motivating power behind it, even though he is involuntarily engaged in dividing and hierarchizing the world when he rewrites the story of creation in *Paradise Lost*, and in illustrating the workings of the social contract when he defines his own inspired stance. Blake, partly because of his reading of Milton and partly because of the different conventions which circumscribe discourse in his time, is much more conscious of, and therefore anxious about, the dichotomy between language which derives its creativity from individual will and language which wields authority by common consent. The evolution of the visionary poet's response to this problematic of Logos, society, and the role of language in constituting or reconstituting reality is the subject of the following chapters.

3

The Language of Inspiration in Milton's Prose

... you [Milton] are very solicitous about [words] as if they were charmes, or had more in them then what they signifie: For no Conjurer's Devill is more concerned in a spell, then you are in a meer word, but never regard the things which it serves to expresse.

The Censure of the Rota

Milton's Word: Theology and Logology

A writer who is going to create his or her own system discovers a matrix of problems inherent in cosmogony and beginnings. So Milton realizes, and Blake after him, when they take on the task of putting the world into words. Whatever the consciousness of being inspired means for these poets on the level of language (and that is one question I will be addressing), it is somehow bound up with the originality of the work and the uniqueness of the message. Being thus engaged, on a fundamental level, with the problem of origin, both poets return to and revise the biblical paradigm of creation through language. Yet the properties of language are often at odds with the idea of origin or free creation, in ways that Milton and Blake intuited and that language theory since Nietzsche has more explicitly addressed.

Milton's narrative of creation by the Word in *Paradise Lost* is founded on his multifaceted understanding of what language is and where it comes from. The Word, in various capitalized and uncapitalized senses, means for him the Son of God; the power by which God creates the universe; the inspired and infallible authority of Scripture; the revelation, comprising both poetic ability and the gift of interpretation, which comes to inspired writers from God; and the instrument which Protestant preachers employ to teach and convert the world. In addition, the word is what twentieth-century readers primarily take it to be, the medium in which Milton enacts his message. Not unnaturally, the most important existing work on these topics has approached them from a seventeenth-century perspective, but I would argue that some of the assumptions behind Milton's use of the inspired and creative Word are most accessible by way of twentieth-century theories of difference, performance, and the autonomy of linguistic systems. Moreover, perhaps because so much contemporary theory developed in conjunction with the study of Romanticism, a twentieth-century perspective helps to expose those aspects of Milton's art that Blake and other Romantics found both fascinating and disturbing.

What I am proposing is, in part, a discussion of Milton's theology in terms of what Kenneth Burke calls 'logology,' or words about words. Burke's premise in putting forward this ungainly but evocative term is that the language we use to talk about God can also tell us something about the nature of language and the basic human attribute which Burke calls *symbolicity* – the structure of logic, rhetoric, and meaning in which we operate. Milton is a logological thinker *par excellence*: when he writes about divine creation, the Holy Spirit, church discipline, and other aspects of theological doctrine, he cannot but write about language as well. The association is necessitated by, among other things, his preoccupation with the theological significance of the word 'Word' and his radical Protestant respect for the exact words of Scripture, demonstrated above all in the project of *De Doctrina Christiana*. The theological episteme of Milton's time, which regarded Nature as the Book of God and took the idea of inspiration literally, made numerous and intricate connections between philology and religious belief. Influenced by such a theological climate, Milton provides a prime example of how a belief in inspired utterance can issue in structures of performative discourse that later poets revise and repeat.

One explicit example of logological criticism is William Shullenberger's reading of *De Doctrina Christiana*, in which he argues that 'the centrality of Christ as both Word and Image makes Milton's theology an explication of both a theory of language and a theory of metaphor' (263). Shullenberger maintains that language is an implicit metaphor for God in *De Doctrina Christiana*, an analogy that seems distinctively Protestant in its avoidance of natural or material imagery, but one which could not receive adequate explication until the development of Saussurian theory. The Father is analogous to Saussure's *langue* and the Son to *parole*; from our experience of the latter, we infer something of the nature of the former. Shullenberger alludes to a further parallel between the Ramist methodology which governs Milton's theology and theory of grammar, and twenti-eth-century structuralist linguistics; thus, 'Milton's theology, as a system of signs organized according to hierarchical sets of binary oppositions, may be read as a language, structured in the way that language is understood to be structured' (266). Unfortunately, Shullenberger never deals with the dis-junction between the Son's uniqueness and the necessary multiplicity of *parole*, though he does hint briefly that *parole* might also correspond to the creatures produced by divine utterance.

While there have been several studies of Milton's philosophy of language in its historical context,[1] few critics have followed up Shullenberger's suggestion that Milton's theology may foreshadow twentieth-century lin-guistics. The readings that follow attempt to extend to some of Milton's prose works and to *Paradise Lost* the basic premise that twentieth-century language theory is a valid vehicle for analysing Milton's assumptions about language. Sometimes by analogy and other times by contrast, speech-act analysis helps to elucidate Milton's ideas about the extraordinary capacities of the divine Word and the way inspiration may offer the human poet access to them. However, using the terms introduced in chapters 1 and 2, we may say that Milton's desire to represent and imitate the phenomenological per-formative, as it appears in divine creation, is repeatedly threatened by the intrusion of the sociopolitical performative. The conventional formulas to which Austin attributes the performative function of words are often the means by which the creative Word achieves its effectiveness in Milton's texts, and these linguistic structures threaten to replace divine, originary power with socially circumscribed norms. If Milton remained oblivious to this ominous institutionalization of the word, Blake at least half realized the possibility and struggled against it. The same is true of the limitation inherent in language, a medium which positions its speaker in a historical and polit-ical scene of discourse, and creates by the setting of bounds. In other words, the language of Milton's claims to inspiration and his re-enactment of divine creation may undermine his intention, ultimately calling into question the possibility of a unique creative voice and consciousness.

1 For Milton's engagement with the seventeenth-century concept of fallen and redeemed language, see Robert L. Entzminger, *Divine Word: Milton and the Redemption of Lang-uage,* and Kathleen M. Swaim, *Before and after the Fall: Contrasting Modes in 'Paradise Lost.'* Georgia B. Christopher, *Milton and the Science of the Saints,* explores the Reforma-tion hermeneutic by which an emphasis on typology and literal meaning shifted to a mode of understanding based on the centrality of the word. Two other works with slightly less direct relevance are William G. Madsen's *From Shadowy Types to Truth: Studies in Milton's Symbolism* and Boyd M. Berry, *Process of Speech: Puritan Religious Writing and Paradise Lost.*

Recognizing how profoundly Milton's sense of his own authority depends on notions of inspiration and prophecy, Milton scholars have adopted the term 'poet-prophet' and identified Milton as a key figure in the 'line of vision' in English poetry. Until the 1970s, the hybrid 'poet-prophet' was particularly common in the extensive literature on Miltonic inspiration. The focus of most mid-twentieth-century criticism on this subject was the identification of the various powers to which Milton appeals for inspiration, chiefly in the invocations in *Paradise Lost*: Heavenly Muse, Spirit, Holy Light, Urania, God the Father or the Son.[2] More recently, the extensive work of J.A. Wittreich in identifying a line of vision which runs from Chaucer, Spenser, and Milton to Blake, Wordsworth, and Shelley has been corroborated by other critics, notably the contributors to the collection edited by Wittreich, *Milton and the Line of Vision*. Most of the work in this vein tends toward an unproblematic acceptance of Milton's visionary role – even if it is willing to confront the complexities of *Romantic* prophecy.

However, William Kerrigan takes the 'bastard word' poet-prophet to task in his introduction to *The Prophetic Milton*, one of two studies to date which has confronted the complexity of Milton's attitude toward inspiration. Traditional Miltonists, according to Kerrigan, replaced the particularity of the historical Milton with abstractions and substituted a 'safe Milton' for a 'dangerous Milton'[3] in an attempt to deflect attention from his prophetic stance, either because a focus on Milton's often objectionable self-image seemed to cater to anti-Miltonists or because twentieth-century readers are resistant to the idea of prophecy (*Prophetic Milton* 3). To counteract these techniques of evasion, Kerrigan focuses on the scene of discourse in Mil-

2 The most significant commentaries on Milton's invocations are James Holly Hanford, 'That Shepherd, Who First Taught the Chosen Seed: A Note on Milton's Mosaic Inspiration'; David Daiches, 'The Opening of *Paradise Lost*'; and Merritt Y. Hughes, 'Milton and the Symbol of Light.' William B. Hunter should also be mentioned for his extensive and vigorous arguments, first that the Son is invoked in book 3 of *Paradise Lost* ('The Meaning of "Holy Light" in *Paradise Lost* III'); then that the Son is invoked throughout the epic ('Milton's Urania'); then, in collaboration with Stevie Davies, that successive invocations in *Paradise Lost* address, respectively, the three persons of the Trinity ('Milton's Urania: "The meaning, not the name I call" '). While I remain unconvinced by Hunter's interpretations, the last of them does begin to address a dichotomy between inspiration by the Holy Spirit and other divine voices which is at least tangentially relevant to my argument about Milton's invocations in chapter 4.

3 A similar point has been made about Blake criticism by W.J.T. Mitchell ('Dangerous Blake'), who argues that the mainstream, professional 'Blake industry' has obscured the more alienating aspects of Blake's character and work, including madness and religious fanaticism.

ton's invocations and attempts to refute the prevalent assumption that these passages constitute formal (i.e., constative) statements on inspiration or prophecy:

[The invocation in book 3] does not communicate with the reader of the poem at all; addressed to God, the language performs a gesture of prayer toward God ... [The invocations] tell who is writing the poem, how he is writing, when and under what conditions he is writing ... As we read the invocations, then, we confront a series of statements that take the form of 'I am writing this poem now.' Through which intellectual and cultural traditions can this kind of poetic statement best be apprehended? (*Prophetic Milton* 7)

The answer Kerrigan offers to his own question is that the most fruitful approach involves a study of theological and literary ideas about prophecy that would have been available to Milton and his contemporaries, combined with a consideration of Milton's work in terms of 'spiritual biography' (which would often like to become psychology or psychoanalysis). My own answer, picking up the terms Kerrigan uses in the passage above, would be to study the invocations in terms of a theory which can accommodate performances such as a 'gesture of prayer,' as well as the sociopolitical, theological, and intertextual contexts in which Milton is writing, and the linguistic presentness and presence contained in the deictic language of '*I* am writing *this* poem *now*': that is, a theory of performative language. It is a commonplace of Milton criticism, arrived at equally by readers who take rhetorical, theological, or formal approaches, that a Miltonic text – *Paradise Lost* in particular, but also the prose – at some point stops arguing with the reader and begins acting on him or her instead, implicating the reader in the work and drawing him or her into a process of conversion. As with many commonplaces, though, the implications of this reading have not been followed through in terms of the critical approach that most directly addresses how we do things with words.

The other study which addresses the complex problematic of Milton, inspiration, and language is John Guillory's *Poetic Authority*, which acknowledges a debt to Kerrigan's book and continues, more explicitly, a Foucauldian genealogy of the idea of poetic authority in the seventeenth century. Guillory's insights into questions of inspiration, intention, and self-representation are particularly relevant here because his approach is heavily rhetorical, exploring Milton's use of tropes such as synecdoche, metonymy, and transumption to build up a sense of his own authority while eliding his own name. Guillory is concerned with the way Milton's language positions the speaker with respect to literary and political history. Analogously, my interest is in exploring the figural language of Milton's invocations and claims to inspiration, the way it positions the speaker with respect to the source of inspiration and the audience and the way it characterizes the qualities of the desired word. In *Paradise Lost* and his later prose, Milton comes to see inspiration as a combined religious and poetic phenomenon which is responsible for rendering language creative and effectual, as is God's language. This concept is bound up with an increasingly strong self-definition by the poet as one who, by contrast with the community of believers who are generally endowed with the Holy Spirit, receives a special gift of inspired speech.

'General' and 'Special' Inspiration

Milton's earliest references to inspiration allude to the classical tradition; he names muses and oracles as sources for poetic ability. In a detailed study of Milton's education, habits of composition, and 'Muse lore,' E.R. Gregory argues that the young Milton distinguished between two classical terms for figures of inspiration. He uses 'Caminae,' which was regarded as a Latin synonym for 'Muses,' to denigrate his own literary efforts in comparison with dignified classical verse, but appeals to 'Musae' when he hopes to achieve greatness in his art (Gregory 45–63). This feature of the early Latin poetry foreshadows the more famous hierarchy of Christian over classical influences in Milton's mature concept of inspiration. There is, however, yet another significant dualism in the idea of inspiration throughout Milton's work. It emerges in Milton's prose works that inspiration can be of a *general* or a *special* type – and only the latter comes to be associated in Milton's mind with the power of performative speech.

The young Milton's experience with special inspiration begins in the *Prolusions*, where he speaks with great respect 'of the [Greek] poets, or (what is almost the same thing) of the divine oracles,' figures whose 'holy' and 'secret' knowledge could not be brought before the public 'unless it be in some way cloaked or veiled' (*CPW* 1:235–6). The origin of modern knowledge is located in the inspired teaching of the Greek poets, who 'have attained an ample meed of honour and of glory ... by being the first to teach, by their divine inspiration, all the sciences which are known today, arraying them in the charming cloak of fable ...' (*CPW* 1:224). Not only do the words of the inspired Greeks still have meaning, but the source of their inspiration can be called on still. In 1628 Milton writes respectfully to his friend and mentor Alexander Gill:

I knew of course how impossible it would be to call you and your genius away from Poetry and to quench those heaven-sent frenzies and the celestial and sacred fire in your inmost heart, since your Being (as Claudian said of himself) 'breathes wholly of Phoebus.' (*CPW* 1:316–17)

Fire and frenzy, nakedness and charmingly beautiful garments – these are strange and dangerous terms for a Puritan to build a concept of divine inspiration on. Kerrigan demonstrates that images of frenzied, pagan prophecy tended to incur the suspicion of Milton's contemporaries with regard to both religious and poetic inspiration. But Milton soon revises these images; by the time he embarks on a poetic career, these oracles are silenced, and he relinquishes the fire and frenzy while retaining ideas of secrecy and special election.

Kerrigan has traced the accommodation of pagan and Old Testament models of prophecy to a Puritan context, a process that begins with the Church Fathers and continues in the work of seventeenth-century Protestants and literary critics. One move in the Christianizing of prophecy is a calming down of the ancient notions of *furor propheticus* and *furor poeticus*. In contrast to the frenzy of pagan oracles, God is said to inspire serenity and tranquillity. The distinction is first made by the Church Fathers in a theological context, then echoed by seventeenth-century critics in terms of poetic inspiration, and finally picked up by Milton: 'Milton, like the early Fathers, associated prophetic inspiration with mental calm' (*Prophetic Milton* 80). Kerrigan's comment relates to Milton's desire for a propitious time in which to write amid an era of political unrest, but the calming of prophetic frenzy can also be observed in his early poetry. In contrast to the *Prolusions*, the muses in the 'Epitaphium Damonis' and 'Ad Patrem' are 'sweet' ('Dulcis ... Musae' [*CP* 132]), or 'sacred' and 'delicate' ('sacras ... Musas,' 'teneras ... Camenas' [*CP* 84]). In 'Elegy VI,' Milton explicitly announces his preference for an abstemious and disciplined poetry over the 'sudden heat' of Phoebus and 'full possession' by Thalia (*CP* 51). Yet the cloaked and secret nature of classical inspiration and the poet's awareness of being the privileged object of divine favour remain and are carried over into the Christianized concept of special inspiration.

While later writings like the *History of Britain* abound with references to oracles, ecstasy, visions, personal revelations from on high, strange thunders and fiery dragons seen in the heavens, the source of these phenomena is inevitably the Christian God. At the same time, Milton's reading of the New Testament leads him to place alongside these extraordinary visitations the more democratic idea that all Christians may be seen as inspired by the

Holy Spirit. When Milton sums up his attitude toward fantastic experiences of divine revelation in *De Doctrina Christiana*, they have been assimilated, historically and theologically, to a Pentecostal doctrine:

And indeed all true believers either prophesy or have within them the Holy Spirit, which is as good as having the gift of prophecy and dreams and visions. (*CPW* 6:523–4)

The 'prophecy and dreams and visions' originate with the prophet Joel, who foretells the outpouring of God's spirit on all Israel on the day of the Lord:

And it shall come to pass afterward, that I will pour out my spirit upon all flesh; and your sons and your daughters shall prophesy, your old men shall dream dreams, your young men shall see visions ... (Joel 2:28)

Joel goes on to prophesy 'wonders in the heavens and in the earth' (2:30) – blood, fire, pillars of smoke, and other terrific events akin to those which signify divine visitation in the *History of Britain* and earlier works of Milton's. In the New Testament, Joel's words are recalled by Saint Peter in a sermon on the day of Pentecost, and he identifies the Holy Spirit that has come upon the apostles in tongues of fire with the outpouring of which Joel spoke (Acts 2:16–21). So the prophet who was visited by the Word of the Lord is replaced by the apostle who has received the gift of the Holy Spirit, and the promise made to the house of Israel is extended 'to all that are afar off, even as many as the Lord our God shall call' (Acts 2:39). Alluding to the words of Peter, Milton picks up their typological and inclusive qualities. The privileged vision bestowed on extraordinary individuals like Alexander Gill or the monarchs and seers who populate the *History of Britain* is now matched by an insight accorded to 'all true believers.' Yet Milton's choice of conjunction in the phrase 'prophesy *or* have ... the Holy Spirit' suggests that he remains aware of the potential for special revelation to chosen individuals. Rather than obliterating the distinction between prophets and spirit-filled believers, he admits only that the believers' abilities are 'as good as' those of the favoured individuals who have received 'the [special] gift of prophecy.'

A more radical figurative reading is involved when Milton extends 'the term *prophet*' to 'anyone endowed with exceptional piety and wisdom for the purpose of teaching' (*CPW* 6:572). This sentence from *De Doctrina Christiana* provides a gloss on the use made in *Areopagitica* of the famous Mosaic utterance that possessed Milton and Blake alike:

For now the time seems come, wherein *Moses* the great Prophet may sit in heav'n rejoycing to see that memorable and glorious wish of his fulfill'd, when not only our sev'nty Elders, but all the Lords people are become Prophets. (*CPW* 2:555–6)

Milton's visionary reading of the Old Testament is not unmotivated by more immediate political and rhetorical considerations. Urging Parliament to free the publication of books from the restraints of the 1643 Licensing Ordinance, Milton argues that all Christians should now share the authority originally granted only to the 'sev'nty Elders' – for which we might read the Stationers' Company, the Archbishops, and the Chancellors of the Universities, those individuals who have been designated as enforcers of the Licensing Ordinance. The democratic spirit that apparently motivates the substitution of a visionary community of believers for a few elect individuals is intrinsically connected with – indeed, essential to – Milton's belief in republican government and presbyterian church order. Yet a special inspired authority seems reserved for '*Moses* the great Prophet,' as marked by the adjective, the definite article, and the fact that Moses is appealed to as the authority for the entire vision. Anticipating the claims he will make in *Paradise Lost*, Milton implicitly casts himself in the role of 'the great Prophet,' inasmuch as he echoes the words first spoken by Moses and announces their fulfilment.

Inspiration again has political significance in the *Defensio Secunda*, where that party of Englishmen which imprisoned and executed the king is described as 'better instructed and doubtless inspired by heaven' (*CPW* 4:552). The notion that all true believers are in some sense inspired is explicitly used to vindicate a popular action of which Milton approves. Yet far more of the proem to the *Defensio Secunda* consists of self-congratulatory remarks, since Milton in particular ('I and no other') has been blessed by God with the gift of 'speaking on so great a theme' and 'publicly defending (if anyone ever did)' the cause of liberty (*CPW* 4:549); the focus is on an inspired voice which will allow Milton to perform things unattempted yet in the oratorical tradition (*CPW* 4:554). Milton needs to retain the concept of special and extraordinary inspiration, both when he turns from government-commissioned defences of national policy to write strong poetry, and when he finds that he and the mass of 'better instructed' Englishmen are no longer on the same side. In the political and ecclesiastical tracts, Milton's argument for freedom of speech and conscience relies on the accessibility of divine inspiration for lay believers, yet even in these texts the language of biblical prophecy tends to attach itself to the recipients of 'the inspired guift of God *rarely* bestow'd' (*CPW* 1:816; my italics).

By the time of Milton's maturity, he has developed a twofold concept of general and particular endowment with divine vision. While these classifications are never made explicit, they correspond to the Ramist logic underlying Milton's theology in *De Doctrina Christiana*, which returns constantly to the opposition of general and particular. For instance:

A DECREE of God is either GENERAL or SPECIAL. (*CPW* 6:153)

Vocation, then, is either general or special. (*CPW* 6:455)

Repentance may be general, in which case it is also called conversion, and this is when a man is converted from a state of sin to a state of grace. Or it may be particular, and this is when a man who is already converted feels penitence for some particular sin. (*CPW* 6:468)

As an implicit organizing principle for Milton's thoughts and pronouncements about inspiration, the separation of general and special suits well the situation of a writer arguing strenuously for republican freedoms, but asserting with equal vehemence his own talent and authority to pronounce on these matters.

Self-Presentation in *The Reason of Church-Government*

Nowhere in Milton's prose is his notion of inspiration more intimately connected with his sense of identity and vocation than in *The Reason of Church-Government*. At the centre of this tract is a testament to the privileges and responsibilities of God-given poetic ability, significantly framed by an autobiographical digression on Milton's own call to a life of writing. Yet the rest of the tract argues for the freeing of the church from the authority of prelates and the giving of church government over to presbyters and deacons who will manage it with reason and sanctity. Milton plainly has an interest in promoting the divine gifts of leadership and right reason possessed by lay believers, yet the biblical and historical precedents on which he grounds his argument for presbyterian church-government repeatedly focus on the inspiration of extraordinary individuals. In describing the qualities necessary in one who would frame a form of government, Milton asserts that the civil virtues of self-knowledge, wit, prudence, fortitude, and eloquence are not enough, but that all the ancient lawgivers were either truly inspir'd as *Moses*, or were such men as with authority anough might give it out to be so, as *Minos, Lycurgus, Numa*, because they wisely forethought that men would never quietly submit to such a discipline as had not more of Gods hand in it then mans. (*CPW* 1:753–4)

Milton's strategy for including great lawgivers of the pagan world is intriguing, as he accords them not a lesser degree or a lower form of inspiration, but the *appearance* of inspiration – suggesting either that there are recognized conventions one may adopt in order to sound inspired, or that a person's office or status in society may bestow the authority which makes that person's words received as if they were inspired. True inspiration remains an exclusive quality of the kind accorded to a few special individuals, above all '*Moses* ... the only Lawgiver that we can believe to have been visibly taught of God' (*CPW* 1:747). In holding up Moses' authority to pronounce on social organization in a tract in which he himself is setting out the acceptable form of church organization, Milton once again aligns himself with the greatest of the prophets.

In Milton's survey of religious history, the successors to Moses and David in the time of the Jews' return from captivity are Haggai and Zechariah –'inspired men, Prophets' who alone directed the actions of the people according to 'divine intimation' (*CPW* 1:757). A line of inspiration is being drawn according to which divine visitation is an exclusive quality, not only because it affects a few chosen individuals, but because it distinguishes allowable from disallowed authority and behaviour. Even when Milton turns to Saint Paul and the organization of the Christian church, the 'gift of the Spirit,' manifested in the ability to preach the Word of God, is distinguished from the practical work of church government:

For publick preaching indeed is the gift of the Spirit working as best seemes to his secret will, *but* discipline is the practick work of preaching directed and apply'd as is most requisite to particular duty ... (*CPW* 1:755–6; my italics)

If Milton's intention is to set the two talents in balance as special and general forms of God-given ability, he does not quite convince. The gift of using language so as to convert others, bestowed according to the Spirit's '*secret* will,' retains a certain mystique and is subtly elevated over the second-order application of that verbal gift in the daily life of the church.

The figural language Milton uses in the autobiographical digression at the beginning of book 2 of *The Reason of Church-Government* locates him firmly in the line of individuals who experience special inspiration.

He appeals to the sympathy of his readership as one who is compelled by conscience to bring an unwelcome message, a situation which elicits comparisons with biblical and pagan prophets, including the 'sad Prophet *Jeremiah*,' John of Patmos, and Sophocles' Tiresias in *Oedipus the King* (*CPW* 1:802–3). But the paradigm of Old Testament prophecy is also more subtly implicated in the language of Milton's autobiographical narrative; for instance, in a word that recurs in several different contexts in the preamble to book 2, the word 'burden.' The opening sentence of book 2 alludes with seeming casualness to a proverb which had recently appeared in a collection of George Herbert's, 'Knowledge is no burden' (Herbert 344); then the word is echoed several times more in an extended metaphor likening those who have spiritual knowledge to impart to traders weighed down by heavy and not easily saleable wares. But the full significance of the metaphor only comes to bear when Milton builds up to the revelation that 'burden,' in the Authorized Version, is the term used by the Old Testament prophets to introduce their troubling visions:

And although divine inspiration must certainly have been sweet to those ancient profets, yet the irksomnesse of that truth which they brought was so unpleasant to them, that every where they call it a burden. (*CPW* 1:802–3)

The image of fire is similarly handled. Milton introduces it with apparent arbitrariness ('they are made ... a very sword and fire both in house and City over the whole earth' [*CPW* 1:802]), then reveals its crucial association with the inspired word (i.e., the burden) of Jeremiah: '*his word was in my heart as a burning fire shut up in my bones*' (*CPW* 1:803).

The more famous allusion to Old Testament prophecy which follows sums up the development of Milton's concept of inspiration. Laying aside pagan models for poetic frenzy – 'the vapours of wine' and 'the invocation of Dame Memory and her Siren daughters' – that held his interest in 'the heat of youth,' Milton appeals instead

by devout prayer to that eternall Spirit who can enrich with all utterance and knowledge, and sends out his Seraphim with the hallow'd fire of his Altar to touch and purify the lips of whom he pleases ... (*CPW* 1:820–1)

The New Testament's prayer for the Holy Spirit, which descended on the apostles and 'gave them utterance' (Acts 2:4), here merges inextricably with the particular circumstances of the call of Isaiah, the most vivid image in the Old Testament of a prophet's special election.[4] It is an appropriate prediction of the genesis of *Paradise Lost*, an epic which combines appeals to a Holy Spirit and a Heavenly Muse with allusions to prophets and patriarchs, and which negotiates between an image of the poet as true, Spirit-led believer interpreting the words of Scripture and a dream of Milton as divinely visited visionary, rewriter of a sacred book.

Milton's Promise

While gesturing toward a more inclusive Protestant doctrine of the ministry of the Spirit, Milton identifies with the recipients of special inspiration as he positions his autobiographical narrative between images of Old Testament prophecy, between the 'burden' and the 'hallow'd fire.' His poetic ability is likened to the 'secret' and special gift of 'publick preaching,' being 'of power beside the office of a pulpit' (*CPW* 1:816). What it means to possess such power is revealed by Milton's use of performative language at this crucial point in his self-presentation. He sets the entire concluding section of his digression in the form of a promise, which frames the description of the work to be produced by the aid of the 'eternall Spirit':

Neither doe I think it shame to covnant with any knowing reader, that for some few yeers yet I may go on trust with him toward the payment of what I am now indebted ... till which in some measure be compast, at mine own peril and cost I refuse not to sustain this expectation from as many as are not loath to hazard so much credulity upon the best pledges that I can give them. (*CPW* 1:820–1)

Milton engages himself to deliver the goods in a few years' time. Using formal legal phraseology, he seals a bargain; indeed, he signs a contract, this being the first of the anti-prelatical tracts to which he puts his name. The

4 Some critics have argued that Milton's 'eternall Spirit' cannot be the Holy Spirit because the dominant context here is an Old Testament one; see Maurice Kelley (110–18) and the commentary of Ralph A. Haug (*CPW* 1:821). Yet Milton's many other references in *The Reason of Church-Government* to the Holy Spirit as an 'inlightning' and instructing power suggest that this passage fits into the same pattern. The angel who touches the prophet's lips with a burning coal in Isaiah 6:1–7 does not, in any case, 'enrich with all utterance,' but only purifies the mouth in the sense of a ritual cleansing; it is the Holy Spirit in the Book of Acts who bestows the gift of tongues and public preaching on the apostles. Although Milton's chapter 'Of the Holy Spirit' in *De Doctrina Christiana* lists several cases in which the term 'Spirit' is used in the Bible to signify God the Father, the Son, or another heavenly minister, Milton's choice of the word in the present context needs to be given its full weight as a revision of the Old Testament image in terms of a Christian doctrine of inspiration.

venture is one in which the reader risks being thought overly credulous while Milton risks his honour and good name should he not deliver what he has promised. Significantly, the bargain is a 'covenant': as if he were choosing his readership the way God chose his people, Milton evokes the Old Testament resonances of an agreement in which both parties have responsibilities to fulfil.[5] The expectations he has of his covenanting partner are made clear by his repeated specification of an 'intelligent and equal auditor' (*CPW* 1:806) and an 'elegant & learned reader' (*CPW* 1:807); he petitions 'the gentler sort' of reader (*CPW* 1:808) and covenants with the 'knowing reader' (*CPW* 1:820).

But 'covenant' is also the term recognized in English common law since its medieval origins to mean 'agreement,' and in issuing his promise Milton is taking upon himself what the law called 'the burden of the covenant.' His promise to the reader actually contains all the elements required by the common law to make a promise actionable; according to William Sheppard in his *Touchstone of Common Assurances*, a treatise published the same year *The Reason of Church-Government* was written, the thing promised in a contract must be 'lawful,' 'possible,' 'clear and certain,' 'serious and weighty,' and it must accord with the consideration or motive the promiser has stated (quoted in A.W.B. Simpson 506). Should Milton not make good on his claim, a reader who had the admittedly aberrant desire to sue him could presumably bring a writ of covenant or breach of promise suit against him, a type of legal action which, according to the legal historian A.W.B. Simpson, was becoming increasingly frequent during the seventeenth century (46–7).

Simpson explains that a covenant had the effect of legally defining a tort or wrong:

... the theoretical function of the covenant was to make future conduct, which would otherwise be lawful, tortious and actionable, in much the same way as an undertaking of responsibility in modern tort law may have the effect of making tortious otherwise lawful future inactivity or carelessness. (19)

5 Milton's concern with the correct use of the term 'covenant' emerges at several points in *De Doctrina Christiana*. He corrects those who would call God's injunction to Adam and Eve a covenant, designating it a command instead (*CPW* 6:352), and he uses the example of God's covenants with Israel to demonstrate that human beings have some say in the organization of the church: 'Obviously if religious matters were not under our control, or to some extent within our power and choice, God could not enter into a covenant with us, and we could not keep it, let alone swear to keep it' (*CPW* 6:398). Both examples demonstrate his conviction that the making of a covenant presupposes free will and responsibility on both sides.

By this definition, God's injunction to Adam and Eve in the Garden of Eden is, as discussed in the previous chapter, a covenant or contract which renders the otherwise lawful activity of eating fruit from a specified tree wrong, and quite seriously actionable. Milton is making the same kind of sociopolitical speech act: in formulating his promise in *The Reason of Church-Government*, he is delimiting the correctness of his future conduct. The comparison with original sin is particularly apt, and Milton's covenant particularly binding, since he offers to seal the bargain with a 'pledge,' a token or symbol exchanged between the covenanting parties. The 'best pledges' that he offers may either be his already existing works, perhaps including the present one, or the verbal assurances he has just given of his talent, ambition, and virtuous intent. One thing the noun 'pledge' does *not* seem to mean here is a vow or verbal commitment; the Oxford English Dictionary does not document this sense of the word until the early nineteenth century. In Milton's time 'pledge' always designated an object handed over as surety, and liable to forfeit if certain conditions were not fulfilled. In Milton's poetry, 'pledge' is normally synonymous with 'symbol' or 'tangible evidence': a child is the pledge of love between its parents (*PL* 2.818); the morning star is the pledge of day (*PL* 5.168); Samson's hair is the pledge of his vow (*SA* 535, 1144); and, significantly, the tree of the knowledge of good and evil is the pledge of humanity's obedience to God (*PL* 8.323–5).[6] The traditionally tangible nature of the pledge ironically highlights the fact that all Milton has to offer as collateral for texts to come are more texts; despite the elaborate fiction of barter and exchange, the entire transaction rests on the reader's willingness to give credit to Milton's words.

In Austin's *How to Do Things with Words*, the promise is a paradigmatic speech act; to utter a promise is, not to describe or report on an action, but to perform the action of committing oneself to do something. Yet the promise is also one of the most problematic of speech acts, since the present utterance remains, in a sense, incomplete until a future fulfilment of the promise renders the speech act totally successful. The legal status of the promise or I.O.U. is historically a vexed question; it defies categoriza-

---

6 Milton also identifies the tree of the knowledge of good and evil as a 'pledge or memorial of obedience' in *De Doctrina Christiana* (*CPW* 6:352). In *The Reason of Church-Government*, he calls on the prelates to 'surrender that pledge which unless you fowlely usurpt it, the Church gave you, and now claimes it againe, for the reason she first lent it' (*CPW* 1:792). The referent seems to be the prelates' power and pre-eminence; while it is probably intangible and hard to identify precisely, the 'pledge' is clearly to something which may be transferred back and forth between parties.

tion as transfer or exchange because of the intrusion of temporality between the making of the promise and its completion. A.W.B. Simpson emphasizes the distinction made in common law between covenants and grants: the latter are contracts which require the immediate transfer of interest in lands or goods and, if violated, are actionable by writ of debt, while covenants, however specific with regard to the future exchange of property, are not understood to involve actual transfer but only promises to transfer, and are only actionable for damages under writ of covenant. Pursuing the theological implications of the temporality of promising, Regina Schwartz has pointed to the underlying affinity between the economic concept of exchange and remuneration and the theological concepts of belief and praise, citing Benveniste's investigation of the etymology of words for belief (*kred, credo*) as the action of giving something away with the certainty of getting it back. Schwartz observes that 'Milton's discussions of praise are dominated by the familiar language of finance, of owing, paying, and reckoning' (68). Financial and legal parlance are equally prevalent when Milton speaks of belief, either in God or, as here, the belief that others may lodge in Milton himself. In his covenant with the reader, Milton asks for a 'credulity' which is both analogous and etymologically related to financial credit; we re-metaphorize the economic frame of reference when we 'give Milton credit' for being sincere in his promise. Michel de Certeau analyses belief as an exchange in which a believer, giving credit to a receiver, 'creates a deficit whereby a future is introduced into the present' (193). As with the pledge, the underlying pattern is that of an object exchanged between parties in a temporal sequence by which a present transaction looks toward a future fulfilment.

In Milton's promise, present *and* future utterances depend on one another and, like his pledge, lack any external validation. This becomes clear when we examine the reason Milton gives for making his self-imposed commitment public:

Although it nothing content me to have disclos'd thus much before hand, but that I trust hereby to make it manifest with what small willingnesse I endure to interrupt the pursuit of no lesse hopes then these, and leave a calme and pleasing solitarynes fed with cherful and confident thoughts, to imbark in a troubl'd sea of noises and hoars disputes ... (*CPW* 1:821)

His anticipation of a greater work in the future reflects back on his disinclination to undertake the present task (of writing a tract on church government), which in turn guarantees the sincerity of what he is now writing – that is, the sincerity of his promise of a future masterpiece. Moreover, the imagery Milton uses foreshadows the analogy to come in *Paradise Lost* between poetic and cosmogonic creation: setting out on a 'troubl'd sea' to compose his tract, Milton resembles the Son of God leaving the calmness of heaven to set forth onto the troubled waves of chaos.[7] Both these aspects of the passage bring Milton's words into relation with the divine Word. The temporal interdependence undermines the causality of logical thought, and therefore perhaps undermines the credibility of Milton's guarantee on the level of human reason. But in doing so, it evokes the perspective of simultaneity which is a feature of Milton's prophetic poetry and of the typological hermeneutic in which he shared. Kerrigan has demonstrated how many of Milton's poems 'dissolved and reordered our literary language to express a prophetic understanding of time fundamentally antipathetic to language itself,' and Kerrigan's summary of the typological understanding of prophetic time might be applied to Milton's use of an unwritten future work to vouch for the sincerity of the present one:

Having escaped from sequence, the Old Testament instant hovers perfected in eternity while the motions of time proceed toward its unveiling ... Christian typology, filling the instant with past and future events, contracts linear time; the future is in the present, the conclusion is in the premise. (*Prophetic Milton* 226)

Legal Contract and Ecclesiastical Oath

In a further defiance of logic, Milton goes on to demonstrate – precisely by speaking out – just how loath he is to break 'the quiet and still air of delightfull studies' (*CPW* 1:821–2). The conflict between speaking and silence is important, and the reason for it emerges at the end of the digression, where the image reappears in an inverted form. Returning to autobiography, Milton affirms his preference for a 'blamelesse silence' over 'the sacred office of speaking bought, and begun with servitude and forswearing' (*CPW* 1:823) – apparently oblivious of the fact that he is by now trumpeting his blameless silence rather loudly. He now informs the reader that he intended to take orders in the Church of England, until he became aware that church government had been corrupted to the extent that one swearing loyalty to the church would be forswearing himself,

that he who would take Orders must subscribe slave, and take an oath withall,

7 Reading *Of Reformation,* Thomas Kranidas discovers a similar analogy between the poet's emergence from studious retirement and God's emergence at the time of creation (499).

which unlesse he took with a conscience that would retch, he must either strait per-jure, or split his faith ... (*CPW* 1:823)

This opens up a new perspective on Milton's pledge to produce a great poetic work. Instead of purchasing the right to preach publicly – that is, to have his utterances supported by the institutional authority of the church – with an oath that goes against his conscience, Milton chooses to barter with the more attractive, though less substantial, currency of his future poetic achievement. He prefers a covenant with a knowing reader over a bond to an authoritarian church that would compel the oath-taker to 'subscribe slave.'

Milton's objection to ordination, or at least to the significance the Church of England accords it, is made clear early on in *The Reason of Church-Government*:

... why should the performance of ordination which is a lower office exalt a Prelat, and not the seldome discharge of a higher and more noble office which is preach-ing & administring much rather depresse him? (*CPW* 1:768)

As Milton's editor notes (*CPW* 1:768), the rhetorical question echoes a com-mon complaint about the lack of preaching being done by prelates in Mil-ton's time and records an expected objection on his part to the ascendancy which some Anglican clergymen gain over others by ordination to a partic-ular office. But a distinction is also being made between the various kinds of performative language at work in church discipline. Here, as elsewhere, Milton identifies the 'higher and more noble office' as preaching; the 'administring' which he joins to preaching is glossed in part by the previous sentence as 'the power of binding and absolving' (i.e., from vows and promises). Preaching the gospel and confirming vows and promises are verbal acts which all ministers have the authority to perform; the ability to preach is not dependent on status in the church, but on special inspiration, just as the making of vows is possible for anyone who is moved to do so by the Spirit. These are also the speech acts which Milton either performs or to which he likens his performance in this tract, as he covenants with the reader and claims inspiration which is 'of power beside the office of a pul-pit' (*CPW* 1:816). Ordination, by contrast, a speech act which depends entirely on the authority vested in an institution for its effectiveness, is the 'lower office' which Milton ultimately declines.

William Riley Parker and others believe that Milton's refusal to take orders is a protest against the oath of ordination as specified in Article

Thirty-six of the *Constitutions and Canons Ecclesiastical* of 1604 (Parker 2:776). In the context of his legal manoeuvring, however, it seems more likely that Milton is referring to the supplemental vow, the so-called 'Et Cetera' oath, which all new and existing ministers were required to take in 1640. The subject of a topical debate at the time Milton was writing the tract, the new oath is considerably more burdensome, not least from a speech-act perspective. The 1604 version required affirmation of belief ('I believe the doctrine of the United Church of England and Ireland ... to be agreeable to the Word of God'), assent to current doctrine ('I assent to the Thirty-nine Articles of Religion, and to the Book of Common Prayer'), and promises of conformity in behaviour ('in public prayer and administration of the sacraments, I will use the form in the said book prescribed') (*Constitutions* 40). The 1640 oath, however, required candidates to bind themselves with regard to future utterances by swearing,

Nor will I ever give my consent to alter the Government of this Church, by Archbishops, Bishops, Deanes, and Arch-deacons, *&c.* as it stands now established, and as by right it ought to stand ... (Quoted in *CPW* 1:990–1; my italics)

This arch-conservative declaration introduces the future into the present in a much more sinister way than an affirmation of belief, compelling an unknown future to adhere to the conditions of a defined and limited present. Milton may well have objected to what amounts to the signing away of *future* rights to performative speech, particularly since he would give up the right to assent to an ominously open-ended 'et cetera' of possibilities. Rather than forswearing this right, Milton prefers a promise which guarantees a future verbal performance – a promise to write inspired poetry.

Milton's decision to decline ordination helps to explain the negative phrasing that characterizes his contract with the reader, in formulations like 'Neither doe I think it shame to covnant' and 'I refuse not to sustain this expectation.' He *does* refuse the oath of ordination, since taking it *would* be shameful to him. The contract that Milton substitutes for the church's oath is, in its negative formulation, a form of protest – protest being both a speech act ('I protest' enacts what it says) and the origin of Milton's preferred 'Protestant' form of church government. We might read the digression as a re-enactment, on a personal level, of what it means to be a Protestant, Protestantism being, from Luther's Ninety-five Theses and the Augsburg Confession onward, intimately involved with performative utterance.

Milton's protest consists in his substitution of a personal agreement, couched in legal and economic terms, for the vows sanctioned by a state-supported institution. Yet the attempt to secure a new basis of convention for one's performative language is risky business, given the heavy reliance of successful speech acts on what is accepted by the community. The situation is akin to what Austin called 'getting away with it,' in reference to procedures which are not yet accepted as conventions but which someone is trying to initiate (*How to Do Things* 30). In order for Milton to get away with substituting a personal promise for an ecclesiastical oath, a community must exist which will consent to such an innovation – and this community is to be found in a Protestant readership which accepts a focus on individual rights and responsibilities, as well as common law and economic transactions.[8] Here Milton's notion of general inspiration by the Holy Spirit comes to bear again, as it often does when he finds that popular opinion is in agreement with him; he can address that group of readers which he identifies as 'better instructed and doubtless inspired by heaven' (*CPW* 4:552).

One might expect Milton also to reject the crass economics of a church that requires its ministers to 'buy' the privilege of speaking – except that the language of the agreement which Milton substitutes is economic through and through. The metaphor of the travelling trader with his burden recurs at the end of the digression; Milton characterizes his opponents, the Anglican divines, as those whose 'packsaddles' are loaded with 'hollow antiquities sold by the seeming bulk' (*CPW* 1:822). The preamble to book 2 is filled with images of economy in both the commercial and the domestic sense: Milton affirms his intention to bestow his commodities 'without any gain to himselfe' and to 'lay up,' instead, 'the best treasure, and solace of a good old age' (*CPW* 1:804); he fears to 'make a thrifty purchase of boldnesse' (*CPW* 1:805); he desires to 'store up ... the good provision of peacefull hours' (*CPW* 1:806) and 'to write as men buy Leases, for three lives and downward' (*CPW* 1:810). Paul Stevens has remarked on this overwhelmingly economic language and associated it with Milton's pangs of conscience over deriving advantage from his father's labour as a tradesman (Stevens 276): 'ease and leasure was given thee for thy retired

---

8 Paul Stevens postulates that a different sense of 'performance' is at work in *The Reason of Church-Government* and reads Milton's self-presentation in terms of a theatrical metaphor. Milton, according to Stevens, writes himself into roles his culture admires, including that of romance hero and religious martyr (268). This would constitute a different but parallel appeal to the conventions accepted by Milton's readership in order to validate the language of the tract.

thoughts out of the sweat of other men' is Milton's wry reproach to himself (*CPW* 1:804). Milton's easy translation of the oath of canon law into the economic and legal contract of common law exposes the extent to which church government and economics share a conceptual and linguistic formula.

The governing metaphor in Milton's self-presentation is Christ's parable of the talents (Matthew 25:14–31), another narrative which weighs present purchase against future pay-off. As a result of Christian exegesis of this parable, the word 'talent,' which originally referred to a Hebrew coin of a certain weight, acquired a secondary meaning as the value of a person's innate ability. In *The Reason of Church-Government*, Milton fully exploits the duality of meaning: the writer's talent is a commodity which can be properly or improperly marketed, or pledged for future delivery, just as oaths can be exchanged for one another. Instead of turning to a purely phenomenological model of creative voice in his discussion of inspired poetry, Milton actually exposes the socioeconomic character of the speech acts required by the church and tries to capitalize on that quality in replacing them with contractual performatives of his own.

The Elision of the Performative

'Throughout his mature existence Milton exhibited a wide, fairly intensive, and highly sentient knowledge of law as both a civil and ecclesiastical entity,' Harris Fletcher remarks, noting the frequent use of legal language and material in Milton's prose (*Intellectual Development* 2:530). Fletcher speculates that, having studied at least some Justinian in the course of his formal education, Milton contemplated following his brother Christopher into the legal profession from the end of his Cambridge career up to the time he left for Italy in 1638 (*Intellectual Development* 2:475, 530–1). Further reasons for and documentation of Milton's legal knowledge are given by J. Milton French, who records Milton's ambiguous response to his father's vocation as scrivener and moneylender, as well as his occasional involvement in legal suits relating to his father's business. The legal instincts thus developed may help to explain the final ironic twist in Milton's covenant with the reader. Notwithstanding the deliberate legal formulation of Milton's promise, it is nicely undercut, in the end, by his use of the subjunctive. In place of the binding 'I go on trust' or 'I will go on trust,' Milton writes, 'I *may* go on trust with [the reader],' a formulation matched in the final lines of the digression by the conditionality of 'hence *may* appear the right I have to meddle in these matters.' The subjunctive could be a courtesy, acknowledging the reader's right to decline the covenant, but it also seems to provide Milton with an out, with the possibility of arguing that he never made a firm commitment. In speech-act terms, a similar loophole is introduced by the seemingly innocuous preamble '*Neither doe I think it shame* to covnant,' which in effect de-activates the performativity of the utterance. In the final analysis, Milton is not concluding a covenant but describing his attitude toward one. Yet both the underlying constative or propositional construction and the potential uncertainty of 'may' are subsumed in the apparent certitude and performativity of the sentence as it culminates in the declaration 'I refuse not to sustain this expectation.' Any awareness that the phrase 'I refuse not' still evades the positivity of 'I sustain this expectation' is almost obliterated by the declarative tone and the legalistic resonances of Milton's rhetoric. Like the intangible pledge and the self-referential temporality of the promise, the grammar of the sentence itself illustrates the ability of language to fabricate a new basis of authority, even out of a series of absences.

The tract as a whole *is* a performance insofar as Milton is using it to transfer the basis for authority and performative language from church officials to inspired individuals, and to accord varying degrees of authority to those who are inspired in the general or the special sense. In the words of the rather obscure closing sentence of the digression, Milton himself assumes 'the right ... to meddle in these matters' (*CPW* 1:823) by rejecting ecclesiastical office as an authorizing power and substituting an individual's legal right to conclude a contract with other members of the community. He is meddling with authority, both in the sense of interfering with recognized power structures (i.e., meddling in authority) and in attempting to secure a new mandate for such interference (i.e., meddling from a position of authority). Revolutionary in its adoption of a new, secular basis for verbal pronouncements, Milton's tract illustrates the way performative language both reflects and creates a communal basis for speech and action. As Sandy Petrey writes:

Revolutionary transformations make apparent what can be concealed when societies are stable: performative language not only derives from but also establishes communal reality and institutional solidity. (*Speech Acts* 21)

With its focus on personal responsibility and individual talent, the digression effectively enacts the foundation Milton is proposing for a reasonable church government. At the same time, it illustrates the extent to which Milton's self-presentation as an inspired poet, and his entire concept of effectual voice, is influenced by sociopolitical uses of performative language, including legal covenants, economic transactions, institutional declarations, hierarchy, and communal expectations. Many of these factors will reappear more subtly in his exploration of verbal performance in *Paradise Lost*.

4

Paradise Lost: The Creation of Poetry and the Poetry of Creation

Er baut seine Welt in diese Lücke hinein.

Friedrich Nietzsche

Creation and 'Firstness' in the Invocations

In the Latin of *De Doctrina Christiana*, Milton follows the tradition of Ficino, Erasmus, Luther, and Calvin in translating *logos* as *sermo*, the spoken word, rather than as *verbum*, the static philosophical idea. The resulting emphasis on orality and communication – that is, on aspects of language which have special relevance for a Protestant poet – is borne out by the analogy between God's use of language and the poet's in *Paradise Lost*. In the invocations, Milton characterizes the inspired language for which he pleads by appealing to the paradigm of creation by the word. Conversely, in book 7, he represents the divine utterances that bring about creation in such a way as to render them models for his own language, which is to bring about a conversion in the reader and the world. Milton rewrites the narrative of beginnings so as to stress aspects of divine creation, such as dividing, naming, and defining, which provide an analogue for his own creation of poetry. Ironically, however, to write about creation in this way is to underscore aspects of the sociopolitical performative, and thus to risk undermining the qualities of transcendence and intentionality that should distinguish God's creative word as the ultimate phenomenological performative. Book 7 of *Paradise Lost*, the epic's resonant centre, is a focal point for questions of inspiration, performativity, and language. The tensions between a transcendent creative voice and a limited, social scene of discourse, between autonomous agency and a subjectivity constructed through language, are at their most explicit in this self-conscious book.

The correlation between inspired language and the language of creation is first formulated by the invocations in books 1, 3, and 7. All these passages reveal a preoccupation with classical and biblical concepts of inspiration, but also with notions of special election to authorial power and a more democratic indwelling of the Spirit, the two types of inspiration distinguished in the previous chapter. All the invocations confront the presumption of beginning, the uncertainty of name-giving, and the persistent problematic of creation in language. Repeated within three relatively short and superficially diverse passages, these themes point to a complex that haunts, for Milton, the writing of visionary poetry.

In his book *Beginnings*, Edward Said unsettles the innocence that would take the inception of a creative or critical enterprise for granted, by exposing the individual and cultural assumptions involved in the decision of where to begin a text and demonstrating that intention and method are necessarily presupposed by the act of beginning. Said reveals how any project that takes place in language, which is to say any project that takes place in history, begins by producing difference, delimiting a frame of reference, and committing itself to a culturally defined position. Most importantly, Said distinguishes between the 'divine, mythical and privileged' notion of origin and the 'secular, humanly produced, and ceaselessly re-examined' one of beginning (xiii). This opposition addresses exactly what is going on in Milton's invocations and his creation narrative. However much he may intend to represent a privileged origin, the conventions of language, particularly the delimiting and categorizing language that characterizes his account of creation, render the divine origin a human beginning which incorporates aspects of sociopolitical performative speech.

The difficulty of approaching origins is readily admitted by both characters and poet in *Paradise Lost*: 'For Man to tell how human Life began / Is hard' (*PL* 8.250–1), and to write of a beginning the poet needs the help of a Spirit who was present from the first. Yet the desire for temporal or conceptual 'firstness' in *Paradise Lost* can be not only difficult but also dangerous, as the example of Satan ('he of the first, / If not the first Arch-Angel' [*PL* 5.659–60]) and all that originates with him aptly illustrates.[1] The invocations in books 1, 3, and 7 all confront the potential presumption of beginning and respond to it by characterizing creative efforts as projects of revision, thus taking a first step toward implicating creative utterance in a structure of repetition.

---

1 For discussions of the anxiety that attaches to ideas of origin in *Paradise Lost*, see Schwartz (40–59) and Kerrigan (*Sacred Complex* 157–70).

It is hardly surprising that Milton's anxiety about beginnings is most explicit in the opening invocation in book 1, which I quote in full:

Of Man's First Disobedience, and the Fruit
Of that Forbidden Tree, whose mortal taste
Brought Death into the World, and all our woe,
With loss of *Eden*, till one greater Man
Restore us, and regain the blissful Seat,
Sing Heav'nly Muse, that on the secret top
Of *Oreb*, or of *Sinai*, didst inspire
That Shepherd, who first taught the chosen Seed,
In the Beginning how the Heav'ns and Earth
Rose out of *Chaos*: Or if *Sion* Hill
Delight thee more, and *Siloa's* Brook that flow'd
Fast by the Oracle of God; I thence
Invoke thy aid to my advent'rous Song,
That with no middle flight intends to soar
Above th' *Aonian* Mount, while it pursues
Things unattempted yet in Prose or Rhyme.
And chiefly Thou O Spirit, that dost prefer
Before all Temples th' upright heart and pure,
Instruct me, for Thou know'st; Thou from the first
Wast present, and with mighty wings outspread
Dove-like satst brooding on the vast Abyss
And mad'st it pregnant: What in me is dark
Illumine, what is low raise and support;
That to the highth of this great Argument
I may assert Eternal Providence,
And justify the ways of God to men.
    Say first ...   (*PL* 1.1–27)

In Milton's first line, we find classically derived epic subjects linked with a first sin. Where Homer sang of 'the anger of Peleus' son' and 'the man of many ways,' and Virgil of 'arms and a man,' Milton combines Man and his actions with the notion of firstness to write of 'Man's First Disobedience.' As if to compensate for the possibility that disobedience and firstness may be connected, these opening lines launch a strategy of displacing and replacing beginnings that will even affect the way Milton represents divine creation. Syntactically as well as thematically and chronologically, Milton's epic begins *in medias res*. He has, of course, a strong precedent for this convention in the epics of Homer and Virgil, but following it necessitates departing from the order of his biblical model. The Bible begins 'in the beginning' and goes on from there; Milton's 'In the Beginning' enters syntactically in the ninth line of his invocation and does not enter thematically until the half-way point of the poem. Starting with a subordinate clause that picks up the course of sacred history from the *second* chapter of Genesis onward ('Man's First Disobedience'), Milton retraces his steps back toward the classical epic beginning ('Sing ... Muse'), and only then toward the Bible's original act of divine creation, which is first broached in an echo or repetition of the words of Moses ('In the Beginning'). 'First' is a prominent word in the invocation, appearing three times in a pattern symmetrical enough to suggest that there is a certain self-consciousness attached to it. Appearing as adjective, adverb, and then noun, at the beginning (1.1), the middle (1.8), and the end (1.19) of the line, the word participates in a reversal that seems to give literal meaning to the prophetic principle that the 'first' shall be last.

Significantly, however, the word 'first' is never attached to Milton himself, but instead to Man, to Moses, to the Holy Spirit, and finally, at the beginning of the second verse-paragraph, to the Muse-Spirit, who is twice enjoined to 'say first' (*PL* 1.27, 28). In terms of the invocation's strategy of deflecting the burden of beginning away from the poet, the adverb in 'say first' can be read with reference not only to the chronological ordering of the narrative, but also to the priority of the Muse's voice in relation to the poet's: the Muse will say first, the poet will repeat after. As the narrative begins, one more damning echo leaves us with the full awareness of what firstness may entail: it was, the Muse answers, 'Th'infernal Serpent' who 'first seduc'd' our grand parents 'to that foul revolt' (*PL* 1.33–4). First cause of the first disobedience, the first of the archangels sets the pattern for all that later projects of beginning must avoid.

Accordingly, the invocation immediately sets up a system that privileges secondary and corrective action. The doubling of epic heroes, of first man Adam with 'one greater Man' Christ, whose purpose is to 'Restore us, and regain,' is clear and canonical. Less immediately obvious is the parallel to this structure in the pairing of Moses and Milton. 'First' and 'In the Beginning' are attached safely to Moses, who originally sang of the origin of the world. Though Milton cannot claim to outdo or correct this inspired model, he can at least voice a displaced desire to better his epic precursor Ariosto, in pursuing 'Things unattempted yet in Prose or Rhyme.'[2] From the outset, Milton puts himself in the position of one who comes second, a reviser and reshaper of received material. As David Daiches has pointed out (67), Milton modifies the classical epic paradigm in displacing the first-person subject who enters in the opening words of Homer's and Virgil's epics ('tell me' and 'I sing'), delaying the introduction of subjectivity into his language until the twelfth line of *Paradise Lost*: 'I thence / Invoke thy aid to my advent'rous Song.'

Milton's address first to the Heavenly Muse, but then 'chiefly' to the Holy Spirit, hints again at this doubling in which the second term is greater than the first. At the same time, the invocation introduces the double sense of inspiration that emerged from Milton's prose works. A model of inspiration that features Moses and a Muse implies that special knowledge is being accorded to a chosen individual, while an indwelling Spirit is accessible to all believers. As the focus of the invocation shifts from the first kind of inspiration to the second, the significance of the creation topos also changes. First introduced as the *matter* of inspired narrative – Moses taught 'In the Beginning how the Heav'ns and Earth / Rose out of *Chaos*' (*PL* 1.9–10) – it becomes a paradigm for the *process* of inspiration itself. The same Spirit that brooded on the abyss is to re-enact creation within the poet, making light out of darkness and raising and supporting the deep. Milton is quite literally casting himself in the role of the abyss, enacting, as it were, a 'mise en abîme' that is repeated in the reflexive structure of his imagery: he asks to participate in a scene of creation in order to describe a scene of creation. The same holds true in all the invocations, as well as throughout book 7: creation is a subject for the narrative as well as being a model for the process of inspiration itself.

The model becomes more problematic when later invocations introduce the possibility of creative failure. In book 3, the poet's meditation on the first created thing, light, entangles him in attendant ambiguities: is the first-day creation of light distinct from the fourth-day creation of the sun, or does Light antedate creation altogether 'since God is Light'? While Milton is less concerned here than his commentators have been with the theological debate these lines might engender, his uncertainty about the naming of

---

2 It is worth noting that even if Milton's intention was to submit to the priority of the biblical text, many readers have remarked that lines 15–16 *sound* like a claim to revise even the Bible. David Daiches, in his influential essay on the book 1 invocation, comments that Milton seems to want to 'overgo Moses' (63); somewhat less convincingly, Said argues that Milton's invocation 'is everywhere characterized by the intention to exceed all previous texts, perhaps not excluding even the Gospels' (212).

light foreshadows the failure he will experience when he tries once again to enact the creative process in his own person. After relating the events of the first day of creation in miniature –

> before the Sun,
> Before the Heavens thou wert, and at the voice
> Of God, as with a Mantle didst invest
> The rising world of waters dark and deep,
> Won from the void and formless infinite   (*PL* 3.8–12)

– the poet himself rises into a light-filled world from the '*Chaos* and *Eternal Night*' (*PL* 3.18) which have been his subject in the first two books. 'Thee I revisit safe,' the poet asserts, having fulfilled his part in the re-enactment of creation, but light has not played the corresponding role that would complete the re-enactment: 'thou / Revisit'st not these eyes' (*PL* 3.21–3). The physical light of the first day of creation is meaningless to Milton, its significance for him eliminated by his blindness:

> for the Book of knowledge fair
> Presented with a Universal blanc
> Of Nature's works to me expung'd and ras'd,
> And wisdom at one entrance quite shut out.   (*PL* 3.47–50)

The external referent of these lines may be Milton's loss of his very mortal sight, but they also embody a theological and poetic principle that is central to *Paradise Lost*. Sanford Budick elucidates the theological analogue, arguing that here and elsewhere in the epic the poet's loss of sight or 'image failure' is 'really the condition of all humanity,' a condition which allows for the development of a compensatory truthful image of reality (71–2). But the lines also imply a compensatory *verbal* creation. Alluding to the commonplace that the natural world is the Book of God, and using diction like 'expung'd and ras'd' that evokes the mechanics of writing, Milton suggests that the world might be rewritten and thus restored. The passage assumes that creation may be brought about through language; in this, it resembles Eve's love lyric in book 4. Telling Adam of her joy in the created world when he is present, Eve runs through the stages of creation – sun, fertile earth, moon, starry train – but then proceeds to 'de-create' the world her words have formed by negating each of its elements in the face of Adam's imagined absence:

> But neither breath of Morn when she ascends
> With charm of earliest Birds, nor rising Sun
> On this delightful land, nor herb, fruit, flow'r,
> Glist'ring with dew, nor fragrance after showers,
> Nor grateful Ev'ning mild, nor silent Night
> With this her solemn Bird, nor walk by Moon,
> Or glittering Star-light without thee is sweet.   (*PL* 4.650–6)

Readers have often noted that, even in denying the attractiveness of nature without Adam's companionship, Eve actually evokes a vivid image of natural paradise. In other words, the ability of language to create a world of phenomena after the model of Genesis 1 appears to transcend the propositional content of the speech.

Through the subtlety of Miltonic negatives, a similar de-creation and re-creation is effected in the invocation in book 3. What do we make of the fact that, in a hymn to Holy Light, poetic inspiration and activity are repeatedly said to take place 'Nightly' (*PL* 3.32), 'darkling, and in shadiest Covert hid' (*PL* 3.39)? Far from being invoked, physical light is being dismissed in favour of a poetic illumination by which the re-creation through Miltonic language takes place. Presented with a 'blanc' page, Milton proceeds to fill it with a rehearsal of the original creative events even as he denies their visible reality for him:

> not to me returns
> Day, or the sweet approach of Ev'n or Morn,
> Or sight of vernal bloom, or Summer's Rose,
> Or flocks, or herds, or human face divine   (*PL* 3.41–4)

The difference between 'holy Light, offspring of Heav'n first-born' (named in the first line of book 3) and 'Celestial Light' (named fifty lines later) is structural as well as semantic. The intervening invocation has expunged the first, physical light and replaced it with a more effective Light, the latter created through Milton's words analogously to the way in which original light was created through the words of God, and through the inspired language of the biblical text. Modelling his poetic re-creation on divine creation in this way, Milton reveals his desire for and faith in what I have been calling the phenomenological performative – the ability of language to create a world of phenomena by reflecting the consciousness and intentionality of the speaker. But the structure of repetition, and the poet's attempts to name and negotiate with the source of his inspiration, also foreshadow a more social and political vision of performative language to come in book 7.

These political aspects – in the broad sense of political, as concerned with relationships of power, knowledge, ascendency, and subordination – begin to emerge in the book 7 invocation. Milton's allusion to the figure of Wisdom and her activities before the natural world was born combines the theme of creation with a concern for knowledge, permitted and forbidden, which becomes ever more insistent until the crisis in book 9. The sisterly duo of Urania and Wisdom repeats the doubling of classical and Christian figures of inspiration as well as the now-familiar distinction between special visitation (Urania is a muse who visits whom she pleases) and general enablement (Wisdom is potentially available to all believers who ask it of the Holy Spirit). As in the book 3 invocation, there is also a doubling of visible objects with a superior imaginative reality. The poet whose Muse existed 'Before the Hills appear'd, or Fountain flow'd' (*PL* 7.8) is now reaching beyond the traditional topoi of poetic inspiration, even if he has employed them in previous invocations ('if *Sion* Hill / Delight thee more, and *Siloa's* Brook that flow'd' [*PL* 1.10–11]; 'pure Ethereal stream, / Whose Fountain who shall tell?' [*PL* 3.7–8]). More explicitly than ever, Milton relies on creation as an analogue for inspiration. He locates himself in a kind of chaos, 'In darkness, and with dangers compast round' (*PL* 7.27), a position for which there are two other analogues in *Paradise Lost*: the figure of Sin, 'With terrors and with clamors compasst round / Of mine own brood' (*PL* 2.862–3), and the faithful angel Abdiel, 'fearless, though alone / Encompass'd round with foes' (*PL* 5.875–6). While Sin, surrounded by monsters which she has engendered, cannot escape, and while the angel has the strength of will to stand alone, the poet must call for divine aid to re-enact the scene of creation around him: 'But drive far off the barbarous dissonance' (*PL* 7.32). Later in book 7 the initial events of the creation – the Son's silencing of the troubled waves and his circumscription of the universe – answer to these lines, the striking image of the Son's golden compasses echoing Milton's already resonant expression 'compast round.'

Golden compasses and encompassing dangers are the positive and negative poles of the image of circumscription or delimitation. By separating off unwanted materials, the Son's compasses describe a space in which creation can occur, but by hemming in and weighing on the poetic self, encompassing dangers threaten poetic creation unless they are driven far off by a defending muse. Milton's opposition of the terms is clear, yet their conjunction reveals a threat inherent in the notion of circumscription. The only way to open a space for creative activity is through an authoritative, even violent, action, one which necessarily sets limits to the space thus created.[3] For Edward Said, the same principle of delimitation is an inescapable part of beginning a text: 'Any worker in discursive language ... must use language to delimit the linguistic object he studies and deals with' (36). The circumscribing action that the poet requires of the Muse, and later attributes to the Son, is essential to the problematic of beginnings in language.

Besides locating Milton at the centre of a scene of creation, the invocation in book 7 intimates a parallel between the poet and Adam, the central figure of the newly created world. Both are receiving narratives from a heavenly source. In the first speech to Raphael in book 7, Adam asks his 'Divine Interpreter,' just as Milton asks his Heavenly Muse, to 'descend' from a celestial to an earthly sphere (*PL* 7.1, 84). Both Adam and the poet are emerging from a situation in which the continuity of their story seems threatened: the 'wild Rout' that Milton asks to be guarded from becomes the equivalent of Satan and his crew, who seemed to threaten Heaven with ruin and horrid confusion in the story which Raphael has just finished relating to Adam and Eve. As that evil was 'Driv'n back' (*PL* 7.57), so Milton asks his Muse to 'drive far off' the dangers around him (*PL* 7.32). Raphael's narrative brings about in Adam a virtual enactment of the process of inspiration, as he is 'fill'd / With ... deep *muse* to hear' (*PL* 7.51–2; my italics). Like the story Milton is told by his divine interlocutor, Raphael's story is to perform a specific function in the hearts and minds of his listeners. Adam and Eve are informed of the 'dire example' of a forerunner who fell from glory, as Bellerophon fell before Milton:

Lest from this flying Steed unrein'd, (as once
Bellerophon, though from a lower Clime)

---

3 Sanford Budick provides a different interpretation of the relationship between circumscription and creativity, arguing that exclusion and disjunction reinstate a 'gulf of the unknown' into creation (120), thus bringing about the preconditions for knowledge and interpretation: 'Just as the deity's creativity revolves around an act of circumscription that culminates in exclusion, so the sustaining virtue of creation is its ability to maintain a space of *in*-coincidentia oppositorum, an interval of unmerged opposition' (114). Although the divisive nature of creation is central to Budick's reading of *Paradise Lost*, his concern with Milton's aesthetic expression in the context of theological and exegetical tradition leads him to a set of conclusions about disjunction, sacrifice, and the renewing of perception that have relatively little in common with the linguistic perspective of this chapter, which is oriented toward the creation of subjectivity and, ultimately, political relations in language.

Dismounted, on th' *Aleian* Field I fall
Erroneous there to wander and forlorn.   (*PL* 7.17–20)

The emphatic repetition of 'fall' and 'befall' (*PL* 7.19, 25, 26, 43, 44), and of
the potential 'error' of Milton and Adam and Eve ('Erroneous there to wander' [*PL* 7.20]; 'thir appetite, / Though wand'ring' [*PL* 7.49–50]), brings
home the fact that heavenly narratives will, ideally, play an effectual role in
the shaping of human life. Yet Adam's imminent failure leaves Milton once
again in the position of a belated hero, with the responsibility of performing a later, corrective 'reading' of divine discourse.

The parallel between Milton and Adam suggests that inspired discourse
in a fallen world may resemble prelapsarian conversation with heaven.
Taking on a visionary role, as Milton does, implies a return to ideal communication. A similar conclusion may be drawn from the morning hymn of
Adam and Eve in book 5, which is described in terms that distinctly resemble the language of Milton's invocations –

Lowly they bow'd adoring, and began
Thir Orisons, *each Morning* duly paid
In *various style*, for neither *various style*
Nor *holy rapture* wanted they to praise
Thir Maker, in *fit strains* pronounct or sung
Unmeditated, such prompt eloquence
Flow'd from thir lips, in *Prose or numerous Verse*

(*PL* 5.144–50; my italics)

– and which goes on to praise all the elements of the created world by
rehearsing the order of their creation in the first chapter of Genesis. If such
parallels sanction the study of Milton's language in relation to the language
of Adam and Eve, there are also other potential analogues for the poet in
book 7. Being 'guided down' after drawing 'Empyreal Air' (*PL* 7.14–15), he
may be like Raphael, who comes 'Down from the Empyrean' (*PL* 7.73);
both Milton and Raphael feel the need to harmonize their sayings to the
ears of their mortal audience. Or he may be like God himself. Milton's plea
for an effective poetic voice stands so close to the supreme example of
effectual language at the creation that it urges readers to examine whether
the relationship between the two is one of disjunction, imitation, or –
though Milton might well have resisted such a suggestion – even identification.

The discovery of parallels between Milton's language and the language of Adam and Eve, or the angelic narrators, or God, is a project related to Stanley Fish's thesis in *Surprised by Sin*, though book 7 is incidental to his argument about how the language of *Paradise Lost* performs the particular function of convicting the reader of sin. Fish's thesis is challenged to a degree by Robert Entzminger, who argues, on the basis of research in seventeenth-century theology and homiletics, that Milton's language at times imitates the qualities of prelapsarian speech. Most recently, John Leonard has written about the way various narrative voices in the epic aspire to, but also deviate from, prelapsarian language. But the comparison is generally confined to Adam's and Eve's language, on the one hand, and Milton's style, on the other. Rarely do critics take into account the possibility that Milton's language imitates the language of God at the creation, even though this event stands at the centre of the poem as a conspicuous paradigm of verbal performativity.

Robert Entzminger has gone furthest toward drawing the parallel between Milton's style and the creative word of God. His argument about the influence of Milton's language on the reader brings together the concepts of inspiration, divine creation, and what Austin would call perlocutionary effect:

... through divine inspiration the style itself is transformed, becoming an instrument capable not simply of persuading or manipulating its auditors but of illuminating them, of engaging them in the same process of revelation begun in the Creation and continued in Scriptures. (Entzminger 139)

Entzminger describes God's language in terms which reveal its performative quality. The words of God, he argues, 'are not only signs but the ontological basis for their referents'; instead of referring back to already existing objects, God's words exist 'both prior to and inclusive of the reality they indicate' (130). It is a type of language which, as an ideal phenomenological performative, enacts what it pronounces:

In God's speech ... the utterance is the virtual accomplishment, its manifestation in human time an inevitable result of God's having spoken. (131)

Entzminger stops short of saying that Milton's language aspires to the same qualities, but that is exactly the conclusion I would draw from a reading of *Paradise Lost*. In the invocations, Milton suggests that inspired language may bring about a re-creation of nature and the human spirit, which follows the pattern of God's original creation, yet is safely insulated from origin or firstness by operating in a repetitive and restorative capacity. In book 7, the qualities that Milton ascribes to divine language, and the events in his cosmogony, seem designed to make divine creation into an analogue for inspired poetic discourse. Paradoxically, perhaps, this involves emphasizing difference, articulation, repetition, and the arbitrariness of beginnings, qualities which are common to an act of world-creation and to the use of language as we understand it from a post-Saussurian perspective. Milton's attempt to capture the qualities of presence and intentionality inherent in the Word may be evidence of a supreme logocentrism, yet his strategy for putting this aim into practice turns divine origins into human beginnings. Beyond his awareness that divine things are only approximately conveyed in human speech, Milton does not seem overly troubled by the limitation and categorization involved in his representation of beginnings. Yet his language lays the foundation for Blake's exploration of the division and constriction that an act of linguistic or cosmogonic creation inevitably involves.

The Performativity of Divine Speech

> And thou my Word, begotten Son, by thee
> This I perform, speak thou, and be it done   (*PL* 7.163–4)

Here, where the creation of the universe begins, language and action are inextricable. The Father addresses his words to his Word, the actant by whom (by whose words and through whom as Word) creation is effected. Centring on the deictics 'thee / This,' which indicate the immediate presence of addressee and object, the lines employ an internal rhyme to enact the closure of the word-event structure: through the Son, God's will is done. At the same time, God's words virtually constitute a definition of verbal performance, as he affirms that the Son's saying is also a doing. In Searle's terms, the lines contain at least two explicit illocutions: the directive 'speak thou,' and the declaration 'be it done.' God's authority to issue these speech acts is of the 'non-institutional' kind that Searle admitted as an exception to the standard sociopolitical declaration. In other words, the language God uses in *Paradise Lost* is representative of the phenomenological performative, the type of utterance which acts and creates because of the transcendent authority of the speaking voice and the creative potential of language itself.

To read in this way is to measure things in heaven by things on earth, or at least to measure theological concepts by a theory of linguistic behaviour within society. God's words are, of course, being conveyed by a poet whose experience of how language operates in a human and social context necessarily affects all aspects of his writing, and what we may discover in a study of God's language is how Milton has tried to represent divine speech as an ideal phenomenological performative. Most importantly, he asks us to identify the Son as God's Word, just as we identify 'This I perform' as God's word. The fact that we perceive the former as an anthropomorphic being and the latter as an audible utterance is due to our sensory and linguistic limitations. Could we transcend these, we would begin to see that these two Words are equivalent, that in some sense God's 'This I perform' already enacts creation. The Son's echo of God's performative utterance, and the physical actions that issue from the Son's words, appear to be multiple and successive events only because of the causality of human logic and the temporality of human speech.

The added dimension of divine performative language in *Paradise Lost* is that the Son's words and actions constitute a repetition of the divine utterance that he himself is. This aspect of the relationship between God the Father and the Son is best illustrated by the divine colloquy in book 3:

> Beyond compare the Son of God was seen
> Most glorious, in him all his Father shone
> Substantially express'd, and in his face
> Divine compassion visibly appear'd,
> Love without end, and without measure Grace,
> Which uttering thus he to his Father spake.
>   O Father, gracious was that word which clos'd
> Thy sovran sentence, that Man should find grace   (*PL* 3.138–45)

The expression or externalization of God in the Son is repeated by the Son's utterance (that is, 'outerance') in words of the grace of his own being. The Father's glory is made visible in the Son, both in that the Son acts out what 'grace' means (since these words foreshadow his sacrifice of himself for humankind), and in his literal utterance. Accommodated to human understanding, this phenomenon is represented by the rhyme between 'his face' and 'Grace,' as well as by the Son's echo, at line 145, of the words God has just spoken at line 131, 'Man therefore shall find grace.' Throughout the epic, the words of God and the Son have a peculiar resonance and meaningfulness, with the presence of the Son a constant reminder that the divine Word has hypostasized being, acting even as it speaks.

The type of performativity ascribed to divine utterance in *Paradise Lost* widens the scope of things that can be done with language in the poem. It has been argued that, in *Paradise Lost* as in other texts of Christian experience, not only the words of God but also the discourse as a whole acquires a special status because of the theological frame of reference: 'religious subject matter place[s] a distinctive logical stress upon language that [has] odd, subtle effects on its structure, its semantics, and the texture of its style' (Merrill, 'Miltonic God-Talk' 298). 'God,' a signifier that cannot be accommodated into discourse by analogy with ordinary, finite signifiers that have demonstrable reference, affects the sense of words around it, putting language 'under logical stress' (Merrill, *Epic God-Talk* 66) and altering the rules of the language game. We assign different values to the verb 'create,' for instance, depending on whether we meet it in the phrase 'Milton creates' or in the phrase 'and God created.' The composers of the 'P' document in Genesis felt this distinction so keenly that they reserved the verb *bara* for God's action of creating new or wondrous phenomena. In English translation, our need to adapt an understanding of 'create' to these circumstances indicates a particular kind of context-dependence that applies to theological language, since the subject matter removes limitations that a secular or sociopolitical frame of reference may place on words like 'create' or 'performative.'

To a certain extent, Milton also attempts to claim the qualities of the phenomenological performative for the language of *Paradise Lost* itself, by assuming that the poem can create and convert by virtue of a transcendent or inspired authority. Part of the poem's premise is that it will effect a variety of purposes, such as justifying the ways of God and bringing about a reconciliation between the reader and God. *Paradise Lost* participates in a greater variety of language games than does a denotative or scientific discourse, or even most fictional discourses. This multidimensional quality is intensified by the superimposition of voices within the poem; one voice may build on the performative qualities of another. In book 7 alone, the reader must attend to the tension and cooperation between the voices of Milton (who may or may not be distinguished from the narrator), Raphael, Adam, God, and God's Word. Thomas Merrill correctly claims that Raphael's words to Adam in books 5 to 8 are 'not informative, but performative, seeking to effect and maintain a "right" relationship between Adam and his Creator,' and that, according to the logic of the creation narrative, 'excellence is measured in performance rather than essence' – that is, by the place and role that each being fills in the created world ('Miltonic God-Talk' 302–3). I would add that Milton is trying to make a world appear that otherwise has disappeared from his sight; that, as narrator, he is concerned to do the same for a contemporary audience for whom 'evil days' have obscured a divinely created nature; that all these voices are echoes of the one truly performative voice, present in the written pre-text of the Bible and imagined as a speaking presence in *Paradise Lost*, which holds the structure of efficacious words together.

For Milton, effective language is not so much language that *completes* an action as language that continues to have an effect; the 'perfect' tense, one might say, is for him the imperfect. The chapter 'Of God's Providence' in *De Doctrina Christiana* explains the working of providence in the ordinary sense, or what 'is commonly ... called Nature,' in terms of the continuing resonance of the voice that brought about creation: 'for nature cannot mean anything except the wonderful power and efficacy of the divine voice which went forth in the beginning, and which all things have obeyed ever since as a perpetual command' (*CPW* 6:340–1). Milton's literalizing interpretation of the commonplace that nature is the visible Word of God is supported by his assumption that the words of God spoken at the creation have not just illocutionary, but an ideal perlocutionary, force. That is to say, they are borne out even when the effective agent is not God himself, as is the case with the divine command concerning procreation. The beginning of the *History of Britain* is predicated on Milton's conviction that the words of God must elicit a response in the physical world: 'That the whole Earth was inhabited before the Flood, and to the utmost point of habitable ground, from those effectual words of *God* in the Creation, may be more then conjectur'd' (*CPW* 5:4). The Miltonic universe is one where God says, '[W]hat I will is Fate' (*PL* 7.173), and where fate is *fatum*, 'that which has been spoken.' In *De Doctrina Christiana*, Milton confirms the identification between fate and divine decree by demonstrating the etymological connection between fate (*fatum*) and the utterance or externalized words of the deity (*effatum*).

In *Paradise Lost*, an analogy to the perpetually effective words of God is provided by voices that seem to continue sounding even after a character has ceased to speak. So of the Son: 'His words here ended, but his meek aspect / Silent yet spake' (*PL* 3.266–7); and later Raphael:

The Angel ended, and in *Adam's* Ear
So Charming left his voice, that he a while
Thought him still speaking, still stood fixt to hear   (*PL* 8.1–3)

More ominously, the divine prohibition continues to resonate, as Adam and Eve both testify:

[Adam:]   Sternly he pronounc'd
The rigid interdiction, which resounds
Yet dreadful in mine ear ...   (*PL* 8.333–5)

[Eve:] God so commanded, and left that Command
Sole Daughter of his voice ...   (*PL* 9.652–3)

Less than a hundred lines later, Eve's imminent fall is signalled by the fact that Satan's words displace God's words in her senses and her heart: 'in her ears the sound / Yet rung of his [the serpent's] persuasive words' (*PL* 9.736–7). Significantly, Eve not only listens to and believes Satan but accords his words the resonant quality which should only belong to heavenly voices.

It is not surprising that the ability to make words reach into the silence belongs to superhuman characters in the poem; the transience of the humanly spoken word has preoccupied Western literary culture from at least Saint Augustine onward. The type of language we *do* expect will survive is written language, and the text of *Paradise Lost might* be expected to 'resound' and retain its efficacy for future generations. By imparting a quality of perpetual presence to certain of the voices in *Paradise Lost*, Milton is actually making them more appropriate as prototypes for his own use of language.

The same is true of the narrative of creation in book 7. The events of creation are presented in such a way as to stress the qualities most relevant to a poet's own linguistic practice: acts of dividing and acts of naming, and the contrast between words, noise, and silence. Readings of Milton's narrative of creation have centred on its theology,[4] its place in the medieval and

---

4 Though it purports to be exploratory and tentative, the essay by A.S.P. Woodhouse, 'Notes on Milton's Views on the Creation: The Initial Phases,' has become the standard discussion of Milton's theology of creation. Similar arguments are advanced by J.H. Adamson in 'Milton and the Creation' (revised as 'The Creation'). Gordon Campbell continues the debate about causality and *ex nihilo* and *ex Deo* creation, while distinguishing between Milton's treatment of the subject in *De Doctrina Christiana* and *Paradise Lost*, in 'Milton's Theological and Literary Treatments of the Creation.'

Renaissance tradition of hexaemeral poetry,[5] and its adaptation of the text of Genesis.[6] The last of these is most relevant to my argument, yet even those critics who analyse Milton's dislocations and reorderings of the biblical narrative do not fully take into account the importance of Milton's reading of Genesis for his perceived task of writing inspired poetry.

Divine Creation and Verbal Performance

If, as I have been arguing, Milton tries to represent God's speech, and to some extent his own, as performative utterance which relies on transcendent authority and the unique qualifications of the speaker, the language of the poem is nevertheless also influenced by the forms of language in society. The account of creation in book 7 reveals the 'post-Saussurian' dimension of God's language and Milton's: both participate in division and articulation, ordering and circumscription. The divine origin is restructured, in Milton's account, as a Saidian beginning; like the invocations, the creation narrative in *Paradise Lost* establishes the arbitrariness of beginnings and deflects an absolute origin. Most explicitly, the scene of discourse into which Milton inserts the biblical account of creation introduces relationships of knowledge and power between the various interlocutors. By employing deictics in his poetry that are absent from the biblical narrative, Milton turns the creation account into a discourse that also explores the creation of subjectivity in performative language.

'Silence, ye troubl'd waves, and thou Deep, peace, / Said then th'Omnific Word, your discord end' (*PL* 7.216–17): the Word's first word is 'silence.' Like the $b^e reshith$ of Genesis 1:1, the command marks a sudden, arbitrary beginning, in a way that must appeal to a poet who feels the threat of the 'barbarous dissonance' that would drown him out. Yet by hav-

---

5 There have been several studies of the relationship between Milton and Du Bartas, considered in terms of influence and imitation; see G.C. Taylor, *Milton's Use of Du Bartas*, and Grant McColley, *Paradise Lost: An Account of Its Growth and Major Origins* and 'Milton's Technique of Source Adaptation.' Two essays by Arnold Williams ('Commentaries on Genesis as a Basis for Hexaemeral Material in the Literature of the Late Renaissance' and 'Renaissance Commentaries on "Genesis" and Some Elements of the Theology of *Paradise Lost*') place Milton's creation account in the wider context of Renaissance commentary and hexaemeral literature. More recently, Jason P. Rosenblatt ('Angelic Tact: Raphael on Creation') has argued that Milton's account of creation owes much less to hexaemeral literature than to patristic, medieval rabbinic, and Reformation commentaries on Genesis.

6 Ernst Häublein, 'Milton's Paraphrase of Genesis: A Stylistic Reading of *Paradise Lost*, Book VII,' and Philip J. Gallagher, 'Creation in Genesis and in *Paradise Lost*,' both offer meticulous comparisons of Milton and Genesis.

ing the Word speak silence, Milton is *breaking* the pre-creationary silence of Genesis, which refuses to discuss anything prior to the beginning demarcated in and by the *bᵉreshith* with which the text opens. The move is consistent with his readiness to put narrative – the entire first half of *Paradise Lost*, in fact – before the biblical beginning. If the Son's initial utterance has any biblical source, it must be the words of Jesus in Mark 4:39 as he stills the storm at sea: 'And he arose, and rebuked the wind, and said unto the sea, Peace, be still.' Milton reverses the sequence of type and antitype, echoing an event in the New Testament as he describes the 'original' act of creating order from a watery chaos.

These first words of the creation have been interpreted as a show of humility, a 'sacrifice' whereby the Son or Word empowers his opposite (Shoaf 124–5), but analogues elsewhere in Milton's prose and poetry suggest that they are rather an appropriation of authority. In *The Doctrine and Discipline of Divorce*, 'the word of God' which 'in one instant hushes outrageous tempests into a sudden stilnesse and peacefull calm' appears as a metaphor for the authoritative, healing 'divine touch' of divorce (*CPW* 2:333). Like the silencing of the pagan oracles in the 'Nativity Ode,' it is a gesture which allows the true word, be it Christ's or Milton's, to sound more effectively. In prefixing this utterance to the biblical narrative of creation, Milton implies that the speaking voice establishes its authority to make performative utterances by first silencing competing voices.

This said, the creative process begins not with a speech act but with an action proper:

> Then stay'd the fervid Wheels, and in his hand
> He took the golden Compasses, prepar'd
> In God's Eternal store, to circumscribe
> This Universe, and all created things:
> One foot he centred, and the other turn'd
> Round through the vast profundity obscure,
> And said, Thus far extend, thus far thy bounds,
> This be thy just Circumference, O World.   (*PL* 7.224–31)

Like the command for silence, the Son's circumscription of the universe separates unwanted material from the significant elements the creator is about to order. The compasses are biblical, alluding to the same passage in Proverbs as the book 7 invocation, a passage in which the figure of Wisdom claims, 'When he prepared the heavens, I was there: when he set a compass upon the face of the depth' (Proverbs 8:27). The Authorized Version, quoted here, has 'compass,' though most of the translations Milton used read 'circle,' a more accurate translation of the Hebrew *hog*. This anomaly has engendered a lively dispute about why Milton intentionally used the less correct and visually cumbersome image of a geometric instrument.[7] Some commentators point out that the compasses were frequently used as a seventeenth-century printer's symbol, and it is this context that they might more readily have evoked for Milton's readers (*CP* 351; McColley, *Paradise Lost* 49). Another contemporary identification for the compasses, one which Blake was to take up, was as a mathematical symbol associated with Isaac Newton (*European Fame* 4–7). In either case, these opening lines direct attention to the scientific and conceptual, if not indeed the literary and textual, forms that creation may take.

For readers like Arnold Williams and A.S.P. Woodhouse, the primary significance of the above passage is to reveal Milton's acceptance of an *ex Deo*, as opposed to an *ex nihilo*, theory of creation. Milton believed, that is to say, that the substance of the created universe was pre-existent and that divine creation was an act of circumscription and ordering, rather than fabrication from nothing. The consequences for Milton's poetics of an *ex Deo* theology, which J.H. Adamson deems 'peculiarly suited to a poetic mind' ('Creation' 81), are as significant as the implications about originality and secondariness that follow from his rejection of creation *ex nihilo*. Milton's belief rests in part on a linguistic argument, to which he alludes in *De Doctrina Christiana*:

In the first place it is certain that neither the Hebrew verb ברא, nor the Greek κτιζειν, nor the Latin *creare* means 'to make out of nothing.' On the contrary, each of them always means 'to make out of something.' (*CPW* 6:305–6)

Milton may also have known, either from rabbinical commentaries or from an intermediary source such as Henry More, that a probable etymological

---

7 Harris F. Fletcher locates Milton's choice of 'compasses' in the rabbinical commentaries printed in Buxtorf's Rabbinical Bible (*Milton's Rabbinical Readings* 100–9). He is answered by George W. Whiting, who feels that a more credible explanation lies in Milton's probable acquaintance with the image of God creating the world with compasses in English church art ('The Golden Compasses in *Paradise Lost*'; *Milton and This Pendant World* 104–18). Grant McColley, in 'Milton's Golden Compasses,' argues that the image of compasses was 'generally accepted and wholly conventional' in Milton's time, though he offers little evidence. The last, quirky word in the debate goes to Joseph E. Morris ('Milton's Golden Compasses'), who speculates that the fabled 'goat and compasses' inn sign may be a corruption of 'God and compasses,' thus offering additional support for the prevalence of the image in the English tradition.

meaning of *bara* is 'divide.'[8] The initial event of the creation narrative in *Paradise Lost* is the division of a chaos which already exists 'outrageous as a Sea, dark, wasteful, wild' (*PL* 7.212). The dividing action is described three times before Milton reaches his scriptural precedent, 'Let there be Light.' The Son's words command an end to discord, his compasses divide world from not-world, and the Spirit separates the four basic elements: 'then founded, then conglob'd / Like things to like, the rest to several place / Disparted' (*PL* 7.239–41).

Milton stresses the role of differentiation more strongly than does his biblical source. Following on the distinction of Word from dissonance and universe from chaos, God proceeds to 'divide' (the word appears often) light from darkness (*PL* 7.250–1), the waters underneath the firmament from those above (*PL* 7.262–3, 268–9), dry land from sea (*PL* 7.283–4), day from night (*PL* 7.340–1), and (once again) light from darkness (*PL* 7.352). Even such a minor departure from the source-text as 'Let there be Lights ... to divide / The Day from Night' (*PL* 7.339–41), rather than 'the day from the night' (Genesis 1:14), may not be 'obviously for metrical reasons' alone, as Ernst Häublein claims in his detailed study of Milton's adaptation of the biblical text (107). Rather, the differentiation of 'The Day' from 'Night' through presence and absence of the definite article distinguishes the privileged, God-created entity from its more amorphous counterpart. '[D]im Night' (*PL* 2.1036), also called 'uncreated night' (*PL* 2.150), 'unessential Night' (*PL* 2.439), '*ancient Night*' (*PL* 2.970, 986), and 'Sable-vested *Night*, eldest of things' (*PL* 2.962), has already been introduced in the chaotic universe of book 2 as the ancestor of Nature. As in the Hesiodic creation myth where Day is born out of an original darkness, 'Night' may be seen as the background against which 'The Day' is defined. A hierarchy is more strongly implied than in the biblical text, which (as discussed in chapter 2) has God divide impartially 'between the day and between the night.'

Whatever it may say about Milton's theology, this strong emphasis on delimitation allows for an analogy with the Saussurian model of language. According to Saussure, in order to make sense of what is in itself a chaotic stream of sound, a hearer divides the sound-mass into units in accordance with the structure of a known language, so that 'the shapeless ribbon [of sound] is cut up into pieces': 'A linguistic entity is not ultimately defined until it is *delimited*, i.e. separated from whatever there may be on either

---

8 'Ibn Ezra renders [*bara*], in accordance with its etymology, to limit, to define, by drawing or incising a line or boundary' (Husik 190). This sentence is quoted by Adamson ('Milton and the Creation' 768); the commentary of Ibn Ezra is also mentioned by Fletcher (*Milton's Rabbinical Readings* 83) and Schwartz (12).

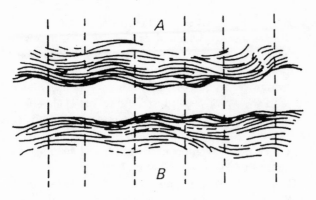

Figure 1
Language as a series of subdivisions imposed on thought and sound. (Ferdinand de Saussure, *Course in General Linguistics*, ed. Charles Bally and Albert Sechehaye, trans. Roy Harris [La Salle IL: Open Court, 1986], 111.)

side of it in a sequence of sounds. It is these delimited entities or *units* which contrast with one another in the mechanism of the language' (*Course* 102). But this process of delimiting sound in order to understand spoken language is only a second-order repetition of the process involved in the creation of the linguistic system itself: 'What takes place, is a somewhat mysterious process by which "thought-sound" evolves divisions, and a language takes shape with its linguistic units in between those two amorphous masses' (*Course* 111). The image is of thought and sound as two chaotic masses, 'the plane of vague, amorphous thought' and 'the equally featureless plane of sound,' between which language acts as an intermediary 'in such a way that the combination of both necessarily produces a mutually complementary delimitation of units,' or a linguistic system (*Course* 110). Saussure's accompanying sketch of the wavy planes of thought and sound divided by vertical marks (fig. 1) might even call to mind the act of dividing the waters from the waters. Language, both as the divine instrument of creation and as a social construct, imposes divisions on chaos: 'Thought, chaotic by nature, is made precise by this process of segmentation' (*Course* 110). In *Paradise Lost*, the creating deity divides the already existing 'raw material' of the cosmos as his words divide what Saussure called 'la substance phonique'; the Son, in Milton's representation, is the Saussurian principle of language which brings about the necessary articulations of chaotic matter.

The argument for creation *ex Deo* is a primary concern in the chapter 'Of the Creation' in *De Doctrina Christiana*. In this text, Milton himself is quick to draw the analogy between the process of creation and rhetoric about creation. Using creation *ex nihilo* as a metaphor, he mocks the supporters of that doctrine for believing in something doubly insubstantial: 'On the whole the moderns are of the opinion that everything was formed out of nothing (which is, I fancy, what their own theory is based on!)' (*CPW* 6:305). His project in *De Doctrina Christiana* manifestly corresponds, instead, to creation *ex Deo*: he works with pre-existing matter, in the form of the biblical text, and his enterprise is one of reordering the parts of that text into an organized doctrine. In both *De Doctrina Christiana* and *Paradise Lost*, the deity's method of creating provides a paradigm for the human poet relying on the power of language to order reality, particularly when that poet's project is to articulate an already existing narrative in new ways.

Delimitation and division are frequently joined with allusions to or images of creation elsewhere in Milton's writing. Not surprisingly, the divorce tracts – which, as Mary Nyquist has shown, rely heavily on the biblical narratives of creation for their argument and imagery – emphasize the role of division in the creative act. Anticipating the phraseology of *Paradise Lost*, *The Doctrine and Discipline of Divorce* makes creation into a prototype for divorce:

... as God and nature signifies ... by the first and last of all his visible works; when by his divorcing command the world first rose out of Chaos, nor can be renew'd again out of confusion but by the separating of unmeet consorts. (*CPW* 2:273)

Regina Schwartz has demonstrated that the overcoming of chaos is a repeated motif in *Paradise Lost*, and that in the epic biblical creation becomes the subject of ritual repetition and commemorative performance.[9] The specifically verbal character of that enterprise is reinforced by numer-

9 Schwartz notes the iterative quality of Milton's account of creation and its consequent fore-shadowing of post-structuralist ideas; these observations lead into a powerful argument about the perpetual need to re-enact creation, or the overcoming of chaos, by ritually commemorating it, and about the way *Paradise Lost* not only records but constitutes such a re-enactment. I am in substantial agreement with Schwartz's observations about the moral, theological, and liturgical dimensions of Miltonic creation, and my exploration of the linguistic dimension complements her study to some extent. However, while Schwartz considers Milton 'our most sensitive reader of the Bible' (30) and interprets his representation of an iterative creation as a faithful reading of Judeo-Christian myth, I would argue that Milton is revising biblical structures, replacing the kerygmatic narrative of the Bible with a discourse of subjectivity.

ous examples from Milton's prose, which suggest that creation by the word is a paradigm throughout Milton's work for the enterprise of shaping an orderly, habitable environment in the face of potentially anarchic forces. Thus chaos comes to be a figure for sin in *Tetrachordon*, and Milton imagines setting limits to it as the creator did: 'But suppose it any way possible to limit sinne, to put a girdle about that *Chaos* ...' (*CPW* 2:658). Significantly, chaos continues to exist at the perimeter of the created universe of *Paradise Lost*, as a place, a living entity, and a potential threat. In a world where chaos can always return in the form of 'evil tongues,' 'darkness,' 'barbarous dissonance,' and sin, it is vital for Milton to hold on to the power of the original divorcing command and to repeat it in his own voice.[10]

Naming and Subjectivity

In order to affirm its own ordering power on the model of the chaos-banishing utterance of God, Milton's poetry emphasizes both divine and human acts of name-giving – a function of language which highlights authority, circumscription, and control. In *De Doctrina Christiana*, Milton recognizes the assertion of sociopolitical authority involved in bestowing a name: 'the giving of a name is always acknowledged to be the function of a superior, whether father or lord' (*CPW* 6:261). *Paradise Lost* reveals at least two levels on which this authority can function. For Milton's God, naming is a method of creation; *Paradise Lost* emphasizes more heavily than does Genesis the way each newly articulated element is incorporated not only into a physical but into a linguistic order. On the human level, naming is a significant expression of subjectivity, as Adam demonstrates when he names his surroundings and thereby defines the place of each element in relation to himself. Subjectivity in Adam's language is the correlative of authority in God's language. In a different context, Benveniste makes the connection between subjectivity and authority when he describes how language 'permits each speaker to *appropriate to himself* an entire language by designating himself as *I*' (226). Appropriating the discourse, or making it his property, is finally also what Milton is doing when he injects markers of subjectivity into the biblical text.

Milton has a scriptural precedent for recounting God's naming of the elements created on the first three days separately from the acts of creation themselves: 'Light the Day, and Darkness Night / He nam'd' (*PL* 7.251–2);

10 Regina Schwartz comes to a similar conclusion with regard to the threat of chaos in the invocations in *Paradise Lost*: 'Milton's epic must do more than epics do: his voice must hold in rapture, not just rocks and woods, but the threatening clamor of chaos itself' (62).

'Heav'n he nam'd the Firmament' (*PL* 7.274); 'The dry Land, Earth, and the great receptacle / Of congregated Waters he call'd Seas' (*PL* 7.307–8). But, given his belief in the pre-existence of matter and his emphasis on division, it becomes more evident than in the biblical account that naming is itself a method of creating. The ability to name, or rename, enables the creator to separate already existing elements and appropriate them for new purposes. The 'hot, cold, moist, and dry' of Chaos (*PL* 2.898) become Day and Night, Seas and Earth. This presents a problem for the poet who would describe Chaos, since he must, in effect, undo the God-created order by removing the God-bestowed names. Hence Milton's Chaos is 'neither Sea, nor Shore, nor Air, nor Fire, / But all these in thir pregnant causes mixt / Confus'dly' (*PL* 2.912–14).[11] When God begins to create entities that require synthesis rather than division, such as heavenly bodies, plants, animals, and human beings, the explicit references to naming stop. In this context, Adam's acts of naming may be understood as a continuation of the divinely instituted process. Adam, presented with (to him) pre-existent 'materials' in the shape of fish, birds, and beasts, bestows names on them by exercising the authority and knowledge that God has bestowed on him ('with such knowledge God endu'd / My sudden apprehension' [*PL* 8.353–4]). While divine naming creates the elements of God's universe, human naming makes them into significant elements of *Adam's* world. God's naming and Adam's both confirm the paradigm inherent in an *ex Deo* theology of creation: that creative effort is equivalent to the fundamentally linguistic process of imposing a differential system on pre-existent matter, such as chaos or chaotic sound.

While the scene of Adam naming the animals (*PL* 8.342–54) has been the most influential passage for critical discussions of Adamic language and naming in *Paradise Lost*, Adam's spontaneous utterance on his first awakening is an equally significant reflection of God's creative naming. Where divine naming creates an objective world, on the human level the naming of one's environment constitutes a creation of subjectivity. When Adam relates the story of his creation to Raphael, he reports that his first words were a spontaneous call to his surroundings:[12]

11 John Leonard discusses the analogous problem Milton experiences when representing the fallen angels, whose original names have been blotted out as a result of their fall and cannot be known by us (67–85).

12 Margarita Stocker, discussing Austin Farrer's theology of creation and its parallels with literary theory, stresses the hermeneutics of human involvement in the process of creation and name-giving. Naming the things in the universe along with the self, the human being becomes aware of difference and otherness, thus bringing about a parallel between the world of created things and the world of linguistic signs, both of which we understand as systems of difference.

> Thou Sun, said I, fair Light,
> And thou enlight'n'd Earth, so fresh and gay,
> Ye Hills and Dales, ye Rivers, Woods, and Plains
> And ye that live and move, fair Creatures ...
> (*PL* 8.273–6)

Adam names elements of the landscape for the first time while placing them in relation to himself as 'I.' In Benveniste's terms, Adam's words are a prime example of the way speakers position themselves in language and in their environment. Benveniste directs the Saussurian distinction between *langue* and *parole* toward a language-user's 'expression of instantaneous and elusive subjectivity,' the ability of language to express subjectivity being an enabling condition of dialogue and indeed of interpersonal relations:

Now a language [*langue*] is a socialized structure which the act of speaking [*parole*] subjects to individual and intersubjective ends, thus adding to it a new and strictly personal design. *Langue* is a system common to everyone; discourse is both the bearer of a message and the instrument of action. In this sense, the configurations of every act of speaking are unique, realized within and by means of language. There is thus an antinomy within the subject between discourse and language. (67)

Discourse, or subjectivized language, is performative, 'the instrument of action'; thus Adam's first words constitute his establishment of a concept of *ego*. Interestingly and by contrast, when Eve recalls her creation she reveals that she did not speak but instead was addressed as 'thou,' first by an invisible voice and then by Adam (*PL* 4.449–91), a difference which seems only to confirm the link between subjectivizing utterance and authority.

Milton's own linguistic positioning is analogous to Adam's: in Benveniste's terms, he turns 'language' into 'discourse' between Raphael and Adam and Eve, and between himself and a reading audience. The *langue* which constitutes Milton's raw material is not only the English language, but specifically the text of Genesis 1 and 2, a privileged and communally recognized order of words which he instantiates within particular scenes of discourse. Address markers distinguish the narrative in book 7 from the biblical version, which has no direct addressee. As told by Raphael, the creation story is addressed directly to Adam and Eve, and its meaning for us as readers depends on a complex of interacting features: the constative dimension of the narrative, or its description of events that are presumed to have objective existence, but also our perception of the relation of these events to Adam and Eve, and of our distance from Adam and Eve and the original scene of discourse. When Raphael compares the rising waves to armies, and adds '(for of Armies thou hast heard)' (*PL* 7.296), we are reminded not only that this creation has a history (the war in heaven), but also that there is an ironic gap between the meaning of Raphael's words to Adam and Eve and the words of Milton as we read them – even if the words themselves are the same. We, like Milton's contemporary readers, hear more than enough of armies, and hardly need to have our memories jogged; Adam and Eve's only experience of armies is from the hearing of a narrative, while for us they have an extra-linguistic reality. Conversely, when Raphael recalls to Adam the heavenly harmony that celebrated the end of creation – '(thou remember'st, for thou heard'st)' (*PL* 7.561) – we find that we lack the memory and the sensory experience of the original addressee. Raphael's entire narrative is, to Adam and Eve, a descriptive history of the world that is present before their eyes. For fallen readers, though, who live in the 'evil days' of a non-Edenic world, as for the blind poet, who faces a 'Universal blanc,' the text cannot be a purely constative description of how things came to be, but must become a performative utterance that re-enacts creation.

When Milton's narrative sets out to perform a creative act on the model of divine creation, it is relying on the phenomenological performative. This dimension of the narrative is evident from, among other things, Milton's placement of his amplifications on the biblical text *between* his paraphrase of the two biblical refrains, 'God saw that it was good' and 'the evening and the morning were the ... day.' By contrast, Milton's most important model in the hexaemeral tradition, Du Bartas, combined both refrains in a concluding couplet:

> *So Morne and Evening the First Day conclude,*
> *And God perceav'd that All his Workes were good.*   (Du Bartas 134)

It is as if Milton prefers to separate God's creative words from his own. Prudently, he has God pronounce judgment only on God's acts of creation, but Milton signals the end of each day when his own creative act is complete. If this ordering gives Milton a measure of creative freedom, it is a freedom he utilizes more and more over the course of the narrative in book 7. By the sixth day, he introduces a preamble that predicts the limit of creation ('The Sixt, and of Creation last arose / With Ev'ning Harps and Matin' [*PL* 7.449–50]), after which the biblical text must be brought in with a subordinating conjunction ('*when* God said'). The constative presence of the biblical text is, throughout book 7, subordinated to the performative function that Milton makes possible when he places that text within a new, dialogical context, in which Raphael addresses Adam and Eve at the same time that the poet addresses the reader.

But the scene of discourse in which Milton locates the creation narrative also exposes the more sociopolitical aspects of his performative language. It reveals that subjectivity is not transcendent, but created through discourse, and that discourse reflects varying degrees of knowledge and authority among the participants. The concluding lines of the catalogue of animals illustrate some of these effects:

> First crept
> The Parsimonious Emmet, provident
> Of future, in small room large heart enclos'd,
> Pattern of just equality perhaps
> Hereafter, join'd in her popular Tribes
> Of Commonalty: swarming next appear'd
> The Female Bee that feeds her Husband Drone
> Deliciously, and builds her waxen Cells
> With Honey stor'd: the rest are numberless,
> And thou thir Natures know'st, and gav'st them Names,
> Needless to thee repeated ...   (*PL* 7.484–94)

The emmet or ant is 'provident / Of future' in more ways than one: commended for its parsimony in storing up provisions for the winter, the creature also serves to foreshadow the political organizations of a time beyond Eden. Its function as an emblem of 'just equality' and 'Commonalty' looks forward to a historical moment, a politicized language, and a hermeneutic of the emblem, none of which yet exists for Adam and Eve. As Stanley Fish observes, 'There are no implications in Paradise' (*Surprised by Sin* 148), and a reading which does not experience Raphael's narrative as an 'objective presentation' of 'cosmic harmony' or participate in the 'spontaneous abandon' of God's creation reveals the reader's own postlapsarian preoccupations (*Surprised by Sin* 151). Raphael's direct address to Adam ('thou thir Natures know'st') confirms our sense that the same language functions differently for us and for the original listeners; we did not name the creatures, and it is because we have no innate understanding of their natures that we must have those natures expounded for us, as they are in Milton's text. Seventeenth- and twentieth-century frames of reference are also superimposed, as when we realize that Milton's concern with the 'Female Bee that feeds her Husband

Drone / Deliciously' as a pattern of domestic economy may outrun his entomological expertise.

Moreover, once attuned to the hint of peril that often accompanies the mention of firstness in the epic, we may be tempted to be suspicious of the emmet which creeps in 'First' so close on the heels of 'some of Serpent kind' (*PL* 7.482–4). The suspicion seems to be borne out by the end of the catalogue of creeping things, where the most dramatic juxtaposition of frames of reference occurs:

> nor unknown
> The Serpent subtl'st Beast of all the field,
> Of huge extent sometimes, with brazen Eyes
> And hairy Mane terrific, though to thee
> Not noxious, but obedient at thy call.   (*PL* 7.494–8)

Fish uses this passage to illustrate the difference in the understanding of book 7 by Adam and Eve and by the guilty reader, whose 'overactive and suspicious intellect' condemns him or her 'to see in this praise of the serpent an ominousness that is simply not there' (*Surprised by Sin* 156). Yet the ominousness *is* there *for us*, because of the echo of biblical language. The irony that is evident to anyone with foreknowledge of the Fall is compounded by an echo of Genesis 3:1 ('Now the serpent was more subtil than any beast of the field'), where the serpent appears for the first time in the biblical text and appears *as tempter*. As if this were not enough, the line 'The Serpent subtlest Beast of all the Field' reappears verbatim at *Paradise Lost* 9.86, when Satan first chooses to enter into the serpent, and again at 9.560, in Eve's first address to Satan ('Thee, Serpent, subtlest beast of all the field / I knew'). Not to notice all of this argues us unmindful of the Scriptures: the circumference of knowledge relevant to our interpretation and appropriation of the narrative is delimited differently from that of the fictional audience. We are simultaneously compelled to read with an awareness of the biblical source-text and to understand that, because we are doing so, the second-person address ('though to thee / Not noxious') excludes us and refers only to Adam or Eve.

The experience of reading book 7 is not, as Fish argued, one of consistently feeling the disjunction between our condition and that of Adam and Eve, but instead of constantly readjusting our perspective according to the relations both of sameness and difference between us and an unfallen audience. When Raphael tells his listeners how God decreed their own creation, his account is a word-for-word conflation of Genesis 1:26–7 and 2:7, with the addition of some crucial demonstratives and second-person pronouns (the added words are italicized below):

> Let us make *now* Man in our image, Man
> In our similitude, and let them rule
> Over the Fish and Fowl of Sea and Air,
> Beast of the Field, and over all the Earth,
> And every creeping thing that creeps the ground.
> *This said*, he form'd *thee, Adam, thee* O Man
> Dust of the ground, and in *thy* nostrils breath'd
> The breath of Life; in his own Image hee
> Created *thee*, in the Image of God
> *Express, and thou* becam'st a living Soul.   (*PL* 7.519–28)

Benveniste identifies the polarity of 'I' and 'you' as 'the fundamental condition in language' (225), and argues that, if language is centred in subjectivity, the third-person verb or pronoun 'does *not* refer to a person because it refers to an object located outside direct address' (229). If this is so, Milton has replaced the 'non-person' of the biblical text with a second-person address that actualizes the discourse and allows the reader (as well as Adam and Eve) to enter into it as 'you.' The effect is to both distinguish and superimpose two scenes of discourse. First, 'thee, *Adam*' reminds us that the subject of Raphael's story is identical with its immediate audience. 'Thee O Man' is on one level a gloss on the preceding phrase, inasmuch as it translates the Hebrew *ha'adam* into English, yet it significantly turns the 'man' of the Bible's 'And the LORD God formed man' from an accusative to a vocative case. The second-person address disrupts the narrative line insofar as it also contains a direct address to the reader; part of the significance of the passage depends on the recognition that we also are the objects of this creative act. As a result, we return to citations of the Genesis text ('Man / Dust of the ground ...') with an altered consciousness that might be termed political, in that it has to do with shifting relations of inclusion and exclusion based on varying degrees of knowledge and control over the discourse. In this text, Adam, like the reader, is being created not only in the image of God but in the image of Milton: that is, as a politicized subject positioned within a discourse and within a set of relations to the speaker and to other groups of addressees.

The creation account ends with an angelic hymn that, having as its subject 'Creation and the Six days' acts' (*PL* 7.601), implicitly recapitulates the preceding narrative while it alludes to the revisionary role of the creation itself:

Great are thy works, *Jehovah*, infinite
Thy power; what thought can measure thee or tongue
Relate thee; greater now in thy return
Than from the Giant Angels; thee that day
Thy Thunders magnifi'd; but to create
Is greater than created to destroy.   (*PL* 7.602–7)

The half-rhymes of the final lines (create/greater/created) stress once more
that ultimate praise goes to a deity who has effected a second, restorative
act of creation after the destruction wrought by Satan's unprecedented act:
the greater creation is the compensatory production of 'another Heav'n /
From Heaven Gate not far' (*PL* 7.617–18). 'Witness this new-made World'
the song continues (*PL* 7.617), a final deictic giving access to three superimposed scenes of discourse. In the angels' celebratory hymn, 'this' is the
newly created universe spread out before the heavenly host; in Raphael's
account to Adam and Eve, 'this' is the Edenic environment that surrounds
them; in the poet's address to the reader, 'this' is the vision his language has
just created. In book 7, the world is made new by being made over in a
subjectivized discourse. We are witnesses not only of a creation *by* the
Word but also a re-creation *of* the Word, the biblical text re-turned into a
history of our own.

I have been suggesting that the language of Milton's creation account
allows for analogies between the process of creation in *Paradise Lost* and
three related twentieth-century models of linguistic structure. First, the
actions performed by the Son as Word dividing chaos and ordering it
into a structure of significantly differentiated units resembles Saussure's
account of the operation of the linguistic system on sound and thought.
Then, just as Benveniste shifts the focus of Saussurian linguistics onto the
speaker's subjectivity, which is both created in and expressed by the
instantiation of *langue* in acts of *parole*, Milton's account of human uses
of language (Adam's and his own) emphasizes the role of subjectivity in
appropriating language and experience. In both these cases Milton renders divine creation and his own textual practice a deliberate, non-origi-
nal, revisionary beginning, as that term was used by Said, whose account
of beginnings derives from the structuralism of both Saussure and Benveniste. Milton's revised narrative of beginnings, or narrative of revised
beginnings, represents a different kind of linguistic structure from the
kerygmatic or proclamatory language of Genesis 1: he inducts us into the
kind of discourse in which performative force depends on the authority
conferred by knowledge and on the construction of subjects within a lin-

guistic and political order. This aspect of his textual practice needs to be recognized, not least because of its implications for the preoccupation with originality, subjectivity, and the politics of discourse in the work of his Romantic heirs.

5

The Circumference of Vision: Blake's *Songs of Innocence and of Experience*

If you have formd a Circle to go into
Go into it yourself & see how you would do

William Blake, 'To God'

Perspectives on Blake's Vision

From his earliest nineteenth-century devotees to present-day academics, readers of William Blake have had to come to terms with his insistent claim that he is an inspired poet. This is a writer whose major epics dramatize the process of his own inspiration, so that he can appropriate for himself the strident bardic cry 'I am Inspired! I know it is Truth! for I Sing / According to the inspiration of the Poetic Genius' (*M* 13.51–14.1, E 107–8), and whose private annotations equally proclaim that 'Inspiration & Vision was then & now is & I hope will always Remain my Element my Eternal Dwelling place' (Ann. Reynolds, E 660–1). In the search for ways to approach Blake's challenging texts, critics have defined various frames of reference for understanding his claim to inspiration and for studying visionary poetry in general. The structure and symbolism of Judeo-Christian tradition has been the most significant general context, as a result of Northrop Frye's masterful systemizations of biblical and Blakean myth. Other critics, including Edward J. Rose and Susan Fox, also base their identification of the characteristics of visionary discourse primarily on formalist studies of Blake's poetry and art, though they concentrate more heavily on imagery, iconography, and narrative organization. Leslie Tannenbaum and Ian Balfour move beyond the Blakean canon to investigate the understanding of inspired language that Blake might have acquired from eighteenth-century biblical scholarship. Finally, Harold Bloom and Joseph Wittreich identify distinctive routes of their own for the transmission of a visionary tradition. Different as their theories are, being based respectively on Freudian and Gnostic principles and on the verbal and visual shape of prophecy in the Book of Revelation, both these critics assign Milton a central place in the line of vision and structure their theories of poetry largely around the problem of Milton's influence on Blake.

The great majority of these readings are sympathetic to Blake's pronouncements about his status as a visionary poet. Blake has had an uncanny ability to seduce critics into accepting the parameters of his universe: his earliest interpreters, from the mid-nineteenth to the mid-twentieth centuries, approached his work as a mystical system, while Frye's success in deriving terms for the study of Blakean and other literature from Blake's own work influenced a majority of scholars until at least the 1970s. More recent criticism has attempted to deconstruct Blake's claims, using the rhetoric of his myth of inspiration to challenge visionary poetry as a critical concept. Reacting to the work of Wittreich and Bloom, David Riede attempts to 'call into question the whole idea of a "line of vision" by rejecting such fundamental romantic mystifications as "inspiration" and "vision" ' (257), and proposes that the 'line of vision' in English poetry may be better understood as a ' "line of reading" descending from St Paul' (258). Based on close readings of Blake's invocation in *Milton* and his account of the way Milton enters into his foot, Riede concludes that the rhetoric of Blake's claim to inspiration undermines itself and 'subvert[s] the very idea of authoritative inspiration' (258). Riede argues convincingly that Blake rejected the body-soul dualism that Milton inherited from Saint Paul, rejecting along with it Milton's belief in a distant, non-human source of inspiration and his unimaginative literal reading of the New Testament; he also makes a case for Blake's concept of inspiration as a type of strong, combative reading displayed by Milton and Paul at their best.

Riede is commendably attentive to the language Blake uses to present himself as a visionary, but his conclusion that Blake himself eventually gives in to a sacralized claim of authoritative inspiration relies on two contradictory tendencies that he finds in Blake's rhetoric, neither of which is fully defensible. On the one hand, he emphasizes the chaotic quality of Blake's language, which 'wanders endlessly,' is 'decentered' and seems to 'spin wildly, out of control,' as evidence that Blake was constantly fighting against the aspersion of madness and attempting to control his own imagination (273–4). Yet there is ample evidence that Blake enjoyed and pandered to his reputation as a madman, perhaps because that reputation is itself a part of the tradition of the inspired prophet from the Old Testament onward.[1] On the other hand, Riede finds in Blake a tendency to reify and eternalize his inspired utterance: 'He wants to establish a voice that *is* the "breath of the Almighty," though he knows the result would be yet another authoritative patriarchal church' (273). But the Blakean image to which Riede refers, the 'breath of the Almighty,' is precisely an intangible image, emphasizing not the message conveyed by inspired language nor the institution which it might support, but rather the process of inspiration itself. The passage from *Milton* in which the image appears not only identifies the language of human beings with the creative language of God but also underlines the performative or productive character of inspired utterance:

> As the breath of the Almighty. such are the words of man to man
> In the great Wars of Eternity, in fury of Poetic Inspiration,
> To build the Universe stupendous: Mental forms Creating

> (*M* 30.18–20, E 129)

Blake's grammar works against the reification of inspired words or the breath of the Almighty, since the 'as ... such' construction deflects attention from positivities to ways of being or acting. The sentence is never completed, but culminates with and remains suspended on the present participle 'Creating,' so as to stress the continuing efficacy of poetic inspiration. It is not certain whether 'Mental forms' is the subject or object of 'Creating,' but in either case the act of creation itself is the main focus of the lines. Riede's analysis of the source of inspiration needs to be supplemented by a study of the extent to which, for both Blake and Milton, inspiration is verbal action, a mode of speaking or writing which has the capacity to alter the poet's surroundings.

1 Cf. epigrams from Blake's Notebook, such as

> Madman I have been calld Fool they Call thee
> I wonder which they Envy Thee or Me (E 507)

or

> All Pictures thats Panted with Sense & with Thought
> Are Painted by Madmen as sure as a Groat (E 510)

as well as extracts from Blake's letters:

> Dear Sir, excuse my enthusiasm or rather madness, for I am really drunk with intellectual vision whenever I take a pencil or graver into my hand, even as I used to be in my youth ... In short, I am now satisfied and proud of my work ... (E 757)

In his ruminative essay on the possibility of applying Derridean strategies to the study of Blake, Dan Miller also concentrates on deconstructing the image of Blake as 'the prophet of eternal vision and transcendent imagination' ('Blake and the Deconstructive Interlude' 155). Analysing the figural language and philosophical assumptions behind Blake's hierarchical distinction of vision from allegory, Miller discovers that

the language of vision is double, at once a discourse of substance, in which the only enduring objects are eternal images, and a discourse of representation, in which images endure because they are sustained by permanent objects. The vision-allegory hierarchy rests ultimately on a seed, which may be either a visionary image or an allegorical figure – or something that cannot be classed conveniently as either. ('Blake and the Deconstructive Interlude' 158–9)

Miller's rigorous reading of *A Vision of The Last Judgment* and his contention that Blake's 'vision' is always already infected by 'allegory,' his idealism by naturalism and sensation, and his ontology by representation, presents a challenge to Blake's concept of vision – at least insofar as vision is something which may be classed as either essence or representation. Miller's analysis, that is to say, assumes an analogy between something called 'vision' and a tree, table, or other element of the phenomenal world which may be said to exist as either Platonic form or perceived object. But vision, as the word suggests, is both an event and an entity, both the act of seeing and the thing seen. When Blake refers to the Bible or his own artwork as 'vision,' he is not only pointing to the text or the painting as a fixed arrangement of words and images, but to a way of perceiving and understanding. 'The Last Judgment begins & its Vision is seen by the [*Imaginative Eye*] of Every one according to the situation he holds,' Blake writes in *A Vision of The Last Judgment* (E 554), while his title identifies the verbal account itself with this *activity* of vision or individual seeing.[2]

Vision as event and entity corresponds exactly to the notion of a speech act, which is both speech, or the process of uttering words, and an act, or the thing which the words accomplish. When, at the end of *A Vision of The Last Judgment*, Blake writes, 'I assert for My self that I do not behold the Outward Creation' (E 565), he is performing the speech act of asserting but his words also constitute a completed assertion, an entity to which he or

2 In a slightly different context, Tilottama Rajan also articulates the idea of vision as both object and process: 'The concept of "visions" suggests ... a form of perception in which the signified does not precede its transcription, and in which what is seen is simultaneous with its seeing, as though things are still in process' (*Supplement of Reading* 266).

we can now refer. Conversely, when we read these words in the text, they *are* the assertion itself since the assertion does not exist apart from the words, yet they also refer or direct our attention to the concept of asserting, which can be conceived of apart from this particular sentence. I am suggesting that both vision, and the performative language which is integral to vision for Blake and Milton, are concepts which indeed combine essence and representation. This does not invalidate the important dehiscences Miller has discovered in Blake's concept of vision; it is still worth exploring why Blake and most everyone else runs up against metaphysical paradoxes when trying to define vision as a concept. However, Miller's reading may be supplemented by a consideration of the active and effectual dimension of visionary art.

One undeniable paradox uncovered by post-structuralist approaches is the fundamental incompatibility between the Blakean ideals of mental fight and active imagination, and the traditional view of inspiration as a kind of double imposition, in which an authoritative voice dictates to the passive poet and the poet, in turn, conveys an incontrovertible message to the reader. There is a single example of a conventional scene of inspiration in Blake's poetry, in the prose fragment 'Samson' included in the *Poetical Sketches* of 1783. Beginning with a formulaic line derived from classical epic ('Samson, the strongest of the children of men, I sing'), this text contains an invocation to an Angel who is identified with Truth:

O white-robed Angel, guide my timorous hand to write as on a lofty rock with iron pens the words of truth, that all who pass may read. (E 443)

Blake soon rejects this Mosaic image of inspired writing, though the figure of Moses continues to play a central role in the development of his idea of vision. Angels become villains in *The Marriage of Heaven and Hell*; rocks, especially lofty ones, become symbols of petrified and oppressive belief; iron pens usually belong to the tyrant Urizen. The circumstances commonly associated with inspired writing – the imposition of an external will on an individual mind, the claim of unambiguous and universal truth, the pretension to a discourse of lasting authority – are in themselves antithetical to Blake's art. By the time he writes *Milton* and *Jerusalem*, Blake has left behind classical muses, Angels of Truth, and anything engraved in stone.

In attempting to define a concept of inspired poetry that is morally and aesthetically acceptable to him, Blake reinterprets inspiration as an expanded form of sensory perception. Perception is again a term that refers to both event and object, to the act of perceiving and the thing perceived.

To the extent that the source of inspiration may still be termed divine, it is a divinity located, as we would expect from Blake, inside the human subject, and expressing itself in the dialogue between the subject and the world. If poetic inspiration is to be located, as Blake says in the passage quoted above, in the words of man to man, we must be particularly attentive to the scenes of discourse in Blake's text, to the events which the speaking of visionary language constitutes and brings about. Just as Blake asserts that the vision of the Last Judgment 'to different People ... appears differently as every thing else does' (*VLJ*, E 555), so the nature of visionary discourse varies according to the situation of speaker and hearer. This helps to explain Blake's concern with address throughout his writing, and it has important implications for the reading of visionary poetry in general.

Yet the performative language which emanates from the Poetic Genius in every individual is often confronted, threatened, or infected by the type of language that Austin identified as explicitly performative: the utterance which derives its power from the authority of an institution or from a set of conventions accepted by a societal group. Thus Blake's poetry challenges our ability to perceive and to create meaning, but also our ability to distinguish the performative authority of the Poetic Genius from that of the social institution. While *Songs of Innocence and of Experience* presents an idealized form of this distinction, even in these poems the 'innocence' of individual expression is threatened by societal discourse, and in Blake's later poetry it becomes increasingly more difficult to draw a dividing line between the two kinds of performative language.

'Introduction' to Innocence: The Performative as Self-Expression

The deceptively simple *Songs of Innocence and of Experience* constitute one of Blake's most fundamental explorations of the relationship between language and action. These texts begin by presenting two contrasting images of inspiration in the figures of the Piper and the Bard, who speak the introductory poems to *Songs of Innocence* and *Songs of Experience*, respectively. The two 'Introductions' have attracted a great deal of critical attention as indices of the way Blake intended the songs to be read, yet they have never been accorded their full weight as utterances that create, in Kenneth Burke's terms, a 'circumference' for the worlds of Innocence and Experience, establishing the conditions of discourse and action that will prevail in each of those worlds. In *A Grammar of Motives*, Burke defines 'circumference' in the context of his theory of dramatism as the set of terms that establish the limits within which a particular project is valid.

We reach different conclusions about the motives of human behaviour, Burke argues, depending on whether we adopt a circumference that includes the idea of a creating God or one limited to a controlling Nature (*Grammar* 77–85). For Blake, the world looks different and functions differently when, as in Innocence, there is a direct correlation between address and reply and between language and action, and when, as in Experience, communication is oblique, interrupted, and generally ineffectual. In a sense not unrelated to Blake's association of outline with inspiration in visual art, the images of inspiration in the two 'Introductions' *outline* the way performative language will work, or fail to work, in Innocence and in Experience. The distinction between these texts has far-reaching consequences for the act of reading and responding to the language of the *Songs*.

Burke maintains that for each choice of circumference there is a corresponding 'representative anecdote,' or functional model; he gives the example of laboratory experiments with the conditioned reflex as the representative anecdote for the behavioural scientist, and drama as the representative anecdote in his own philosophy of actions and motives (*Grammar* 59–60). In keeping with the idealistic tendency that governs his work, Burke then postulates a paradigm or ultimate example for every representative anecdote. As the paradigm for his philosophy of dramatism, he chooses the divine act of creation, which he regards as 'the logical prototype of an act' (*Grammar* 64). In the same vein, we may read the following 'Introduction' as the paradigmatic representative anecdote for the state of Innocence – and as, in its way, an act of creation:

Piping down the valleys wild
Piping songs of pleasant glee
On a cloud I saw a child.
And he laughing said to me.

Pipe a song about a Lamb;
So I piped with merry chear,
Piper pipe that song again –
So I piped, he wept to hear.

Drop thy pipe thy happy pipe
Sing thy songs of happy chear,
So I sung the same again
While he wept with joy to hear

Piper sit thee down and write
In a book that all may read –
So he vanish'd from my sight.
And I pluck'd a hollow reed.

And I made a rural pen,
And I stain'd the water clear,
And I wrote my happy songs
Every child may joy to hear   (E 7)

The introductory quality of this poem involves not only its presentation
of a pastoral landscape and a set of images that will recur throughout *Songs
of Innocence*, but also its presentation of a mode of discourse. It is primarily a model of clear communication and comprehensible relationships, the
delineation of which can best be appreciated through a comparison with
the 'Introduction' to *Songs of Experience*.[3] In contrast to the Bard of Experience, who will combine echoes from ancient texts with imperative and
prophecy that reach into present and future, the Piper relates a personal
experience using direct reports of discourse and simple past-tense verbs.
Grammatical and metrical features both contribute to the regularity of the
poem. Almost every noun has exactly one appropriate adjective. The
rhyme scheme is constructed around long vowel sounds and a few
repeated words, particularly the 'chear/again/hear' sequence that appears
in the second and third stanzas and is recalled in 'clear/hear' at the end.
Even the spelling of these rhyme-words contributes to the echo effect; we
note the persistence of 'hear' in 'chear,' as the rhyme appeals to both aural
and visual perception.

Repetition is the central principle of the poem. The Piper pipes twice;
the Child weeps twice. As the Piper's activity modulates from piping to
singing to writing, each event still echoes the one before: when the Piper

3 The question of whether *Songs of Innocence* and *Songs of Experience*, originally com-
posed and etched five years apart, should be considered separately or in conjunction, continues to be a point of critical debate. While some have argued that Blake's production of
the *Songs of Innocence* in 1789 without any apparent intention to produce a corresponding volume of *Songs of Experience* should be respected, most major interpreters of the
Songs, from Frye and Bloom to, most recently, Zachary Leader and Harold Pagliaro, have
emphasized the fact that *Songs of Experience* was almost always printed in conjunction
with *Songs of Innocence*, and that the two sets of songs came to represent for Blake 'the
Two Contrary States of the Human Soul' (E 7). Since my argument has much more to do
with contrary states than with the original context of production, I have followed this tradition of interpreting the volumes in relation to one another.

sings 'the same again,' the Child again responds with tears of joy; and when the Piper writes, it is once more his 'happy songs' that reach children's ears. Repetition governs the relationship between request and response, in that each time the Child speaks, his words result in immediate action. The perfect correspondence of language and action and the almost formulaic repetition of phrases recall the ideally performative language of magic or ritual. We may hear, in fact, an echo of the phenomenological performative in the first chapter of Genesis. Just as the Bible's 'And God said' is invariably followed by 'and it was so,' the repeated formula '*so* (I piped),' '*so* (I sung),' here underlines the continuity of each command with its immediate fulfilment in action.

The repeated syntactic and semantic structures sublimate the transition by which wordless tune becomes written text. We are led to believe that the song sung in words is the same as the piped tune, since the Child's response ('he wept') is the same, and the songs in their final written form are still things we 'hear' as in the beginning. The crucial moment of transition occurs in the fourth stanza, where the homonymic rhyme 'read/reed' associates reading with the instrument of writing and links the Child's utterance ('sit thee down and write / In a book that all may read') with the Piper's active response ('And I pluck'd a hollow reed'). At this moment, the poem enacts the movement from oral to written communication and elicits our cooperation in it. The difference between 'read' and 'reed' cannot be heard, but depends on visible signs: the traces of writing are deliberately inscribed even in a poem which seems, up to this point, to favour oral communication. Before we are fully aware of it, by reading 'reed' we have participated in the transition from hearing to reading that the text both describes and enacts.

Like the other songs of Innocence, the 'Introduction' has been subject to revisionary readings which question whether it really conveys the purity, simplicity and straightforwardness that it has traditionally been taken to represent. The most significant revisions are the result of historicist approaches, sometimes in combination with a Derridean assumption that, since the poem involves a movement from voice to writing, it must also reveal anxiety about that movement. The two most extensive and convincing revisionary readings of the 'Introduction,' which I address here in order to examine how they are affected by an awareness of verbal performance, are those of Edward Larrissy and Heather Glen.

The 'Introduction' figures prominently in Glen's study of the *Songs* and Wordsworth's *Lyrical Ballads* in the context of the literary, philosophical, and social conventions of their time. In keeping with her argument that

Blake, like Wordsworth, employed but parodied and subverted current literary fashions by producing children's books which declined to inculcate a clear lesson or moral direction, she reads the 'Introduction' as an ambivalent and disturbing poem. Its subject, according to Glen, is 'the gap between actual experience and cultural definition,' or between free expressiveness and the constraints of a fixed written text (65); the poem moves from free-roaming energy toward delimitation, the laborious process of book-production, and the unpredictability of a text's reception and interpretation. Larrissy, working within a frame of reference that is part Marxist and part Derridean, develops an even darker interpretation of the poem as 'a descent from the formless to the formed' and a corruption of original inspiration (26).

Though readings of the 'Introduction' as an innocent text have been all but outlawed,[4] I would argue that a counter-reading to the recent ironic ones needs to be more fully developed in order to appreciate what speakers are doing with language in *Songs of Innocence and of Experience*. The vision of the 'Introduction' may seem limited when judged in terms of our everyday world, but when read in the context of the *Songs* the text establishes an alternative reality characterized by ideally performative language, as a necessary counterbalance to the failed performatives and institutionalized language that cast a shadow on other poems in the collection. Indeed, the 'Introduction' solicits the reader's cooperation in validating its claim for the effectiveness of spoken *and* written language. If we accept the affirmation that all may joy to hear the songs the Piper has written, we have simultaneously demonstrated the validity of the claim *by* accepting what we read – by reading, as the Piper composes, responsively.

Yet the movement from oral to written, marked by details such as the 'staining' of the clear water and the disappearance of the child on the cloud, is the most disturbing element of the poem for Glen, Larrissy, and others who read it ironically. Larrissy considers the Piper's act of writing a sign that 'the state of Innocence is already fallen': 'we are alerted to the possibility that writing down the songs has corrupted the original inspiration by the idea of the staining of the clear water, as well as by the disappearance of the child, and, of course, the mere contrast of voice and writing' (26). Larrissy offers no additional evidence as to why the 'mere contrast of voice and writing' should in itself be suspect, but the reason

4 Larrissy claims that 'among critics the idea that there is an ironic element [in *Songs of Innocence*] commands almost universal assent' (38), and W.J.T. Mitchell believes that 'no critical reader of this poem ... has been able to avoid the ironic undertones' ('Visible Language' 55).

why he would 'of course' be alerted by this contrast is not far to seek. His discussion of the 'Introduction' is itself introduced by an analogy between Blake's framing of speakers in the *Songs* and the Derridean *parergon*; his concern over writing has the flavour of a Derridean anxiety imposed onto a Blakean text. Glen, on the other hand, offers a much more extensive analysis of why Blake might have had reservations about written language, tracing his distrust of book-learning to the Swedenborgians and back through Boehme to Plato (57–64).

Yet if the poem demonstrates phonocentrism in the value it places on presence and the origin of the songs in a face-to-face encounter, it lacks the suspicion of and hostility toward writing that Derrida has associated with the phonocentric tradition. Surveying the 'politics of writing' during the Romantic period, W.J.T. Mitchell distinguishes Blake's attitude from the dominant prejudice against written and printed texts and identifies him as 'graphocentric' because of 'his tendency to treat writing and printing as media capable of full presence, not as mere supplements to speech' ('Visible Language' 51). The graphocentrism of the 'Introduction' is warranted for the same reason that Stanley Fish gives to justify his reading of book 7 of *Paradise Lost.* Just as that text can refer to a subtle serpent without evoking demonic allusions in the minds of the angelic speaker or the prelapsarian auditors, so this poem takes place in a scene of discourse within which there is as yet no reason to connect writing with anxiety. Any uneasiness we feel in reading about a 'fall' into textuality says more about our own experience than about the state of Innocence.

By the same token, this poem in which literal meaning predominates offers us no reliable precedent for imposing a moral dimension on the line 'I stain'd the water clear.' Rather, the context is action- and object-centred ('pluck'd' and 'made,' 'reed' and 'pen'), arguing for a more empirical reading of 'stain' as a colorant that tints more transparently and penetrates more deeply and evenly than paint or dye. The syntax of the line allows for almost contrary interpretations, in that the water may be 'clear' either before or as a result of the staining process. While we may not be familiar with a world in which it is possible to stain something so as to render it clear, the suggestion is present because 'clear' gets the emphatic line-end position and echoes in the reader's mind. Both the coloured water and the rural pen emphasize the continuity of the writing process with the natural setting; the poem depicts a remarkable connection between the natural and supernatural environments and the human activity of writing. Nature provides the instrument of literary production, the 'rural pen' of reed and water, which we may also identify with the unnamed instrument of music if it is a shepherd's reed- or Pan-pipe.[5] The effect of the Child's disappearance, finally, is minimized by the continuity of his vanishing with the other actions in the poem. The echo of 'so I piped' and 'so I sung' makes 'so he vanish'd' sound natural and expected, and the connection with the previous line is maintained visually by the long punctuation mark conspicuously repeated after the seventh and the fourteenth lines: 'Piper pipe that song again – / So I piped' parallels 'In a book that all may read – / So he vanish'd.' The final line, while returning to the timeless perspective suggested by the present participles at the beginning of the poem, expands the poem's audience from one Child to 'every child.'

The text brings about one final conflation of oral and written language when it ends with the word 'hear': not only are the written songs still perceived in the same way the piping was in the beginning, but the latent homonym 'here' maintains the sense of immediacy. The syllable 'ēr' is the dominant sound of the 'Introduction,' and it encapsulates the bond between aural and visual perception. Even though the word never actually appears in the poem, 'ear' echoes when we hear it aloud as a subliminal reference to the organ of hearing. When we read the printed page, not only is the allusion reinforced by our seeing 'e-a-r' combinations (made more conspicuous by Blake's unconventional spelling of 'chear'), but we also discover the anagram 'r-e-a.' The interdependence of h*ear*ing and *rea*ding is confirmed both by the constative statement of the poem and by the performative moment in which we apprehend it.

Although the text finally invites us to participate in its performative dimension, its presentation of an idealized scene of discourse also depends on the balance and closure of the dialogue between Piper and Child. On the frontispiece to *Songs of Innocence*, the two characters are focused on one another (fig. 2). We imagine that a story will be told *about* them; the scene implies an objective narrative that does not involve the reader directly. This is the story of an inspired origin, an idyllic parable that identifies a conversation with heaven with an act of writing. Only at the end does this narrative expand into a context in which we recognize our own situation: the series of transitions from voice to writing and word to action culminates in the relationship between the narrated experience and the present text. The 'book that all may read' is

5 Compare Yeats's 'Sad Shepherd,' in a poem written while Yeats was intensely involved with Blake's poetry, who finds that his natural instrument (a seashell) turns his song into 'inarticulate moan' (69). The cooperation between nature and human voice in the 'Introduction' contrasts sharply with many examples in Romantic and post-Romantic poetry of their complete disjunction.

Figure 2
Frontispiece to *Songs of Innocence* (copy A). Department of Prints and Drawings, British Museum.

Blake's book, and the poem tells how it came to be; its ending implies the directive 'you are here' – or perhaps, proferring the volume, 'here you are.'

Relations in the State of Innocence

As a story – or an act – of creation, the 'Introduction' traces the circumference of the state of Innocence by demonstrating what that state means in terms of language and identity. In her thematic study of Blake's poetry, Alicia Ostriker describes Innocence as 'a world of plain identities, progressions, and contrasts' (57). In terms of language theory, we may identify it further as a world of answerable and answered questions, of symmetry between request and response, of stable identities that allow for meaningful interaction between an 'I' and a 'you,' of performatives felicitous in their illocutionary and perlocutionary effect. The 'Introduction' inaugurates these relations and establishes for Innocence a type of linguistic behaviour which reflects the fact that identities are defined by essence and relationships by reciprocity. Kenneth Burke calls the act of delimiting such a scope 'a kind of "partial Creation" ':

For its terms, in being restricted to the nature of the thesis, will thereby establish a circumference, marking the outer boundaries of the ground that is to be covered. As agent, the writer will have acted creatively – and the motives and motifs featured by his terminology will fix the nature of the constitution which he has enacted. (*Grammar* 86)

Burke's term 'constitution' refers both to a body's structure or conformation and to the act of setting up a state, and it is a paradigmatic performative: a constitution creates a state by setting out its rights and practices in verbal form. In all these senses, we might speak of the state of Innocence as being *constituted* by the linguistic order of the 'Introduction.' Innocence, like most states, consists in relations rather than positivities. Images such as the lamb and the child may help us to recognize Innocence when we see it, but the state itself is constituted by a set of relations – between human and divine, speaker and addressee, I and Thou – which are reflected in verbal performance. It may even be possible, and productive, to identify Innocence *as* a distinctive mode of language.

The songs of Innocence reinforce these linguistic relations, sometimes through familiar and well-documented patterns such as the refrains and the balanced question-answer structure of 'The Lamb.' Here, the child's question is answered by an act of naming which establishes the identification between speaker and addressee and God:

> He is called by thy name,
> For he calls himself a Lamb:
>
> ...
>
> I a child & thou a lamb,
> We are called by his name.   (E 9)

The prevalence of echoes in Innocence is also relevant, not only when they are explicit as in 'The Ecchoing Green,' 'Nurse's Song' ('And all the hills ecchoed'), or the 'Laughing Song''s chorus of 'Ha, Ha, He,' but also in the many poems in which speakers and their environment respond to one another. In the second stanza of 'The Shepherd,' a world is evoked through the call and reply of lambs and ewes, a reciprocity which calls the shepherd to participate by moving him to praise. His watchfulness – that is, his identity as a shepherd – is dependent on the sheep's being 'in peace,' but their peacefulness is in turn a result of the shepherd's proximity:

> He is watchful while they are in peace,
> For they know when their Shepherd is nigh.   (E 7)

In fact, the frequency of formulations with 'while' in *Songs of Innocence* ('While he wept with joy to hear,' 'Thou dost smile. / I sing the while,' 'While our sports shall be seen / On the Ecchoing Green') may be considered a reflection in grammar of the dependence of subject and environment on one another.

Apart from the 'Introduction,' the poem that most clearly presents the ideal speech act characteristic of the state of Innocence is 'Infant Joy.' In this I-Thou dialogue question is immediately followed by response, and the poem centres on the discovery of a name which reflects the subject's essence. Like the Piper, the infant takes on a name which expresses its major attribute and activity, in the manner of motivated or Adamic language. The congruence is expressed in the lines 'I happy am' (or, 'I "happy" am') and 'Joy is my name' (or, '"Joy" is my name'), in which adjective is never quite distinguished from proper noun, nor language from metalanguage. The equivalence of attribute and name is intensified by the parallel performative utterances 'Sweet joy I call thee' and 'Sweet joy befall thee.' Joy is both an impression and an expression of the infant's: it is called joy because it is happy, and, as in a culture in which sympathetic magic

plays a part in the naming of children, it will have joy because it is felici-
tously named.

While my reading of *Songs of Innocence* stresses felicitous speech acts,
I do not mean to deny all irony to these poems. There is, in fact, an inherent danger in the very echoes, responses, and repetitions which render the
dialogues of Innocence so successful. This has to do with the fact that
innocent speakers respond not only to their dialogue with individuals or
the natural environment, but also to utterances which have a less candid
and less stable source, such as those which emanate from social authority.
The beginnings of this process may be seen in 'The Little Black Boy,'
where, as in so many of the songs of Innocence, the speaker responds to
the words of another by repeating them in a new context. But the boy
learns his lesson too thoroughly, picking up not only the mother's myth
about earthly life as a way of learning to bear the beams of love, and
about a future existence in which we will play like lambs around the tents
of God, but also the prejudicial connotations of her imagery: that light is
good, that not merely bodies but '*black* bodies' are like a cloud and a
shade, and that conformity is a virtue. The child's response to adults' language is more sinister still in those cases – 'The Chimney Sweeper' and
'Holy Thursday' – in which the original source of the utterance remains
anonymous. The last line of each of these poems leaves us with the
uneasy sense that the speaker's words are a faithful echo of something he
has heard before, but their origin remains (ominously for Blake) abstract
and unidentified. Harriet Kramer Linkin maintains that syntactic structures
in the *Songs* reveal the way speakers have assimilated the ideolects,
vocabulary, and false logic of their society, an interpretation supported by
the first lines of the 'Motto to the Songs of Innocence & of Experience' that
Blake scribbled in his Notebook:

> The Good are attracted by Mens perceptions
> And Think not for themselves   (E 499)

Ironically, to the extent that this assimilation of the words and world-views
of others occurs in Innocence, it is the result of a verbal order in which
communication, and hence illocutionary and perlocutionary effect, are successful and complete.

'Introduction' to Experience: The Performative as Institutionalized Utterance

Experience, by contrast, is a state of failed speech acts, or else of utterances which are felicitous not by virtue of an individual's capacity to affect his or her environment, but because the language sanctioned by societal institutions successfully imposes on its auditors. Perlocutionary effect is never immediate in a world of Experience; if it follows at all, it depends on a difficult and precarious process of interpretation. Rather than I-Thou dialogues, Experience consists of adjacent monologues in which speakers never really interact with one another, as well as of unanswered and unanswerable questions, anonymous interlocutors, and utterances co-opted by characters to whom they were never addressed. These patterns of verbal behaviour are established by the 'Introduction' to *Songs of Experience*, particularly when it is considered alongside 'Earth's Answer':

> Hear the voice of the Bard!
> Who Present, Past, & Future sees
> Whose ears have heard,
> The Holy Word,
> That walk'd among the ancient trees.
>
> Calling the lapsed Soul
> And weeping in the evening dew:
> That might controll,
> The starry pole;
> And fallen fallen light renew!
>
> O Earth O Earth return!
> Arise from out the dewy grass;
> Night is worn,
> And the morn
> Rises from the slumberous mass.
>
> Turn away no more:
> Why wilt thou turn away
> The starry floor
> The watry shore
> Is giv'n thee till the break of day.   (E 18)

The 'Introduction' to *Experience* is a poem about the breakdown of relationships which, at the same time, foregrounds the relationship between speaking voice and reading audience. The infinitive 'to hear' at the end of the 'Introduction' to *Innocence* is picked up as an imperative at the beginning of *Experience*: 'Hear the voice of the Bard!' It is tempting, once again, to hear a subliminal 'here'; but rather than evoking the mythical immediacy of *Songs of Innocence*, this poem is demanding our present attention – even though its setting in place and time remains abstract. Visually, the frontispiece to *Songs of Experience* conveys the same change in address (fig. 3). Now the poet-figure and the child are no longer involved with each other; instead, both are confronting the reader with a disconcerting stare.

The attempted act of communication between Bard and reader is much more disturbed and disturbing than the Piper's conversation with the Child. The Bard's opening command to 'Hear' echoes a standard formula for public announcements, including the biblical 'Hear, O Israel.' But on a strictly literal level it is a disturbing imperative, impossible to follow inasmuch as we must always already be hearing the Bard's voice in order to obey his command. If the 'Introduction' to *Innocence* stressed the interdependence of aural and visual perception, the relationship between voice and vision in this text is troublingly confused. The Bard's authority rests on his ability both to see and to hear: 'Who Present, Past, & Future sees / Whose ears have heard, / The Holy Word.' His perspective seems at first to transcend time, yet this transcendence is at once called into question by the definite pastness of 'Whose ears *have heard.*' Moreover, the 'Word' suddenly turns into a visible being, challenging our assumptions about what words are and demanding that we be ready to see as well as to hear. This doubleness may be traced back to the ambiguous syntax of Genesis 3:8 in the Authorized Version, the biblical source-text for these lines:

And they *heard the voice* of the LORD God *walking* in the garden in the cool of the day: and Adam and his wife hid themselves from the presence of the LORD God amongst the trees of the garden. (my italics)

Like Adam and Eve, the Bard and the reader of the poem are uncertain as to whether they should be hearing a voice or seeing a walking presence. Our insecurity is only intensified when we realize that, in Genesis, the divine voice is accusing and the presence a threat to fallen humanity. On another level, the very fact that diction like 'The Holy Word, / That

Figure 3
Frontispiece to *Songs of Experience* (Copy A). Department of Prints and Drawings, British Museum.

walk'd among the ancient trees' sends us in search of allusions to prior texts distinguishes the language of Experience as what Northrop Frye would call centrifugal: it cautions us that we may not be able to interpret correctly unless we bring specialized knowledge from outside the poem. By contrast, the 'Introduction' to *Innocence* is fundamentally centripetal in that the words do not send us anywhere but inside the text itself for their primary meaning (though, of course, external elements may be brought to bear in later stages of interpretation). It may be significant that the only figure pictured on the illuminated plate of the 'Introduction' to *Experience* is looking away from the poem and toward the remainder of the book (fig. 4).

In the history of its reception, the 'Introduction' to *Experience* has indeed prompted critics to search out a wide range of mystical and sectarian sources, and the confusion and contradiction it has engendered forms part of the circumference of verbal behaviour which the text marks out. In the New Critical era, René Wellek's insistence that the poem has 'only one possible meaning,' to be arrived at by decoding its images according to 'the whole of Blake's symbolical philosophy' (24), gave F.R. Leavis occasion to accuse Wellek of reading poetry like an abstract philosopher. Leavis himself, reading as 'a literary critic' and interpreting 'the precision of a poet working as a poet,' defends the poem's richness of association within a context of Miltonic, Christian, and Druidic imagery (*Revaluation* 140–2; 'Reply' 35–7). Two decades later, Northrop Frye's analysis of the poem ('Blake's Introduction to Experience'), in terms of Blake's prophetic books, Milton, and the Bible, proved persuasive to many readers. In regarding the 'Introduction' primarily as a dialogue between characters – between the Bard, the Holy Word, and Earth, as well as between poet and reader – Frye's analysis set a pattern which many other critical readings have followed.

In other words, most readers of the 'Introduction' to *Experience* concentrate on the identification of the various speakers and their parts in the dialogue and action of the poem. Robert Gleckner, in an essay published in 1957, claims that a 'faithful interpretation' of Blake's *Songs* depends on 'a correct determination of speaker and perspective' ('Point of View' 533), and Michael Ackland, more recently, agrees that 'our central problem' in reading the poem is (still) to 'assess[ ] the personae' and 'establish the nature and scope of their roles' (3). Struggling to assign lines to different voices, critics have constructed several mutually contradictory narratives about the Bard, the Earth, and a

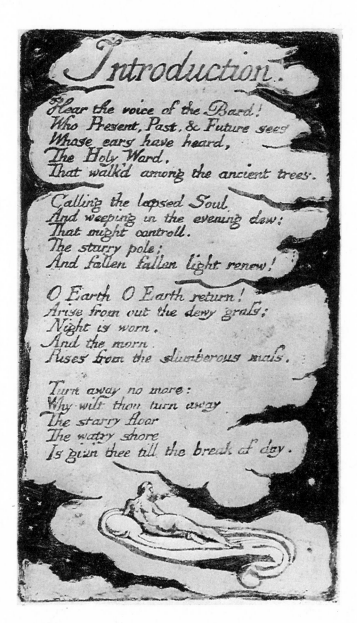

Figure 4

'Introduction' to *Songs of Experience* (Copy A). Department of Prints and Drawings, British Museum.

deity.[6] Yet clear characterization and a determined dialogical structure is precisely what the 'Introduction' to *Experience* resists.[7] In effect, the poem postulates a number of different speakers and actants while refusing to make clear who does or says what. Various methods of determining, for instance, who is calling to the earth or who 'might controll, / The starry pole' will produce plausible, though incompatible, interpretations. Seen in this light, the 'Introduction' almost looks like a primer in structuralist, or post-structuralist, analysis – *yet undecidability is crucial to the experience that the text represents.*

If the identity of speakers and actants is one locus of uncertainty in the poem, the figural dimension of the language also disrupts our attempts at interpretation. The phrases 'fallen light' and 'evening dew' in the second stanza introduce an analogy with the natural cycle that has variously been

6 A survey of the major critical readings of the 'Introduction' to *Experience*, and especially of opinions on who is speaking in the last two stanzas of the poem, will demonstrate the general orientation toward speakers and their roles. René Wellek (24) and Nelson Hilton (*Literal Imagination* 48) both assume that the last two stanzas are addressed by the Bard to the Earth, though for Wellek the Bard is inspired by the voice of God and identical with the poet, while for Hilton he is a tragic character who enacts the Romantic dilemma of nature and consciousness. D.G. Gillham believes the Bard is speaking to the Earth 'on his own behalf, as a lover would' (*William Blake* 53); similarly, Harold Pagliaro concentrates on the psychological and sexual relationship between the Bard and Earth. D.W. Harding, however, claims it is the Holy Word who is pleading with Earth, 'wooing her to come to him' (76). Frye hears the last two stanzas as spoken 'by Jesus through the mouth of his "Bard"' ('Blake's Introduction' 27), Jesus being the Holy Word of stanza 1, and he reads the poem as an introduction to the redemptive mythology of Blake's prophecies. Harold Bloom follows Frye in identifying the Holy Word as 'God-as-Man, Jesus' but strives to distinguish the Bard from both the Holy Word and Blake himself (*Blake's Apocalypse* 130–1). Michael Ackland also agrees with Frye's identification of the speakers ('it is His [the Holy Word's] direct speech which is "heard" and reported by the Bard' [6]), but for him this identification confirms that the Holy Word is a malicious, repressive God. For Robert Gleckner, an accurate interpretation of the poem depends on the realization that 'the last two stanzas are the words of both voices [the Bard's and the Holy Word's],' though the meaning the speakers give to the same words is crucially different ('Point of View' 535). Hazard Adams (*William Blake* 24–5) and John Beer (80), on the other hand, argue that the words and intentions of the Holy Word and the Bard are identical in these stanzas.

7 Tilottama Rajan has proposed that over the course of Blake's canon there is a development from characters represented 'phenomenologically as selves' to ones who function 'structurally as actants.' This argument might be adapted to describe the shift in characterization and representation between Innocence and Experience: the 'Introduction' to *Experience* anticipates Blake's later prophetic books in that, to use Rajan's terms, 'these characters function allegorically ... in the sense that their referent is an argument (however self-complicating), and not an "inside," a personality' (*Supplement of Reading* 200).

interpreted as the redemptive crux of the poem and as a denigrating literalization that proves the malicious intent of the Holy Word. This disagreement between two of the most influential interpreters of the 'Introduction' (Frye, 'Blake's Introduction' 29; Gleckner, 'Point of View' 535–7) hinges on whether the references to Earth and the natural cycle are understood literally or metaphorically. The question of literal and metaphorical meaning is at the heart of the poem and its intertextual language, as we discover by, once again, tracking allusions. The Bard's cry, 'O Earth O Earth return!' echoes Milton in *The Readie & Easie Way to Establish a Free Commonwealth*, who in turn echoes Jeremiah 22:29. In Jeremiah's original utterance, 'O earth, earth, earth, hear the word of the LORD,' the prophet is not addressing a planet but a human audience; 'earth' refers metonymically to 'inhabitants of the earth.' Milton undoes the trope in his allusion to the biblical verse:

Thus much I should perhaps have said though I were sure I should have spoken only to trees and stones; and had none to cry to, but with the Prophet, *O earth, earth, earth!* to tell the very soil it self, what her perverse inhabitants are deaf to. (*CPW* 7:462–3)

Milton's ironic literalization of the call to earth is a reproach to his readers, implying that they are less responsive than soil, stones, and trees. In Blake's poem, however, it is impossible to decide for either a literal or a figurative reading. If we take the Bard's call as addressed to 'inhabitants of the earth' alone, the irony and bitterness of the poem turns on our unimaginative willingness to regard the earth as Milton did, as an image of deafness and deadness. Yet if we believe the Bard's call is literally addressed to Earth, as the Child's was to the Piper, we surely neglect the urgent appeal the Bard is making to his readers. In contrast to the 'Introduction' to *Innocence*, which concerns itself with literal meaning and physical objects, this poem opens up a circumference within which metaphorical readings of the songs of Experience become crucial, although the literal dimension can never safely be ignored.

While most critics have interpreted the poem based on their identification of actants, what is really at issue is a mode of understanding. In this world of Experience, even inspired language fails to provide a reliable transition between writing and action; ironically, it is when the Bard takes on a self-consciously prophetic role and seeks to convey an urgent message that structures of dialogue and referentiality begin to fail, making communication difficult and unreliable. Instead, the language of the 'Introduction' hovers between literal and figurative and requires interpretation if it is to be effective.[8] In a strictly literal sense, the cry 'O Earth O Earth return!' is intelligible but redundant: according to our knowledge of the natural world, the earth will surely 're-turn' or turn again, thus renewing light. But 'O Earth O Earth return!' is also the call to a 'lapsed Soul,' and 'turn away no more' is a plea to a personified Earth who has a moral choice to make about turning. Read figuratively and with attention to intertextuality, the second half of the poem turns into a prophecy of apocalypse. The image of morning arising from a 'slumberous mass' implies a Genesis-like re-creation of light; the oxymoronic 'starry floor' and 'watry shore' are liminal points that remind us of the threat of chaos, but may also represent the transition into a new order. In this double literal and figurative reading, the 'break of day' with which the poem concludes is both morning and the end of time.

There is a further cause for uneasiness in the Bard's strident claim to inspiration, which may well make us suspicious about the authority behind his utterance. A 'Holy Word' is, at least for Blake, a very different source of inspiration from a human form appearing on a cloud, and we are never certain who or what has bestowed on this voice the ideological epithet 'Holy.' While the Bard explicitly claims to have heard the Holy Word, his implicit claim is that he shares the perspective of God in *Paradise Lost*, who, Milton says, beholds 'past, present, future' from his 'prospect high' (*PL* 3.77–8), but who was for Blake a figure of tyrannical authority. By his very name, the Bard summons up a historical and ideological context that contrasts with the timeless realm of the 'Introduction' to *Innocence*. Frye points out that, in assuming the title 'Bard,' the speaking voice draws on a particular tradition of British poetry, which, especially after the appearance of Gray's 'The Bard,' carried nationalistic and revolutionary connotations ('Blake's Introduction' 27). Zachary Leader, after an extensive investigation of the connotations of 'Bard,' adds that, for Blake's contemporaries, Bards would be associated with Druids and with 'a Dark Age of religious and military barbarism' (139). Their narratives draw on the socially constructed field of 'fact, legend, religious precept, law, genealogy, and prophecy' (137), and, significantly, they 'address nations not individuals' (139). The speaker here is committed, and limited, with regard to an ideological con-

---

8 W.J.T. Mitchell comes to a similar conclusion about the contrasting modes of understanding required by the two frontispieces, arguing that in the frontispiece to *Songs of Experience* Blake 'challenges us to fill the void, and places us in a position analogous to that of his Bard ..., making us work for our meanings rather than passively receive them as we do in the frontispiece to *Innocence*' (*Blake's Composite Art* 8–9).

text as the Piper was not. The Piper is defined and named by his activity; the Bard must name and define himself in order that he may speak and act effectively. The Bard's is the first of many voices in Experience which derive their authority from ideology, in the sense defined by Frye in *Words with Power* (13–29): they are voices which draw attention to the process by which social authority rationalizes its power in words.

Relations in the State of Experience

The Bard's call is answered only insofar as the adjacent poem, 'Earth's Answer,' imitates or parodies the verse-form of the 'Introduction' and echoes some of its diction: 'light,' 'wat'ry shore,' 'weeping,' 'ancient,' 'night.' Yet the expected response in terms of action is denied. Despite an encouraging beginning, 'Earth rais'd up her head,' the poem makes clear that Earth is bound to one time (night) and one season (winter), and cannot or will not 'return.' The pair of poems together subverts the model of communication set up in the 'Introduction' to *Innocence*. That primary dialogue is replaced in *Experience* by two monologues, of which the 'answer,' to add to the irony, was written first. The immediate stimulus-response relationship of the Child and the Piper degenerates into a structure of false assumptions, accusations, and misconceptions, the respondent being able to speak – and curse – but not act. The 'Introduction' to *Innocence* achieves a transition from the moment of inspiration to the written text, but, despite the urgency of the bardic voice, the return from prophetic language to action seems defeated. If the *Innocence* poem provides a myth of origins, the *Experience* poem strives for a prophecy of apocalypse. Yet the prophecy can only be realized by intense interpretive effort, it never seems to escape ambiguity, and its performative force is finally disabled. In the 'Introduction' to *Experience* and 'Earth's Answer,' the syllable 'ear' is obtrusive, being repeated in 'earth,' 'heard,' 'dread and drear,' 'hear,' 'fear,' and 'bear.' Significantly, 'e-a-r' is no longer always pronounced 'eer,' as it was in the 'Introduction' to *Innocence*, but lapses (with the assistance of rhyme-words such as 'Word' and 'turn') into 'err': shorter, more abrupt, indicative of error.

Other songs of Experience recall the various verbal infelicities that occur in the 'Introduction.' 'The Clod and the Pebble' repeats the situation of two speakers who fail to respond to one another: the utterances of clod and pebble are syntactically and metrically parallel – 'metres meet' – yet they do not constitute a meaningful dialogue. 'Holy Thursday,' 'The Tyger,' and 'The Fly' are full of unanswerable or rhetorical questions, the term 'rhetorical' pointing to the way language in Experience ceases to be a means of communication between individuals and instead becomes conscious of its own operations, including its potential to sway a society or nation. The identity of speakers often remains uncertain, as is the case with the little boy's anonymous interlocutor in 'The Chimney Sweeper.' Elsewhere, as in the final stanza of 'Holy Thursday,' it is the logical source of an utterance which defies identification. This stanza suddenly presents us with a land where the sun shines and the rain falls, a welcome vision of renewed innocence, but it is not in any way responsive to the rest of the poem. Vision, it seems, is possible within the world of Experience, yet discontinuous with that world; it breaks unpredictably into Experience's same dull round. 'London,' as Gavin Edwards has noted, provides the most fully developed representation of the often disembodied speech acts which circulate in Experience, and the double incursion by which these utterances constrain the speaking subject while the subject imposes his discriminating mark on the environment.

The infelicities of other songs of Experience emerge when we reflect back on the correponding songs of Innocence. In contrast with the motivated act of naming in 'Infant Joy,' 'Infant Sorrow' is full of not only uncommunicative but inarticulate noises: the mother groaning, the father weeping, the infant piping loud. Whereas joy was an instinctive and spontaneous condition for the child of Innocence, this child's sulking is a meditated act – 'I thought best / To sulk upon my mothers breast' (E 28). To use the terms Blake would later adopt in *Milton*, sorrow is a temporary state the child has entered, not an individual identity by which it may be named and its essence known. This accounts for the asymmetry in the two titles, whereby 'Infant Joy' simultaneously names the poem and the infant which is its subject, while 'Infant Sorrow' designates more obliquely the state that the infant has entered.

Among the most disturbing poems in both *Innocence* and *Experience*, finally, are the 'Little Boy Lost' songs. 'The Little Boy Lost' and 'The Little Boy Found,' with their narrative of a child whose father is absent and unresponsive to the little boy's call, may seem to participate only marginally in the structure of successful speech acts that governs *Songs of Innocence*. But the two poems at least answer to one another, and if the mortal father is unresponsive, God takes the father's place and answers the boy's cry. In 'A Little Boy Lost' from *Songs of Experience*, however, we are immediately alerted by the indefinite article and the absence of any corresponding poem about a little boy found. Typically for a song of Experience, the speaker and context of the opening lines are at first unclear. But by the time we are able to surmise that this is a boy's address to his father, and thus potentially the beginning of a face-to-face dialogue, the boy's utterance is intercepted by a

Priest who 'sat by and heard,' and who steps into the father's place in a demonic parody of the way God substituted for the absent father in the song of Innocence. We do not know enough about the context of the boy's utterance to determine what it was meant to express, but it is likely that his words, not unlike Cordelia's to Lear, are a childishly candid assessment of human relationships and the sense of self as he understands it. The Priest, however, apprehends the illocutionary force of the boy's statement on his own terms, taking it as a defiance of the theological principles the church has instituted and the familial relationships it has sanctioned.

'A Little Boy Lost' offers the clearest example in the *Songs* of how the language of social authority, which is often, for Blake, the language of Priesthood, may usurp the force of individual utterance. The Priest's declaration from the 'altar high' drowns out the voices of some individuals ('The weeping child could not be heard') and renders the cries of others impotent ('The weeping parents wept in vain'). The priestly definitions of 'fiend,' 'reason,' and 'holy' prevail, and the most insidious aspect of the poem may be that the language of the Priest is not restricted to his actual speech in the fourth stanza but penetrates into the rest of the text, as when the scene of the boy's martyrdom is called 'holy':

And burn'd him in a holy place,
Where many had been burn'd before:
The weeping parents wept in vain.
Are such things done on Albions shore.   (E 29)

The language of the institution has even influenced the title of the poem, and thus coloured our understanding of the narrative from the beginning. Whereas the little boy in *Songs of Innocence* was lost in a literal sense (at least, he and the other characters and the reader tend to agree on the sense in which he is 'lost'), this boy's lostness is not only a metaphorical but an ideological condition: he is 'lost' in a way which the church alone defines.

The poem's anonymous narrator adds a final question, 'Are such things done on Albions shore' – though the lack of a question mark emphasizes the fact that there is really no question about the tyranny of priestly language. The allusion to Albion refers us to a more nationalistic context than is usual in the *Songs*, although such a context has been hinted at in the epithet 'Bard.' 'A Little Boy Lost' thus begins to set up a context for Blake's early prophecies, which explore with greater intensity and self-consciousness the confrontation between the language of individuals and that of institutions, or the things done with words on Albion's shore.

6

Binding the Infinite: Blake's Brief Epics

Es ist gleich tödlich für den Geist, ein System zu haben, und keins zu haben. Er wird sich also wohl entschließen müssen, beides zu verbinden.

Friedrich Schlegel

Bounding and Binding

The equivocal allusions to Genesis in the 'Introduction' to *Songs of Experience* foreshadow Blake's rejection of most aspects of biblical cosmogony in his later works. With greater deliberateness than Milton in *Paradise Lost*, Blake unseats divine creation from its position as originary act and reassigns the central images of the opening chapters of Genesis a place within the larger myth he himself has organized:

Albion was the Parent of the Druids; & in his Chaotic State of Sleep Satan & Adam & the whole World was Created by the Elohim. (*J* 27, E 171)

According to Blake's radical, fundamentally Gnostic interpretation of Genesis, creation and fall are a single event, an act of mercy performed by a sympathetic God for the sake of human beings who need to have limits set to their physical and mental space. More explicitly than in *Paradise Lost*, creation is, for Blake, a moment in the ongoing history of the cosmos and consciousness. The danger lies in taking the compromise solution for ultimate reality, and regarding this non-eternal world as eternal. Milton's creation may not occur at the beginning of his story, but it retains logical priority for him, being, as it is for Kenneth Burke, 'the logical prototype of an act' (*Grammar* 64). In Blake's mythology, though, divine creation is only a particular instance of creative action:

Many suppose that before [*Adam*] <the Creation> All was Solitude & Chaos This is the most pernicious Idea that can enter the Mind as it takes away all sublimity from the Bible & Limits All Existence to Creation & to Chaos To the Time & Space fixed by the Corporeal Vegetative Eye & leaves the Man who entertains such an Idea the habitation of Unbelieving Demons Eternity Exists and All things in Eternity Independent of Creation which was an act of Mercy (*VLJ*, E 563)

The physical creation is contained within Eternity, which Blake conceives of as a state of never-ending creativity effected by the 'words of man to man' (*M* 30.18, E 129). Our tendency to idealize the creation of the world as a unique act must give way to the awareness of a creative mode of being, 'the Eternal Creation flowing from the Divine Humanity in Jesus' (*DLJ*, E 554).

Yet Blake's work is constantly under stress from the paradox inherent in the ideal of an 'eternal' and 'flowing' creation. Few writers have been more aware than Blake of the limitation, separation, and ordering inherent in any creative act. Few writers, that is, except Nietzsche, whom Blake anticipates in the awareness that cognition requires restriction and knowledge is never knowledge of a whole ('Alles Wissen entsteht durch Separation, Abgrenzung, Beschränkung; kein absolutes Wissen eines Ganzen!' [*Philosophenbuch* 122]). Locating the notion of limits in cognition itself, Blake explores the individual's need to separate himself or herself from others in order to forge an identity, and the writer's need to reduce a subject in order to put it into a book.

Many critics (not least those who read the 'Introduction' to *Songs of Innocence* as a fall from wordless song into written text) have commented on Blake's anxiety about the restrictive power of the word. Yet at least as many have called attention to his ardent defence of definite form and the strict bounding line over chiaroscuro and blurred colouring, and demonstrated that his preference for outline is extreme even in the context of late-eighteenth-century artistic theory and practice. To a certain extent the latter position may be associated with Blake as draughtsman and engraver (and thus with critics who have a particular interest in his visual art),[1] the former with Blake as poet (and with literary critics).[2] But the neat separation can-

---

1 In chapter 1 of *William Blake's Theory of Art*, Morris Eaves provides a thorough analysis of Blake's unwavering preference for outline in the context of eighteenth-century neoclassicism and the Greek Revival.
2 Anya Taylor's argument that Blake, unlike other Romantics, rejected the reliance of the occult tradition 'on the magical power of language as an agent for effecting the transformations of the world' because he recognized the Urizenic, restrictive element in lan-

not be maintained: for an artist who insists that execution is inseparable from conception, and a poet who describes manacles as mind-forged, the origin of both positive outline and negative limit, as of both image and word, is in a mental act. Bounding, and the suggestively homophonous binding, needs to be identified as a locus of undecidability in Blake's art.[3]

In beginning a study of language and limitation in *The Book of Urizen* and *The Marriage of Heaven and Hell*, it is worth taking another look at Blake's pronouncements on the bounding line. Though most of these are drawn from his aesthetic theory, the terms in which they get articulated demonstrate that language as well as visual art is inevitably implicated in both positive and negative aspects of outline. The 'great and golden rule of art' passage in *A Descriptive Catalogue* establishes the importance of the bounding line in virtually all spheres of human life. It sets out causal connections among outline, moral action, and identity, metaphorical connections between outline and divine creation, as well as subliminal connections between outline and language:

The great and golden rule of art, as well as of life, is this: That the more distinct, sharp, and wirey the bounding line, the more perfect the work of art; and the less keen and sharp, the greater is the evidence of weak imitation, plagiarism, and bungling. Great inventors, in all ages, knew this: Protogenes and Apelles knew each other by this line. Rafael and Michael Angelo, and Albert Durer, are known by this and this alone. The want of this determinate and bounding form evidences the want of idea in the artist's mind, and the pretence of the plagiary in all its branches. How do we distinguish the oak from the beech, the horse from the ox, but by the bounding outline? How do we distinguish one face or countenance from another, but by the bounding line and its infinite inflexions and movements? What is it that builds a house and plants a garden, but the definite and determinate? What is it that distinguishes honesty from knavery, but the hard and wirey line of rectitude and certainty in the actions and intentions. Leave out this l[i]ne and you leave out life itself; all is chaos again, and the line of the almighty must be drawn out upon it before man or beast can exist. (E 550)

The uncompromising link between art and morality is startling, even though Morris Eaves has usefully placed Blake's beliefs within an artistic tradition in which the hierarchy of outline over colouring is dependent on

guage, is perhaps the most explicit treatment of this topic (75). Taylor's argument is supported and extended by Kathleen Lundeen ('Urizen's Quaking Word').

3 For discussions of these terms, see Larrissy, chapter 4 ('The Ambiguity of Bound'), and Paul Mann.

hierarchies of intellect and social class (*William Blake's Theory of Art* 11–20). In Blake's logic, the use of sharp outline equals good art – yet the lack of outline is not equated with poor art or *aesthetic* failure, but rather with imitation and plagiarism, or *moral* failure. This conclusion follows from Blake's concept of outline as an expression of imagination, which is individual identity. If an artist is not using a strong outline to express his or her own imagination, that artist must be imitating someone else's imagination, and therefore counterfeiting someone else's identity. Blake's understanding of outline incorporates a twofold sense of identification: objectively, we use outline to distinguish what is being represented in art (for instance, a horse or an ox); subjectively, we identify ourselves by the lines we draw as we do by our signatures, which is why great artists know each other by their line. Like vision and speech acts, self-expression through the bounding line occurs in the relation between subject and object: it is a process of expression or recognition that defines the subject *and* the phenomenal world.

The second half of the passage raises the vexed questions of Blake's idealism and his theory of perception. When we distinguish the oak from the beech and the horse from the ox, do we do it, like the slave-boy in Plato's *Meno*, by comparing the outlines of those animals to their ideal forms (forms being, so to speak, pure outline without substance)? And are the outlines properties of material things which exist independently of us, or do we bestow the outlines in perceiving them? The latter possibility arises if we read Blake's verb 'distinguish' in a causal rather than a deductive sense, so that his question becomes something like: 'How do we distinguish [i.e., make distinguishable] the horse from the ox but by [imposing] the bounding outline?' This reading suggests that when we draw a bounding line we are helping to create the empirical world, a suggestion followed up by Blake's allusion to the act of building a house and planting a garden. Definite form is the means by which we create a habitable human environment, a 'here' in place of an 'out there.'

The allusions to creative action culminate in Blake's almost Miltonic assertion that God separates cosmos from chaos with a bounding line. The line that the Almighty draws is both a mark such as Blake the draughtsman makes, and the measure or 'line' that the creating deity stretches over the earth in Job 38:5: 'Who hath laid the measures thereof [i.e., of the earth], if thou knowest? or who hath stretched the line upon it?' While Blake's phrase recalls the Lord's rhetorical question to Job, it is, ironically, a more exact echo yet of Isaiah's prophecy against the nation of Edom, when he foretells that the Lord 'shall stretch out upon it the line of confusion' (Isaiah

34:11). Isaiah's phrase contains a significant intertextual allusion of its own: it is one of a very few verses in the Hebrew Bible to use the expression *tohu wabbohu* 'without form, and void,' an echo of the way chaos is described in Genesis 1:2. The Lord will return the sinful nation of Edom to the state of pre-creationary chaos, by reversing the effect of the measuring line he used to divide the quadrants of the universe: this is what Isaiah's terrible prophecy intimates. Isaiah 34, a chapter to which Blake directs his reader on plate 3 of *The Marriage of Heaven and Hell*, is filled with demonic counterparts for the images of line and book. Isaiah's prophecy is all about the return of chaos, brought about not only by the Lord's line of confusion but also by his curse (34:5), by what is written in his book, and by the divine word ('for my mouth it hath commanded' [34:16]).

Once the context of performative utterance is evoked through the allusion to divine creation and the echo of Isaiah, we may go on to identify an analogy between Blake's aesthetic theory and the structure of language. While Blake claims that the bounding line allows us to distinguish oak from beech, for Saussure the distinction would be brought about by the significant differences between the sound-patterns *ōk* and *bēch*, and between the outlines of the letters in the written form of these words. As we read Blake's text, it is Saussure's distinctions that we are applying. Blake's two examples of tree and horse are the same ones used by Saussure to introduce his concept of the linguistic sign; in an ironic reversal, Saussure's text even includes outline drawings of a tree and a horse to reinforce the distinction between *arbor* and *equos* (*Course* 65). In both cases, there is a distant recollection of Genesis, where the tree is the marker of difference and the horse or animal is the symbol of effective language as it is used by Adam in bestowing names. Blake's point, which is also Saussure's, about the way significant marks and differences control representational and conceptual chaos, is ironically illustrated in *A Descriptive Catalogue* when Blake (or his printer) writes 'lne' for 'line.' The absence of the line and the mark – the 'i' – that would make 'lne' into a meaningful word draws attention to the lines and marks that organize the potential chaos of written language, and which distinguish, for instance, 'line' from 'life.'

Blake's recognition that language is as much in need of the bounding line as are visual images is implicit in the parallel construction of statements like 'Every line of his [Michelangelo's] has Meaning' (E 512) and 'Every word and every letter is studied and put into its fit place' (*J* 3, E 146). In *A Vision of The Last Judgment*, Blake attempts to complete the analogy between painting and poetry as methods of particularizing and organizing the world:

not a line is drawn without intention & that most discriminate & particular <as Poetry admits not a Letter that is Insignificant so Painting admits not a Grain of Sand or a Blade of Grass <Insignificant> much less an Insignificant Blur or Mark> (E 560)

Yet one might say that the line of creation in Blake's text has become a line of confusion. In the Erdman edition quoted here, the words in angle brackets are additions to the original text (or the original 'intention'), which at some points *has* disappeared into an 'Insignificant Blur' and often needs to be deciphered by Erdman and others through a laborious process of infrared photography. Elsewhere in *A Vision of The Last Judgment*, Erdman uses italics to identify words and phrases that have been deleted but remain legible, so that they exist, in effect, *sous rature*. The very text that argues for the necessity of the determinate demonstrates Blake's reluctance to impose definitive form, and so shadows forth his conflicted concept of limit or bound.

Creation, for Blake, is restrictive but also necessary; it guarantees the immanence of God but also sets aside a space for humankind separate from the realm of the Eternals. Similarly, determinate writing or art overcomes chaos and vagueness, but at the cost of restricting significance. In the course of his reading of *The Book of Urizen*, Blake's most explicitly cosmogonic poem, Paul Mann comments, 'Simply to repeat Blakean maxims about firm bounding lines and minute particulars as if they were purely benevolent is to avoid the persistent threat implicit in bounding and particularization. Bounding is binding' (59). To bounding and binding we may add bands, as in the 'swadling bands' with which the speaker of 'Infant Sorrow' is 'bound,' which grow to cosmic size and significance in *Europe*: 'And who shall bind the infinite with an eternal band? / To compass it with swaddling bands?' (*Eur.* 2.13–14, E 61). The words are those of the nameless shadowy female, despairing at the readiness of the world of nature to give form to her seemingly infinite progeny. But she is also echoing God's words to Job; the voice from the whirlwind has a great deal to say about binding and bounding in the creation and control of the world. The Lord tells Job how he made a 'swaddlingband' for the sea when it broke forth 'as if it had issued out of the womb' (Job 38:8–9). *Europe* makes this image more explicit, more literal, and more sinister; the poem begins the process, to be continued in Blake's later epics, of demonstrating that the creation of the physical universe is complicit with human generation.

The same poem also gives us 'bands of iron' around the necks of the citizens of Europe as a compelling image of oppression (*Eur.* 12.29–30, E 64), along with a pun on 'bands' as armies:

> Shadows of men in fleeting bands upon the winds:
> Divide the heavens of Europe:
> Till Albions Angel smitten with his own plagues fled with his bands
>
> (*Eur.* 9.6–8, E 63)

Describing bands as fleeting and fleeing, the lines almost seem to associate them with release – yet these bands belong to Albion's tyrannical Angel, and they continue to be restrictive and destructive. As all these quotations suggest, the period from 1790 to 1795, when Blake wrote *The Marriage of Heaven and Hell* and the shorter prophetic books, is for him a period of obsession with the dilemma that bounding, binding, and banding are necessary features of world-making. Latent in the tradition of Genesis, Job, *Paradise Lost*, and other texts which put the beginnings of the world into words, in Blake's epics these restrictive elements are drawn into the light.

Naming in *The Book of Urizen*

In *The Book of Urizen* Blake rewrites Genesis with the aid of *Paradise Lost*, and rewrites *Paradise Lost* by conflating the account of creation with the generations of Hell. The Miltonic echoes in this poem are so dense and complex that some critics, like W.J.T. Mitchell, believe Blake must have known *Paradise Lost* as well as substantial amounts of the Bible by heart. Mitchell's analysis of implicit and explicit allusions to *Paradise Lost* brings out the way Blake has not only conflated creation with the Fall but intermixed elements of Exodus and Revelation, and the way his inversion and displacement of the characters and roles in *Paradise Lost* calls Milton's moral binarism into question (*Blake's Composite Art* 122–37). The Miltonic echoes in *The Book of Urizen* identify the fallen Eternal, Urizen, as often with Satan as with a tyrannical, world-ordering God. When Urizen's realm is described in the opening plates by a series of negations and paradoxes – 'unseen,' 'unknown,' 'unprolific,' 'no light from the fires' – it sounds like Milton's Hell. But when we read that, in the Urizenic space, 'Earth was not' (*BU* 3.36, E 71) and 'Death was not' (*BU* 3.39, E 71), we must think of the first day of creation in *Paradise Lost*, when 'yet the Sun / Was not' (*PL* 7.247–8). Like Milton's pendant world, the universe of Urizen hangs 'self balanc'd stretch'd o'er the void' (*BU* 4.18, E 72), and the allusions to the Miltonic and biblical creator become more and more pointed as Urizen forms 'golden compasses' and plants a 'garden of fruits' (*BU* 20.39–41, E 81). Urizen's activity of dividing and measuring, separating and setting bounds, is the activity of Enlightenment scientists, whom the poem is often assumed to be satirizing, but it is equally the *modus operandi* of the creating deity in *Paradise Lost.*

Urizen's first speech, in which he proclaims his achievement in organizing the four elements, brings the combative element in the cosmogony of *Paradise Lost* to the surface:

> 5 First I fought with the fire; consum'd
> Inwards, into a deep world within:
> A void immense, wild dark & deep,
> Where nothing was: Natures wide womb
>
> And self balanc'd stretch'd o'er the void
> I alone, even I! the winds merciless
> Bound; but condensing, in torrents
> They fall & fall; strong I repell'd
> The vast waves, & arose on the waters
> A wide world of solid obstruction   (*BU* 4.14–23, E 72)

Although the echoes of primordial chaos and the early stages of creation in *Paradise Lost* are too numerous to mention, it is not at first clear that Urizen is creating a world by much the same process as the Son in Milton's epic. Urizen conceives of his activity more as a heroic struggle to master the elements than as a teleological process of ordering the cosmos. He reports fighting with fire until it is interiorized within the void, binding the windy air until it condenses, thrusting away the waters until, almost as an unintended side-effect, a dense earth arises. In Milton's account the production of a habitable earth is the motivating force of the narrative, yet the effects of the Son's words, which 'far remov'd' chaos (*PL* 7.272) and 'such flight ... impress'd' on the waters (*PL* 7.294), are not too far different from Urizen's acts.

Urizen's recasting of biblical cosmogony as an aggressive act implies that God's creation through language involves similar constraint. In place of a creator whose spoken words articulate the cosmos, *The Book of Urizen* portrays a demiurge whose written decrees establish a restrictive world-order. To put it another way, while Milton represented God's words as phenomenological performatives emanating from a transcendent authority, Blake's poem exposes and ironizes the extent to which Milton's God also participates in a sociopolitical form of utterance, by having his deity engage in arbitrary naming and issue oppressive speech acts. Blake's epic will not allow us to transcend the political constraints of performative language.

The first and, for a while, the only words spoken in the poem are 'It is Urizen':

1. Lo, a shadow of horror is risen
In Eternity! Unknown, unprolific!
Self-closd, all-repelling: what Demon
Hath form'd this abdominable void
This soul-shudd'ring vacuum? – Some said
'It is Urizen,' But unknown, abstracted
Brooding secret, the dark power hid.   (*BU* 3.1–7, E 70)

This utterance, issuing from an anonymous 'Some,' constitutes a tentative answer to the narrator's question at the outset of chapter 1: 'what Demon / Hath form'd this abdominable void / This soul-shudd'ring vacuum?' By analogy with *Paradise Lost* and other epics, the question occupies the place of the conventional query addressed by the poet to the muse after an invocation in order to get the action of the poem under way. Yet the answer implies that any verbal response to such a question – that is, any epic poem – may limit as much as it advances knowledge. In pronouncing, 'It is Urizen,' the mysterious 'Some' first objectify the 'unknown' phenomenon as 'It,' then enclose that object within a proper noun in what is, intentionally or not, the poem's primal act of naming. The utterance 'It is Urizen' corresponds to (and either repeats or prefigures, depending on our reading of the poem's convoluted temporality) Urizen's own act in removing and closing himself off from Eternals; the fact that it is presumably uttered by some of the Eternals makes them complicit in the catastrophe of Urizenic existence. Acts of naming are certainly not always demonic in Blake – on the contrary, there are highly positive scenes of naming at the beginning and end of his canon in *Songs of Innocence* and *Jerusalem* –but in the context of language and action in *The Book of Urizen*, this initial utterance sets a restrictive pattern. In the next chapter we learn that Urizen is 'so nam'd / That solitary one in Immensity' (*BU* 3.52–3, E 71): it is tempting to connect the attribute of a name, which Urizen alone among the Eternals bears at this juncture, with the condition of being a solitary one.

Like God in *Paradise Lost*, Blake's Eternals create by naming. When, at the sight of the sleeping Urizen, they utter, 'What is this? Death / Urizen is a clod of clay' (*BU* 6.9–10, E 74), Death, as a concept and a state, immediately comes into existence. When the narrative voice refers to Urizen a few lines further on as 'cold, featureless, flesh or *clay*' (*BU* 7.5, E 74; my italics), it seems as if the Eternals' utterance has had the perhaps unintentional effect of making clay a part of what Urizen is. *The Book of Urizen* adds another dimension to our awareness of what is going on in figural language. 'Urizen is a clod of clay' sounds like a metaphoric way of describing Urizen's lack of emotion or expression; it is only when a voice other than the Eternals' testifies that Urizen is indeed 'flesh or clay' that we begin to wonder what effect metaphors have in permanently imposing attributes on their objects.

The puzzling 'Preludium' to the poem, in which the poet echoes both Homeric and Miltonic invocations in asking the Eternals to 'dictate swift winged words' (*BU* 2.6, E 70), must already make us suspicious about the extent to which (inspired) words will be instruments of imposition on a passive audience. A word less often noted in the 'Preludium' is the 'call' of the Eternals (*BU* 2.5, E 70) – seemingly a neutral or even desirable summons at this point, but over the course of the poem 'call' becomes firmly implicated in restrictive acts of naming. Deliberate echoes of *Paradise Lost* suggest that Blake is again challenging the effects of naming in Miltonic language. Milton's repeated reminder that the names of his fallen angels are not the names they bore before their fall is parodied in Blake's contrary insistence that the names he uses *are* eternal ones: 'Urizen (so his eternal name)' (*BU* 10.11, E 75). Blake's inversion of the Miltonic parenthesis in, for instance, '*Satan,* so call him now, his former name / Is heard no more in Heav'n' (*PL* 5.658–9) implies that Urizen could have had no other name before the Eternals imposed one on him, since names are antithetical to the state before the creation-fall. We may also read Blake's line as a parody of Milton's sense of sacred mystery, for a name that is unknowable in a human context is meaningless, or no name at all.

Yet the ending of *The Book of Urizen* sets the parenthetical phrase ('so his eternal name') in a new context, as the poet specifies that the sons of Urizen built cities in a place 'now call'd / Africa: its name was then Egypt' (*BU* 28.9–10, E 83). Blake now seems to be doing precisely what Milton did in admitting that names change as states and conditions change. Significantly, though, in Blake's version 'Africa' and 'Egypt' are both names imposed by human societies at different historical junctures. 'Egypt' is, as Blake implies, the older, probably indigenous name, while 'Africa' was imposed by the Romans when they captured Carthage in the second century B.C. and established a new province on the southern continent. While Blake may not have known the origin of the names, it is clear from his use of 'Africa' in *The Song of Los* and the 'Preludium' to *America*, and from the awareness of the slavery issue that underlies *Visions of the Daughters of Albion*, that he associates Africa with oppression by the imperial powers of

Europe. To both eighteenth- and twentieth-century readers, 'Africa' may be more meaningful in specifying geographical location and connoting imperialistic oppression, 'Egypt' in understanding the significance of the place in terms of biblical history and typology. The situation is reminiscent of Austin's phrase 'France is hexagonal,' as an example of an utterance which is dependent on the speech situation: the statement may be true for a general, false for a geographer (*How to Do Things* 143). We are made aware that place-names are dependent on context, on shifts in human civilization, and on whether the group doing the naming regards the place as part of an empire, or as its home.

The beginning of *The Book of Urizen* contains, as we have seen, only isolated acts of naming performed by Eternals whose utterances are ambiguous yet authoritative. But it is surely no accident that references to naming become increasingly frequent toward the end of the poem, beginning on plate 19 after the first female is created, and continuing as the narrative moves into the realm of human rather than cosmic history. At the sight of the 'first female form now separate,' the Eternals 'call'd her Pity, and fled' (*BU* 18.15–19.1, E 78). Besides an echo of the words of Sin in *Paradise Lost* ('back they recoil'd afraid / At first, and call'd me *Sin*' [*PL* 2.759–60]), we may also hear a more contemporary echo of interest groups which accuse their society's administrators of labelling a problem only in order to pigeon-hole and thus forget about it. Naming, for the Eternals, is a way of making something into an object and distancing that object from themselves. Their intention is all too clearly articulated in their immediate command that Los and Enitharmon be veiled and confined 'that Eternals may no more behold them' (*BU* 19.4, E 78). Yet this move is already implicit in their naming of the female form: 'They call'd her Pity' is, in some sense, equivalent to 'and fled.'

The significance of this paradigm for human behaviour is confirmed by the next two speech acts in the text. Establishing parental right and tradition, Los and Enitharmon name their child Orc (*BU* 20.6, E 80). Since the only other act they perform on him is chaining him to a rock, there is a strongly implied identification between naming and chaining. Urizen also echoes the Eternals' naming of the female form when, seeing 'that life liv'd upon death' (*BU* 23.27, E 81), 'he wept, & he called it Pity' (*BU* 25.3, E 82). Given the paradigm of the Eternals who called Enitharmon 'Pity' in order to remove her from their sight, this speech act implies that the naming of Pity plays the same role in Urizen's inauguration of societal ethics. He names pity in order to be able to close himself off from it; his tears, which 'flowed down on the winds' (*BU* 25.4, E 82), betray the vanity of his nominative compassion.

Once Urizen has introduced naming into the sphere of ethics, the remaining speech acts of the poem concern themselves with the way the descendants of Urizen – early human societies – solidify their moral and institutional structures by giving them names: 'all calld it, The Net of Religion' (*BU* 25.22, E 82); 'their children ... form'd laws of prudence, and call'd them / The eternal laws of God' (*BU* 28.4–7, E 83); 'They called it Egypt, & left it' (*BU* 28.22, E 83). These utterances lie entirely within the realm of sociopolitical speech acts. The first two examples, while insidious in the manner of the priest's utterance in 'A Little Boy Lost,' are recognizable as the acts of an institution which imposes a moral structure by designating what is and is not sacred. This move itself might be described as an appropriation of the phenomenological performative by the sociopolitical performative. Societal institutions take words like 'God' and 'eternal,' which in other contexts would convey transcendent authority and evoke a realm of language in which saying and doing are the same, and appropriate them into a logic of human laws and conventions. The lack of individual voice and the collective tyranny in this kind of naming is emphasized by the hollow assonance of 'all calld it' (echoed, though with a different sense of 'call,' in 'So Fuzon call'd all together' [*BU* 28.19, E 83]).

The final act of naming, in the penultimate line of the poem, is the most complex, though it seems to involve the straightforward assignment of a proper name: 'They called it Egypt, & left it.' On one level, this line marks the poem's arrival at the beginning of recorded history, Egypt being the land which the Israelites leave in the Book of Exodus. But a figurative reading of 'Egypt' as an archetypal place of bondage vies with the literal meaning. Leslie Tannenbaum hears an echo of Revelation 11:8, where the corpses of the two prophets are said to lie 'in the street of the great city, which spiritually is called Sodom and Egypt' ('Blake's Art of Crypsis' 160).[4] Spiritually or metaphorically, Egypt designates an alien and oppressive environment; calling a place Egypt has the perlocutionary function of identifying it as a place hostile to the namer. The referent's lack of fixity exposes, in turn, the fictionality of history. In the same manner as the signifiers 'Satan' and 'Messiah' in Blake's famous misreading of *Paradise Lost* in *The Marriage of Heaven and Hell*, 'Egypt' can designate any number of physical or spiritual states, depending on the speaker's perspective. If

4 Tannenbaum addresses some of the same passages and issues discussed in this chapter; his main conclusion is that naming in *The Book of Urizen* inverts the function of naming in Genesis so as to 'describe a perverted creation' and bring about an identification between creation and the Last Judgment.

Blake's parody of a sacred book is about the laying down of the law, it also demonstrates how the history of origins can be adopted, or co-opted, by different parties.

Finally, the text embodies Blake's awareness that language is prone to be equally restrictive when he himself uses it as when his characters and precursors do. Hence the self-conscious designation of the poem as the 'Book' of Urizen and the visual imitation of biblical form in Blake's chapter and verse divisions and double-columned printing. The multiple analogy between a sacred book, the created world as book, the 'Book / Of eternal brass' in which Urizen writes his laws (*BU* 4.32–3, E 72), and *The Book of Urizen* itself, is encapsulated in the illumination on plate 5 (fig. 5). The image of Urizen offering, or imposing, his open book marks the nadir of Blake's attitude toward verbal bounds. In most copies, the contents of the book are identical to the chaotic material world of Blake's large 1795 paintings, including *Newton* and *Albion Rose*. In setting a limit to chaos, the illustration suggests, Urizen also preserves chaos, and indeed proffers it to the reader.

If Urizen's world comes to resemble a brass-bound volume, Blake's poem grows more formal and formulaic and imitates a sacred book. Blake's relationship to Genesis is the reverse of Milton's in *Paradise Lost*. While Milton becomes more individualistic in his ornamentations of Genesis over the course of book 7, Blake begins to cite the biblical text more insistently, but with bitter irony:

> 3. Six days they shrunk up from existence
> And on the seventh day they rested
> And they bless'd the seventh day, in sick hope:
> And forgot their eternal life
> (BU 27.39–42, E 83)

At the end of the poem, Urizen, shackled and confined by the poet-figure Los, remains a symbol of his own bound book. *The Book of Urizen* is an indictment of language as it is used in sacred books, and in religious and political institutions, to authorize and designate the activities of a society. By taking the dividing and denominating power of language and creative action to an extreme, Blake explores the negative potential of creation by the word. True, positive creativity remains the goal of his later prophetic poetry and art.

The 'Argument' of *The Marriage of Heaven and Hell*

With reference to the beginning of *The Marriage of Heaven and Hell*, Mark

Figure 5
The Book of Urizen, plate 5 (copy D). Department of Prints and Drawings, British Museum.

Bracher has described the shifting of the referent in Blake's work in terms which parallel my reading of *The Book of Urizen*. Bracher maintains that the 'Argument' makes a reader aware of the necessity of choosing a position, while simultaneously demonstrating that the same story may be appropriated by parties who hold opposite positions (177–8). This is one way in which the opening plate of the *Marriage*, if it refuses to outline the plot of the book in the manner of a traditional 'Argument,' at least introduces us to the way in which the text will operate as a critique of authoritative language. The various sections of *The Marriage of Heaven and Hell* imitate and parody what might be called, after Wittgenstein, the Bible's various language games, including prophecy, wisdom literature, law, and history. By virtue of its position and imagery, the 'Argument' corresponds to a myth of beginnings; as such, it provides an ironic commentary on inspiration and creation, the familiar components of beginnings in sacred books.

Disturbing echoes make it difficult to deny a parodic relationship between this poem and the opening chapters of the Bible. 'Hungry clouds swag on the deep' (*MHH* 2.2, 22; E 33) reads like an ironic reminiscence of Genesis 1:2, 'the Spirit of God moved upon the face of the waters' – with the benevolent but formless 'Spirit of God' replaced by ominous 'hungry clouds,' and 'moved' by the unwieldy 'swag.' Yet the imagery of the 'Argument' comes, for the most part, not from Genesis but from Isaiah's and Ezekiel's prophecies about the renewal of the land and its people after the judgment of the Lord has passed. Isaiah 35, to which Blake directs his reader on the facing plate of the text, is a prophecy of the return of the Lord's people to Zion, and contains references to the desert blossoming as the rose, to streams of water breaking out in the wilderness, to lions, and to a highway where villains will not walk. The 'bleached bones' in the 'Argument' are reminiscent of the vision in Ezekiel 37, where, in another prophecy of renewal, dry bones are reanimated through the prophecy of Ezekiel in obedience to the voice of the Lord. 'Red clay,' the literal translation of the Hebrew *adamah*, is habitually associated by Blake with the creation of Adam, as in *Milton* where the hero tries to use red clay to form Urizen into a new Adam (*M* 19.10–14, E 112). All these allusions establish that creation, in this text, can only ever be re-creation: the 'Argument' denies the possibility of transcendent origins by representing a creation that is always already dependent on a (last) judgment.

Unlike the biblical narrative, this text refuses to mark off an absolute beginning. There is a world of difference between Blake's opening line, 'Rintrah roars & shakes his fires in the burden'd air' (*MHH* 2.1, E 33), and the Bible's paradigmatic sentence, 'In the beginning God created the heaven and the earth.' The extra-biblical and extra-linguistic associations we have for the word 'God' alter the parameters of the biblical text, obliging us to accept, among other things, the arbitrary *b^ereshith* as an absolute beginning to world and text. As Geoffrey Hartman observes, the Bible's 'in the beginning' is 'a limiting concept, which tells us not to think about what went before' (*Fate of Reading* 119). By contrast, 'Rintrah' as a beginning is absolute only in its inscrutability. The name seems to require readers to ask what went before, and what comes after, in terms of Blake's canon, since the signifier has no meaning apart from what may be inferred from texts in which it appears. As the first word in the poem, 'Rintrah' both sets a limit (because it closes the door on conventional referentiality) and abolishes a limit (because it sends us beyond the text in search of potentially infinite associations for this undefined name); in either case, it defies the traditional closure of the sacred book.

The Intersection of Will and Act

In calling his text *The Marriage of Heaven and Hell*, Blake inadvertently refers to what will become the primary example of a speech act in twentieth-century language theory. Austin uses the words uttered during a marriage ceremony as his first example of performative utterances in *How to Do Things with Words:*

'I do (sc. take this woman to be my lawful wedded wife)' – as uttered in the course of the marriage ceremony. (5)

There is a footnote to this example, provided by Austin's editor after his death:

[Austin realized that the expression 'I do' is not used in the marriage ceremony too late to correct his mistake. We have let it remain in the text as it is philosophically unimportant that it is a mistake.] (5)

Some have doubted the correctness of the editor's correction, though the Book of Common Prayer confirms that 'I will' is the appropriate liturgical response. In any case, far from being 'philosophically unimportant,' the confusion between 'I do' and 'I will' points to one of the major sources of disagreement between speech-act theorists: the relationship of act, or performative utterance, to will, or spiritual commitment. Austin maintains that we must assume the utterer of a performative takes responsibility for having the appropriate beliefs and intentions; for all practical purposes, we can 'exclude such fictitious inward acts' from our analysis and hold by the convention that 'our word is our bond' (*How to Do Things* 10). He suggests that this attitude might bring him into conflict with moral philosophers who give priority to spiritual intention; on the other hand, post-structuralists like Derrida claim that Austin's description of the performative still does not recognize that intention can never be fully present. Blake's illuminated title pages of the early 1790s, which read 'Printed by *Will* Blake,' seem to allude provocatively to the debate over intention and will which, in a more theological context, was equally relevant to the eighteenth century.

The distinction between utterances produced by individual will and utterances that do things by virtue of collectively accepted conventions corresponds to the difference between the phenomenological performative and the sociopolitical performative. *The Marriage of Heaven and Hell* represents a confrontation between the two kinds of utterance, making it the text of Blake's which most invites a speech-act reading – though this approach is also encouraged by the dialogical and dramatic qualities of the work. While the *Marriage* is made up of prose and poetry, it is dominated by voices which 'interpellate' the reader (to use the term favoured by Mark Bracher in his Lacanian reading), casting him or her in a variety of dramatic situations. Blake lets devils and angels speak and stage-manages encounters with angels and prophets. In consequence, language is not primarily used to tell a story or express feelings, as it might normally be in narrative prose or lyric poetry, but for proclaiming, protesting, promising, prophesying, judging, choosing, cursing, calling, and playing games.

Yet in most of *The Marriage of Heaven and Hell*, the requisite societal context for Austinian speech acts may still seem to be missing. Rather than operating according to Austin's prime directive, that 'there must exist an accepted conventional procedure having a certain conventional effect, that procedure to include the uttering of certain words by certain persons in certain circumstances' (*How to Do Things* 14), the utterances of the narrator in the *Marriage* emulate the phenomenological performative of divine pronouncements. 'For Every thing that lives is holy' is the cry of a visionary isolated from a community: the speaker may feel he has a divinely bestowed right to make such a pronouncement, but few members of his audience would agree in according him that right. There is no institution which qualifies him to dictate to the community what is to be regarded as holy; figures who do have that right are the Priest of 'A Little Boy Lost,' the Bard of Experience, or the collective race of Urizen as they identify the 'eternal laws of God.' Yet many verbal formulations in the *Marriage*, including the title, reflect an awareness of the power of institutionally sanctioned language. Sociopolitical speech acts have imposed on the individual language of vision, but Blake seems ready to negotiate between both forms of utterance in order to establish the effectiveness of his words.

Plate 11 of the *Marriage* offers two contrary examples of effective language. The first comes from individuals, 'the ancient Poets,' who

animated all sensible objects with Gods or Geniuses, calling them by the names and adorning them with the properties of woods, rivers, mountains, lakes, cities, nations, and whatever their enlarged & numerous senses could percieve. (*MHH* 11, E 38)

I take it that the 'sensible objects' *are* what we know as woods, rivers, mountains, and other elements of the natural environment. The ancient poets, like Adam in *Paradise Lost*, 'nam'd them ... and understood / Thir Nature' (*PL* 8.352–3), endowing the objects with divine souls in that, and so that, they become meaningful elements of the created order. Blake's unusual syntax reflects an attempt to echo the ancient poets in their acts of naming: after describing the effects of names on sensible objects, he demonstrates by calling a selection of objects by their names so that we may see how names convey the proper attributes. He highlights the fact that 'woods, rivers, mountains,' and so on, are *names* – but since we think of them also as *things*, the name and the thing seem to come together in the articulation of the catalogue.

Hazard Adams, in whose philosophy of literary symbolism this passage plays a seminal role, subtly rewrites Blake in order to get him to say that the words of the ancient Poets are literally creative, making empirical phenomena of what are originally only 'potential possibilities of vision' (*Philosophy* 5–6, 105–7; 'Blake and the Philosophy' 2–5). The creative aspect of the Poets' language is, however, more akin to the creativity of Adam, who does not produce the animals but rather creates a habitable environment by bringing them into a relationship with himself as subject. The corresponding situation in this passage suggests a muted allusion to Adamic naming, a biblical paradigm that was almost inevitably referred to in seventeenth- and eighteenth-century theories of the nature and origin of language. In his act of naming, Adam, like the ancient Poets, sees into the nature of things and preserves the essence in the name; this becomes the prototype for a theory of language that stresses the mystical power of individual words, rather than seeing words as the arbitrary products of communal consent.

The second verbal act on plate 11, however, is performed by a collectivity, 'Priesthood,' which forms (and was formed by) a system, abstracts deities from objects instead of confirming their immanence, and usurps divine voice:

Till a system was formed, which some took advantage of & enslav'd the vulgar by attempting to realize or abstract the mental dieties from their objects: thus began Priesthood.

 Choosing forms of worship from poetic tales. (*MHH* 11, E 38)

As Dan Miller has noted, the conjunction in '*Till* a system was formed' makes the Priesthood's behaviour dependent on that of the ancient Poets ('Blake and the Deconstructive Interlude' 161). For Miller, this dependence undermines Blake's notion of visionary poetry, but I would see in it Blake's recognition of the continuity and interdependence of the phenomenological and the sociopolitical performative. Still, there is a series of significant oppositions between the two instances of verbal performance. While the Priesthood's pronouncement brings about restriction, the Poets' acts of naming animate or cause to move; one language game enslaves and causes forgetfulness, while the other liberates and brings about expanded awareness. Both legitimate themselves by an appeal to the divine – only the earlier type of utterance results from a perception of the gods' presence and confirms that presence, while the later one uses conventional language to replace or reconstitute gods who are absent. Ultimately, the passage establishes a continuity between the two kinds of performatives, revealing Blake's awareness that all creative language potentially wields political power, but also, conversely, that the language of tyrannical institutions originates in creative expression.

 Plate 11 parallels the 'Argument' in providing a perspective on human history, as we recognize from the progression of conjunctions introducing successive sentences: 'till,' 'at length,' 'thus.' Here this development is understood in terms of the evolution of language from a motivated to an artificial phenomenon, or from words which reveal the essence of their objects to words which betray the sociopolitical status and agendas of their speakers. This history of linguistic practice and religious belief is elucidated by the following 'Memorable Fancy,' in which the narrator dines with Isaiah and Ezekiel. Their dialogue begins on the subject of poets, expanded senses, mountains, first principles, geniuses, and origins; it ends with priests, codes, and subjection. The conversation is filled with speech acts, but again there is a distinction between the speech acts of the prophets (who are, of course, ancient poets) and the belated ones of priests. The narrator's initial question to Isaiah concerns the effects of words:

... I asked them how they dared so roundly to assert. that God spake to them; and whether they did not think at the time, that they would be misunderstood, & so be the cause of imposition. (*MHH* 12, E 38)

There are two possible moments of imposition in prophetic discourse: if God's words do not impose on the prophets, the prophets' words may still impose on their audience; both utterances are subject to misapprehension and misappropriation. Isaiah's answer is that his type of utterance, like that of the Poets on plate 11, results from his senses discovering the infinite in every thing, a state of conviction which he calls a 'firm perswasion.' His honest indignation and firm perswasion place him on the side of those who believe that words must be backed up by spiritual commitment; it is intention and will that give this kind of utterance its force. In Austin's speech acts, saying makes it so; in Isaiah's, will makes it so.

While Ezekiel, for his part, provides the best example of an Old Testament prophet who used both word and action as prophetic media – as Blake vividly puts it, he 'eat dung, & lay so long on his right & left side' in order to express the word of the Lord (*MHH* 13, E 39) – his speech introduces increasingly conventional examples of performative utterance. Echoing the previous plate, Ezekiel reveals how an utterance motivated by firm persuasion may collaborate in the establishment of a monotheistic state religion:

... we of Israel taught that the Poetic Genius (as you now call it) was the first principle ... it was this. that our great poet King David desired so fervently & invokes so patheticly, saying by this he conquers enemies & governs kingdoms; and we so loved our God. that we cursed in his name all the deities of surrounding nations, and asserted that they had rebelled ... (*MHH* 12–13, E 39)

In Ezekiel's story, the illocutionary act of invoking is performed by a great poet, King David, who is also an imperialistic king and conqueror, and the act of cursing is performed by those seeking to institute a dominant and nationalistic religious tradition. These are societally authorized speech acts performed by specially appointed (or anointed) individuals; they bring about subjection to statehood, priesthood, an abstract deity, and an institutionalized language.

When the narrator (in another explicit performative) now confesses his own conviction, what is it that has 'convicted' him – the intentionality of prophetic persuasion, or the political and religious order to which he has been subjected? Perhaps both, since what he seems convinced of is the necessary intersection of these two types of performative utterance. The following plate shows him applying the lesson he has learned from his dinner companions by using conventional speech acts in the service of his own conviction. On plate 14, Blake first attempts to bring about apocalypse by pronouncing an explicit, official-sounding performative:

For the cherub with his flaming sword is hereby commanded to leave his guard at the tree of life, and when he does, the whole creation will be consumed, and appear infinite. and holy whereas it now appears finite & corrupt. (*MHH* 14, E 39)

The self-referential first clause ('is hereby commanded') issues in a prophecy of future events ('the whole creation will be consumed'). The two utterances correspond with impressive accuracy to the paradigms of Austinian performative and biblical proclamation, respectively. '[T]he cherub is hereby commanded' conforms to Austin's definition of what he calls 'a very common and important type of ... indubitable performative,' the type which has a verb in the second or third person and in the passive voice (his examples are 'You are hereby authorized to pay ...' and 'Notice is hereby given that trespassers will be prosecuted'). Especially in writing, Austin adds, ' "hereby" is a useful criterion that the utterance is performative' (*How to Do Things* 57). '[T]he whole creation will be consumed,' on the other hand, echoes biblical prophecies of apocalypse and fulfils what Blake describes as the true sense of prophecy, by which the prophet, acting on a firm persuasion, tells a society 'If you go on So / the result is So' (Ann. Watson, E 617).

In the following lines, the order of the two utterances is reversed, so that prophecy leads to a kind of performative writing:

This will come to pass by an improvement of sensual enjoyment.

But first the notion that man has a body distinct from his soul, is to be expunged; this I shall do, by printing in the infernal method, by corrosives, which in Hell are salutary and medicinal, melting apparent surfaces away, and displaying the infinite which was hid. (*MHH* 14, E 39)

The product of Blake's resolution to print 'in the infernal method' is the illuminated book we are reading, a book which denies both in words and by the manner of its production – both constatively and performatively –

that 'man has a body distinct from his soul.' Prophecy and performativity interconstitute one another; what the poet predicts will happen *is* happening in and through his writing, and vice versa.

In the final 'Memorable Fancy,' Blake's Devil sends his angelic interlocutor into a chromatic fit by naming Jesus Christ as the greatest man and asserting that he broke each of the ten commandments. When the Devil details the ways in which Jesus broke the law, it turns out that most of his acts were speech acts: he mocked at the sabbath, turned away the law, bore false witness, prayed for his disciples, and bid them shake the dust off their feet. 'Jesus was all virtue, and acted from impulse: not from rules,' the Devil concludes (*MHH* 23–4, E 43), articulating another confrontation between individual will and language endorsed by church and state. Christ's greatness consists in opposing individualistic, impulse-driven speech acts to a code of law, where law is the epitome of formulaic, institutional, socially legitimated linguistic practice. Blake emulates the verbal performance of Jesus when he offers, as a challenge to the institutionally sanctioned language of the Bible, his idiosyncratic and subversive 'Bible of Hell.' In a speech act that Austin would call infelicitous, since the speaker himself undermines the conditions for a valid promise by spurning the audience's consent, Blake wills us this text. The world shall have the Bible of Hell, he pronounces, 'whether they will or no' (*MHH* 24, E 44).

'A Song of Liberty'

Despite its later date of composition, 'A Song of Liberty' is representative of the *Marriage* as a whole in linguistic practice as it is in theme. The text alternates past-tense narrative with vivid evocations of the present situation brought about by the narrated events; this much is clear from the grammatical structure and verb tenses. Thematically, though, the allusions to the prophetic text of Revelation, on the one hand, and to the historical events of 1792 and 1793, on the other, generate a more complex temporality. The first verse already conflates history with prophecy:

1. The Eternal Female groand! it was heard over all the Earth: (*MHH* 25, E 44)

A reader sensitive to biblical echoes might identify Blake's 'Eternal Female' with the 'woman clothed with the sun' of Revelation 12, and thus align Blake's narrative perspective with that of John, who describes a vision seen in the past that is provident of future events.

Ending with a colon, the verse leaves us in a state of expectancy: and indeed the next five verses describe the effects of the universal groan as if they were immediately present. The illocutionary force of the voice changes, as the text incorporates imperatives and direct address:

3. Shadows of Prophecy shiver along by the lakes and the rivers and mutter across the ocean! France rend down thy dungeon (*MHH* 25, E 44)

The fall of France's dungeon is the first historically locatable event, and with it the paradoxical time-frame is reversed. Beginning as past-tense narrative that must be read as prophecy, the text turns into future-oriented imperative that refers to an event in the past.

'A Song of Liberty' divides into three approximately equal units of narrative, each of which begins in the past tense but slides irresistibly into the present. The first unit ends abruptly at verse 6 – 'And weep!' – with a full stop and the first full rhyme in the text (weep/deep). Verse 7 returns to the narrative of past events, but once more builds to a climax at which the sense of immediacy is intensified by repetition, present progressives, and direct address to the reader:

11. The fire, the fire, is falling!
12. Look up! look up! O citizen of London. enlarge thy countenance; O Jew, leave counting gold! return to thy oil and wine; O African! black African! (go. winged thought widen his forehead.) (*MHH* 26, E 44)

In the final unit, which begins at verse 13, the distinction between past and present is obliterated altogether. The 'new born wonder' is cast down, the sea flees, the starry king falls with his retinue – and the grammatical structure begins to deteriorate accordingly. It is as if the ruin of the tyrant who upheld moral law brings with it the ruin of expository language, which is founded on laws of grammar and reference. The mock-epic catalogue in verse 15, intended at first to ridicule the obsolete trappings of tyranny, gets out of control in the verses that follow:

15. Down rushd beating his wings in vain the jealous king: his grey brow'd councellors, thunderous warriors, curl'd veterans, among helms, and shields, and chariots horses, elephants: banners, castles, slings and rocks,
16. Falling, rushing, ruining! buried in the ruins, on Urthona's dens.
17. All night beneath the ruins, then their sullen flames faded emerge round the gloomy king,

18. With thunder and fire: leading his starry hosts thro' the waste wilderness he promulgates his ten commands, glancing his beamy eyelids over the deep in dark dismay (*MHH* 26–7, E 44)

Up to verse 14, despite the randomness of verse divisions, grammaticality has been upheld. Now verb tenses, after a period of confusion, change to present, and referentiality breaks down. The text admits, on the one hand, an inscrutable signifier like 'Urthona'; on the other hand, there are recognizable but paradoxical identifications between the starry king and Satan in *Paradise Lost*, as well as between the king and Moses. As the imagery leads us into a more distant biblical past than that of Revelation, we seem also to have reached the present of the prophecy.

This convoluted temporal structure, in which past, present, and future seem interdependent, is reminiscent of Milton's language in passages which critics have identified as distinctively visionary.[5] But the illocutionary structure also suggests that 'A Song of Liberty' cannot rest content with constative statement but constantly breaks into explicit performatives: commands, exhortations, declarations. In one sense, this is a myth about the emergence of the declarative speech act. Just as constation gives way to explicit performatives, Rintrah's inarticulate roar and the Eternal Female's groan are superseded by the triumphantly articulate cry of the 'son of fire':

20. Spurning the clouds written with curses, stamps the stony law to dust, loosing the eternal horses from the dens of night, crying

Empire is no more! and now the lion & wolf shall cease. (*MHH* 27, E 45)

At first glance, 'A Song of Liberty' appears to distinguish between oral and written forms of performative language as those which Blake approves and condemns. Here voice is the privileged medium; writing, and moreover engraving, are explicitly devalued, associated with curses and tyrannical laws. But the *Marriage* as a whole does not allow for such a straightforward division; Isaiah and Ezekiel are among the writing prophets, and the material production of a written text is central here as it is throughout Blake's work. The more valid distinction is between language that restricts – laws and curses – and language that animates and expresses individuality. In 'Spurning the clouds written with curses' and stamping the tables of the law to dust, the son of fire is rejecting oppres-

5 See chapter 3 above, and Kerrigan (*Prophetic Milton* 226).

sive and institutionally sanctioned speech acts. What is substituted for these is a declaration which, as Searle would say, fits world to words *and* words to world: 'Empire is no more! and now the lion & wolf shall cease.' The utterance is, in fact, as illegitimate a declaration as Searle's infamous 'Let there be light.' Blake, or his mythical revolutionary, usurps the voice of a political leader who might be expected to legitimately and effectively declare the end of empire, while utterly lacking the authority and societal consensus that would give him the right to make such a pronouncement. The intersection of Logos with sociopolitical speech act that disrupts Searle's taxonomy is precisely what Blake relies on to express his visionary stance.

The subjunctives of the concluding 'Chorus' again oppose the curses of the priesthood with the blessing of a visionary:

Let the Priests of the Raven of dawn, no longer in deadly black, with hoarse note curse the sons of joy. Nor his accepted brethren whom, tyrant, he calls free; lay the bound or build the roof. Nor pale religious letchery call that virginity, that wishes but acts not!

For every thing that lives is Holy (*MHH* 27, E 45)

All of the poet's speech acts are in the form of negations; they seek to bring about a state in which certain things are no longer done. With his characteristic suspicion of limits, Blake represents the essence of liberty, not as rules for a new order, but as a breaking of the old bounds (or bonds). He rejects the authority of church and state to perform speech acts, like cursing and calling (i.e., naming), that impose on their objects. Instead, Blake arrogates to himself the power of calling religious and secular authorities by new names – 'Priests of the Raven of dawn,' 'tyrant,' 'pale religious letchery' – thus undermining their attempts to declare who is free and to define what virginity is. In rebaptizing the objects of the curse as 'sons of joy,' and redefining virginity as that which 'wishes but acts not,' Blake flouts the apparent authority of Priesthood. Insofar as he (and like-minded readers) constitute the community which must ratify the Priests' speech acts, he withholds his acceptance of the necessary conventions and renders their performative utterances, to use Austin's term, 'misfires.'

Blake's coda is overlaid on the conclusion of the Book of Revelation (11:1–2, 21:15–17), which in turn founds itself on the ending of Ezekiel (chapters 40–3). Both texts describe the measurement and construction of a restored temple. In *The Reason of Church-Government* (a text in which Milton, just like Blake in the *Marriage*, is taking stock of his artistic career at

the Christological age of thirty-three), Milton provides a typological interpretation of the rebuilt temple:

... should not he ... have cast his line and levell upon the soule of man which is his
rationall temple, and by the divine square and compasse thereof forme and regen-
erate in us the lovely shapes of vertues and graces, the sooner to edifie and accomplish that immortall stature of Christs body which is his Church, in all her glorious
lineaments and proportions. (*CPW* 1:757–8)

The 'rationall temple' is variously identified with the human soul, the body
of Christ, and the reformed church. Blake, for his part, declines even such a
fluid reinterpretation of the image. He declines the whole project of rebuild-
ing a temple, implying by his refusal that, although Christ claims to make all
things new, this prophecy is put off in the Book of Revelation into an indefinite future while, for the present, the writer can only reiterate Ezekiel. For
Blake the temple is an image of restriction, constructed by arbitrary measurement ('lay the bound') and a hard covering ('build the roof'). The restrictiveness is not only physical but spiritual, insofar as a temple authorizes
oppressive pronouncements, and indeed stands for the decree that one
place is holy but another is not. The parallelism of Blake's sentences in the
'Chorus' renders the building of a temple equivalent to repressing one's
desires and to cursing or inhibiting the livelihood of another.

Both Ezekiel and John make much of the instrument with which the
temple is measured, a carpenter's rod, which in Greek (though not in the
vocabulary of Revelation) is a *kanon*, the source of our word 'canon' for a
body of writings. In Revelation, the measuring of the heavenly temple goes
hand in hand with the sealing off of the scriptural canon. The text concludes famously – and, for a sacred code, quite conventionally – with a
curse on anyone who alters the prophecies in the book, threatening to
excommunicate such a person from everything holy:

And if any man shall take away from the words of the book of this prophecy, God
shall take away his part out of the book of life, and out of the holy city, and from
the things which are written in this book. (Revelation 22:19)

As Randel Helms has pointed out, the definition of what is holy is, at one
point in Revelation, restricted to a single being: 'for only thou art holy,' the
redeemed sing to the Lord in heaven (Helms 291). Spurning the curse as he
rewrites the prophecy, Blake changes this into a supremely inclusive blessing: 'For every thing that lives is Holy.'

The 'let-for' structure of the 'Chorus' reads like an adaptation of the liturgical form of a service of worship. Just as he declines to rebuild the temple and denies the authority of priestly pronouncements, Blake draws the language of liturgy into an extra-institutional or anti-institutional context. It is reminiscent of the syntax adopted by a poet Blake admired, in a work Blake did not know: 'For every thing that lives is Holy' might easily be a verse out of Christopher Smart's *Jubilate Agno*, another text bound up with performative utterance from the title onward. Like Smart, Blake attempts to cancel curses and bestow blessings, a move that above all requires faith in the power of language to alter reality by animating rather than by codifying or delimiting.

The deceptively simple title 'A Song of Liberty,' like the title 'Marriage of Heaven and Hell,' leaves open the question of whether the song is historical, prophetic, or performative. We may elect to read it as a song which commemorates the achievement of liberty in the past, one which predicts the coming of liberty in the future – or else one which brings about liberty, the way a Charter of Rights or a Declaration of Independence brings those rights, or that independence, into existence by virtue of being an established type of linguistic act. Similarly, in offering us 'The Marriage of Heaven and Hell,' Blake might be reporting on an event in the past; he might be announcing an upcoming event (in the manner of a wedding invitation, which the script on the title page may resemble); or he might be performing the marriage in and by the words of the text. *The Marriage of Heaven and Hell* presents itself as a substitute for the conventional speech acts that constitute the performance of a marriage. My reading has stressed this last alternative, in an attempt to argue that Blake tries to turn the language game we are playing when we accept the declarative authority of priests and legislators into a language game in which the term 'marriage' still has meaning as a fundamental change in condition, even though the required words are not uttered by a properly ordained official. The author of Revelation only went so far as to announce an upcoming marriage between Christ and the church; Blake performs one in the writing of the poem itself, and we instantiate it in reading.

Extra-institutional performatives, or speech-act formulas without their sanctioning sociopolitical authority, play a crucial role in the later poetry of Blake. *The Marriage of Heaven and Hell* is often regarded as a turning point in Blake's art, and I would argue that it is so in his use of performative language as well. There have been repeated attempts to identify Blake's target audience for this tract, but such attempts generally end with the critic's conclusion that whatever audience has been suggested will not fit the bill.[6] *The Marriage of Heaven and Hell* is addressed neither to the members of the Swedenborgian New Jerusalem Church, nor to the writers and artists who frequented the house of Blake's publisher Joseph Johnson, nor to the members of the radical societies that sympathized with the revolution in France, though a full understanding of the text's implications requires a knowledge of all these positions. In the 1790s and early 1800s, Blake was becoming progressively more alienated from potential friends and patrons, prompting his friend John Flaxman to write to William Hayley in 1805, 'I very much fear [Blake's] abstracted habits are so much at variance with the usual modes of human life, that he will not derive all the advantage to be wished from the present favourable appearances' (Bentley, *Blake Records Supplement* 30). In terms of authorial voice and perspective, this means that Blake was losing whatever interpretive community he was ever able to address. From here on, he would continue to use the forms of performative language, but these conventions have a different kind of meaning outside of the social contexts in and by which they were formed.

6 See John Howard, 'An Audience for *The Marriage of Heaven and Hell*'; Michael Scrivener, 'A Swedenborgian Visionary and *The Marriage of Heaven and Hell*'; and Morris Eaves, 'Romantic Expressive Theory and Blake's Idea of the Audience.'

7

Blake's *Jerusalem*: Statements and States

Es ist diese bindende Notwendigkeit, die Welttotalität für jeden Einzelfall und individuell für jeden Einzelmenschen neu zu erstellen, die als der wesentliche Grundzug der Romantik gelten kann.

Hermann Broch

Vision, Prophecy, Reading, and Performance

The claim that Blake's texts do things or create worlds is in itself hardly revolutionary. Even a quantitative analysis of the type undertaken by Josephine Miles four decades ago encourages an emphasis on the relative and dynamic, rather than the constative and static, elements of Blake's poetry. While Blake inherits the eighteenth-century predilection for 'physical, descriptive, onomatopoetic, invocative, and declarative' language, Miles concludes, he tends to bring out these qualities through verbal forms, favouring 'the participial sort of meaning' which reveals 'the motion observed in process' (85). The participle, a verbal form that commonly functions as an adjective ('the laughing child') yet can also be a substantive ('his laughing') or an adverb ('he laughing said to me'), illustrates the fluidity of grammatical categories that is vital to Blake's poetry and underlies its illocutionary effect. Ronald Clayton Taylor takes Miles's stylistic observations a step further, concluding that Blake's heavy use of the progressive or 'ongoing' aspect of verbs throws into relief the verbs of definite change in the first-person present, investing those verbs, by contrast, with quasi-performative force. Blake's poetry employs present participles to create background states; these are punctuated by utterances – like 'I go to Eternal Death!' – which daringly 'force a mere verb of motion into performative use' (R.C. Taylor 46–7).

Other critics begin with Blake's thematic emphasis on dynamism and transformation and explore the way this theme is reflected in his fluid, idiosyncratic grammar. Thus, to say that 'a perceiving subject becomes what it beholds' is equivalent, according to Edward J. Rose, to saying or demonstrating that 'a subject can be simultaneously the subject and the object of the same verb,' as in the constructions 'blackning church' or 'darkning man' ('Visionary Forms Dramatic' 118). On a more radical plane, Peter Middleton proposes an inclusive critical approach that would give full weight to elements of the text that the critical tradition 'censors,' elements which generate 'distance, contention, intervention or re-examination,' including 'the ungrammatical syntax of the poetry, the specific perceptual elements of the illuminated texts, the refractory elements of the narrative ..., the use of repetition, the use of proper names, and the refusal to grant the reality of narrative existence to the figures which bear many of those names' ('Revolutionary Poetics, Part I' 114, 117).[1] Middleton is essentially challenging criticism to take account of a certain performative dimension of Blake's poetry. A reading that recognizes 'ungrammatical syntax' and 'refractory elements' does not approach the text as constative statement, but rather as a performance where meaning emerges in and through the encounter between reader and text. Blake's 'writerly' poetry involves the reader in performativity by requiring his or her participation in the creation of new interpretive strategies, in the making of sense.

If Blake's texts challenge us to create what we read, this challenge corresponds to the creative force of language as it is demonstrated by the actions and responses of characters in the texts. Many critics have recognized the creative potential of language as a central element in Blake's concept of the prophet and poet; also, and often in consequence, many associate the creativity of language with particular characters in his epics, of whom Los is the most significant. W.J.T. Mitchell specifically relates the creative effect of Blake's language to his rejection of a Miltonic model of inspiration: 'Without the Miltonic assumption of an untouched, perfect divinity in the heavens, the prophet cannot simply serve as the mouthpiece of God; if he is to be a seer, he must create what he sees' (*Blake's Composite Art* 169). A seer with the power to create what he or she sees would be one who has appropriated the phenomenological performative epitomized

1 Middleton's essay gives a specifically linguistic slant to W.J.T. Mitchell's prediction of the recovery of a 'dangerous Blake,' in an article ('Dangerous Blake') which appeared, like Middleton's, a decade ago. The reconsideration of disruptive aspects of Blake and his work now seems well under way; two of several examples that could be cited of the fulfilment of Mitchell's and Middleton's predictions are Paul Youngquist's work on Blake's madness and V.A. de Luca on the intransigence of his language.

by God's 'Let there be light.' According to most critics, the character in Blake's mythological universe who comes closest to imitating this type of performative utterance is Los, the Eternal Prophet, who creates time because he embodies time and thus radically recasts the prophet's relation to history. Los illustrates the visionary's need to preserve the dynamic power of words and struggle against their petrification; he must continually destroy and recreate his works, Leopold Damrosch argues, since 'it is the activity, not the product, that matters' (325). Leonard W. Deen adds that Los himself, and his characteristic activity of forging and building, are both fundamental metaphors for speech becoming act, as evident from the way Los's song is ' "utterd with Hammer & Anvil" ' (226). All these critics in some way identify Blakean song, text, and language as act; though none of them uses the vocabulary of speech-act theory, they effectively lay the groundwork for an account of the illocutionary force of the text.

Recent critical studies have increasingly been employing the terms 'performative' and 'performance' to describe Blake's art. From the viewpoint of textual criticism, G.E. Bentley, Jr., and Jerome McGann both characterize the illuminated books as performances. For Bentley, the term conveniently sums up the features that render the Blakean text unique: the variant copies, the indeterminate ordering of plates, the fact that Blake did everything but manufacture the paper himself. McGann, with his characteristic conflation of textual scholarship and new historicism, interprets the term 'performance' in a way that is at once more specific with regard to features of the text and much broader in its implications for historical criticism. *Jerusalem*, according to McGann, 'calls attention to itself as gestural, performative,' because it incorporates corrections, emendations, deletions, gougings of the copper plate – not as stages in the production of a work, but in the 'finished' work itself (*Towards a Literature* 12). The performative or processive character of Blake's art mirrors his belief that imagination reveals itself as action in the world: 'The work of art is the display of the artist's imaginative energy. It is fundamentally an action, and to the degree that the "completed" work reveals it *as* an action, the work is successful' (*Towards a Literature* 13). Blake's text is a performance in two senses: as a work which shows forth the labour that went into it, and as communicative action in a social context. These two dimensions together reveal his dynamic conception of knowledge: 'The *truth* of Blake's poetry emerges as the textual "performances" of his imaginative communications' (*Towards a Literature* 32).

McGann's conflation of textual performativity and social action provides the most relevant context for my own study of speech acts in *Jerusalem*. Yet while McGann regards the text itself as the primary 'utterance' or communicative act, I begin with a consideration of some of the speech acts which take place within a text like *Jerusalem*. Once we analyse the way speech acts operate in Blake's major epics, we may recognize those utterances as paradigms for the kind of speech act the poetry itself represents. Blake's epics negotiate the dichotomy between phenomenological performatives and societally authorized pronouncements which was implicit in the *Songs* and encapsulated in plate 11 of *The Marriage of Heaven and Hell*. *Jerusalem* recognizes a type of speech act, the best example of which is the act of 'creating states,' which compromises between transcendent and convention-based performativity: it is both phenomenological and sociopolitical; it may be spoken by the Divine Voice, but it is understood by Albion in terms of, one might say, the Austinian performative. At the same time, *Jerusalem* is itself an example of such a speech act. The title, at once the name of a city, a community of people, an individual ('The Emanation of The Giant Albion'), a state of consciousness, and a poem, already evokes the problematics of naming, reference, and performative utterance. If the opening word 'Jerusalem' immediately achieves the naming of Blake's text, according to the literary conventions which allow us to recognize it as the title of the book, the sociopolitical and psychological resonances of the name are only established over the course of the poem, which closes with a 'Jerusalem' rediscovered and legitimized. This re-established 'Jerusalem' is a hybrid of the phenomenological and the sociopolitical performative, a 'state' created by Blake's text analogously to the way states are created by characters within the text. The epic thus represents not only the conflation of the two types of speech acts distinguished in the first chapter of this book, but also authorizes a reading which combines the two forms of speech-act criticism that were distinguished there, the study of performatives in the text and the study of the text as performative.

Adamic Language and Blakean Naming

By the mid-eighteenth century, a sincere belief in the Adamic origin of language had long since given way to linguistic theories, like that of John Locke, which were oriented toward arbitrary representation and toward mentalism, or the belief that words correspond to ideas and not to things themselves. Yet eighteenth-century philosophy continued to be preoccupied with naming, reference, and the problem of achieving an exact correspondence between signifier and signified, and the myth of Adamic naming was eventually revived in a different context, as an element of the emerging Romantic myth of poetic creation. Johann Gottfried Herder is a primary spokesperson for the analogy between the poet, the naming subject, and the divine creator, an analogy resurrected and invested with new vigour by pre-Romantic philology and by Romantic devotees of the imagination:

Light is the first uttered word of the creator, and the instrument of Divine efficiency in the sensitive human soul ... In giving names to all, and ordering all from the impulse of his own inward feeling, and with reference to himself, [man] becomes an imitator of the Divinity, a second Creator, a true *poietes*, a creative poet. Following this origin of the poetick art ... we might still more boldly place it in an imitation of that Divine agency, which creates, and gives form and determinateness to the objects of its creation. Only the creative thoughts of God, however, are truly objective and have actuality in their outward expression, and stand forth existent and living in the products of creative power. Man can only give names to these creations, arrange and link them together ... (Herder 2:7–8)

Walter Benjamin, the heir of eighteenth-century and Romantic theories of language, also makes Adam's acts of naming into a reflection of God's creative activity. 'Der Mensch ist der Erkennende derselben Sprache, in der Gott Schöpfer ist' (Benjamin 149); God and Adam speak the same language. But Benjamin also draws the significant distinction between creator (*Schöpfer*) and knower (*der Erkennende*), or between the ideal performativity of divine language, which matches a world to the words, and the ideal correspondence of Adamic language, which matches words to the world. In contrast to God's arbitrary speech acts at the creation, Adam's use of language is motivated by his recognition of the essential nature of the animals on which he is bestowing names.

Given the contemporaneous interest of philosophers and philologists in exact designation, and of poets in the way the poetic mind imitates the example of Adam by naming a world as its own, there is ample reason to consider Blake's work in light of the paradigm of Adamic naming.[2] The model seems particularly appropriate in cases where Blake invents names which, like those Adam gives to the animals, were previously unknown in the world. Thus

2 The most extensive study of Blake's work in relation to Adamic language is Robert Essick, *William Blake and the Language of Adam*; my discussion of naming may be read in part as a dialogue with Essick's work. Essick's primary context is philosophy, philology, and theory of art during and prior to Blake's time; this context leads him to distinguish between Blake's recognition of a concrete, motivated, and expressive language and an abstract or differential language. My study, which recognizes two types of performative language, is in general agreement with Essick's analysis though it has a different basis in twentieth-century philosophy and linguistics.

Daniel Stempel argues that Blake inherits from the classical episteme of the eighteenth century a commitment to naming as 'the interplay of imagination and resemblance' (391), or a compromise between the properties of the human mind and the properties of the natural order. Even though names are prone to the corruption brought about by linguistic change, Blake strives to recover an ideal of exact designation as the interaction of nature and imagination: 'Blake's names are natural in the sense that they attempt to restore each name to its proper place, but they are also arbitrary because they are deliberate coinages' (Stempel 394). As a compromise between appropriateness and arbitrariness, Blake's names encourage readers to reflect on the problematics of naming in general. A proper name, as the adjective suggests, can designate with ideal accuracy only once, and with additional use must betray or gloss over the differences between the objects to which it refers. Nietzsche's complaint that all concepts falsify individual experience by equating dissimilar experiences and objects could also be used to expose the inherent metaphoricity of every name, insofar as its individual referents are at best related by resemblance and not by identity.[3] Names come to us overloaded with semantic content and overdetermined by other roles they have played. If Blake attempts to reduce the element of misrepresentation involved in the use of names by making up fresh names for many of the characters and places in his epics, he nevertheless exploits to the fullest the ability of names to bring with them evocative syllables, morphemes, homonyms, and even significant single letters. As the work of Nelson Hilton demonstrates, each of Blake's multidimensional words calls up a wealth of possible significations, while avoiding the direct path to a distinct referent; Blake's texts expand our perception of language to the point where the referent of his words is 'the entire vision of words in which each particular exists' (*Literal Imagination* 237).[4]

3 'Every word becomes a concept as soon as it is supposed to serve not merely as a reminder of the unique, absolutely individualized original experience, to which it owes its origin, but at the same time to fit countless, more or less similar cases, which, strictly speaking, are never identical, and hence absolutely dissimilar. Every concept originates by the equation of the dissimilar' (*Friedrich Nietzsche* 249).

4 In a more specialized study of morphemic patterning in Blake's language, Aaron Fogel relates the play of phonemes and morphemes to the dialogical function of Blake's names, by which they 'direct[ ] us to types of mutual speech more than to simple categories' (217). As Fogel recognizes, his discovery that names and sound patterns in Blake's poetry contribute to the evocation of 'pictures of speech,' or models for dialogue conceived in a context that is both poetic and social, has fundamental relevance for the study of speech as act. However, Fogel dismisses the potential parallel with Austinian theory because he believes such a parallel would commit him to an alliance between poetry and ordinary language which he is unprepared to defend.

Without denying the originality of Hilton's approach, it is possible to align it with a traditional critical assumption about Blake's naming. Despite vast methodological differences, critics have generally acted on the assumption that Blake's names *are* ultimately referential – that their purpose is to reveal referents that perhaps can be evoked in no other way. Blake's names, that is to say, are attempts to fit words to *his* world; like Adam, he invents a new language to describe a new creation. In the spirit of S. Foster Damon's *Blake Dictionary*, twentieth-century critics have expended a great deal of energy decoding Blake's symbolic system and his arcane vocabulary, as if it were a language cognate with but different from our own. From a post-structuralist perspective, this critical approach, which sees Blake's corpus as a 'poetry of nouns' that must be translated back into ordinary language, has been called a 'vision of Blake as a poetic Adam naming his creatures' (Hilton and Vogler, *Unnam'd Forms* 6).[5] By contrast, the past decade and more has seen a dramatic increase in the exploration of non-nominal, non-referential, and non-univocal elements in Blake's poetry, with two results: the signifying power of Blake's names may be de-emphasized and even denied, and Blake may come to seem more like God creating the animals than like Adam naming them.

While Robert Essick's primary argument, in *William Blake and the Language of Adam*, involves the relation of Blake's linguistic practice to theories of Adamic naming, he intimates more than once that there is a continuity between Adamic naming and God's creative use of language (11, 123). However, a distinction between God's language and Adam's, as between creativity and correspondence, emerges more fully in recent work which regards Blake's language as fundamentally non-referential. V.A. de Luca concentrates on those points at which Blake's text itself becomes iconic, demanding that we look *at* the words rather than beyond them. Catalogues of names, or resistant masses of familiar and unfamiliar signifiers (which are especially common in *Jerusalem*), represent one form of what de Luca has called a 'wall of words.'[6] Arguing that Blake's names ultimately refuse to legitimate any etymologies that commentators may suggest for them, Peter Middleton contends that Blake is singularly un-Adamic in his name-giving, since he is unconcerned with knowing the natures of

---

5 Cf. Robert Gleckner, referring to Blake's evocation of Eternity: 'He describes it, names it (precisely as Adam names the creatures in Genesis), talks about it ...' ('Most Holy Forms' 101).

6 De Luca's perceptive and detailed argument for considering Blake's names as a principle of structure, rather than conceptual reference, is begun in 'Proper Names in the Structural Design of Blake's Myth-making' and continued in 'A Wall of Words: The Sublime as Text' and *Words of Eternity: Blake and the Poetics of the Sublime.*

the things he names: 'The effect of Blake's neologistic naming is to call into question the whole practice of naming as a referential gesture pointing out some thing that is named' ('Revolutionary Poetics, Part II' 40–1).[7]

A mode of designation which does not seek correspondence with already existing referents is a central aspect of the theory of fictional discourse put forward by speech-act philosophers. According to John Searle, a certain kind of non-referentiality is common to all imaginative writing, since the writer of fiction does not refer to an existing fictional person, but *creates* a fictional person (*Expression and Meaning* 71–2). This is one aspect of Searle's theory of fictional discourse, which holds that writers of fiction are simulating the illocutionary acts found in 'serious' discourse. The fiction writer pretends to perform the speech act of referring, and accordingly pretends that there is an object to be referred to, since the existence of such an object is normally a necessary condition of reference. As a universal theory of fiction, Searle's analysis has been influential, but it carries implications that many literary scholars have trouble accepting: that the text can be portioned out into 'serious' and 'pretended' statements, and that the entire responsibility for determining what is and is not fiction lies in the writer's intentions. In the case of Blake, however, Searle's claim that the imaginative writer's use of names is fundamentally creative rather than referential helps to define one of the performative aspects of a text like *Jerusalem*. Like the deity in book 7 of *Paradise Lost*, Blake, with his unusually frequent use of neologisms and imaginative names, uses naming as a method of creation.

When a writer of fiction introduces names like 'Marianne Dashwood' and 'John Willoughby' into an early nineteenth-century British context, she may indeed be said to feign referentiality while actually creating characters, and this is the type of example on which Searle's theory is based. But when Coleridge uses the name 'Kubla Khan,' or Byron uses 'Don Juan' and 'George the Third,' or Blake uses 'Luther' and 'Milton,' are they referring to

7 Middleton's argument is not only that Blake subverts reference, but that he calls into question 'the transcendence generated by naming in the ideology of divine power' ('Revolutionary Poetics, Part II' 41) – that is, Blake (like Middleton) subverts precisely the privileged model of reference which the myth of Adamic language would support.

A final variant on the subversion of Adamic language in Blake's work comes from Leslie Brisman, who interprets Blake's rewriting of the Garden of Eden story in *The Four Zoas* as an exposure of the representational or fictional nature of any myth of origins. The fall brings a consciousness of metaphoricity, and Blake's characters find that the only name-giving they can engage in is objectification, a fallen parody of Adam's creative activity: 'When Adam named the animals he knew a creative power that preceded fall. But when Blake's Albion "called them Luvah & Vala" he read the signs, as it were, that barred his way back to paradise' (' "The Four Zoas" ' 150–1).

characters or creating them? In Blake's case, his use of historical names is unavoidably influenced by his admixture of names like 'Los' and 'Enitharmon,' which flaunt the fact that they do not refer, at least not to any referent the reader has experience of. Blake's use of unfamiliar names defamiliarizes the whole concept of naming, exposing the fact that names in imaginative literature do not function the way they are supposed to in real-world discourse. This is not just to say that Blake's fictional entities are previously unknown to the reader, but even to deny that they are pre-existent for Blake. Rather, the manner in which Blake's names re-shape or re-create existing words and names suggests that the referent comes into being in the act of applying the name. Blake's naming of characters, in other words, is *not* analogous to the baptizing of a baby, who exists as an autonomous being even before the name is bestowed.

Yet it is also true that names in the real world do not always exhibit referentiality in the way they are supposed to, and there is a sense in which an infant *does* come into being – as an accountable member of society – when he or she is given a name. Baptizing an infant, generally with a name made up of a certain number of words in an order appropriate to the socio-cultural group into which the infant is born, brings that person into existence as, so to speak, an institutional fact, entitled to a birth certificate and a family allowance cheque. Blake's Los, as several critics have noted, is 'Loss' which has lost an 's'; the name performs itself, and the character takes shape as an incarnation of this linguistic effect of loss. Los's existence, as an embodiment of desire and the architect of a city of art which is provisional and yet offers hope that the spiritual world may be recovered, is inextricably bound up with the condition of being and not being 'loss.' The same may be said of his identity as a reversed 'sol' or an embodiment of the German *Los*, 'destiny.' The name and its connotations so strongly condition our (and Blake's) understanding of what the character *is* that he does not really exist apart from the name. Though it is an un-Blakean way of putting it, there is a sense in which Los exists purely as an institutional fact.

The process by which identity evolves out of the name is displayed in Vala's speech at the beginning of chapter 2 of *Jerusalem*, where she identifies herself to Albion, who has failed, in his error, to recognize her. Her speech moves toward the declaration 'I am Love' (*J* 29.52, E 176), where the word/name 'Love,' capitalized and distinguished as the final word on the plate, evolves out of her initial self-identification as 'the loveliest of the daughters of Eternity' (*J* 29.40, E 175), and out of her history, as she claims that she 'loved ... Jerusalem' (*J* 29.43, E 176) and 'loving create[d] love' (*J* 29.45, E 176). The activity of loving generates a reified and abstracted con-

cept of love, which is then elevated into a proper name and an identity, difficult to separate, once the declaration is made, from the name 'Vala' itself,
a reversed echo of 'Love' with altered vowels. Vala's statement is, of
course, delusive, intended to seduce Albion into believing that the imaginative human being is a product of the Female Will and that her love is an
attractive alternative to the ideal of brotherhood in Eternity. Yet the fact
that her words do not correspond to the ultimate reality of the poem's
world only exposes more clearly the way naming functions as an authoritative speech act. Defining herself as a linguistic effect (in terms of the cog-
nates loveliest/loved/loving/Love/[Vala]) and as the reified form of her
actions in history, Vala effectively makes herself into the Love of Albion's
life. By contrast, the later epiphany of Vala in chapter 3 allows Los to rede-
fine the name and the identity she has assumed: 'Without Forgiveness of
Sin Love is Itself Eternal Death' (*J* 64.24, E 215).

Tempting as it is to search out puns and etymological clues in Blake's
names, these self-definitions and re-definitions suggest that the significance
of names also lies in the declarative rhetoric with which they are bestowed,
by characters themselves or by the poet. When Blake has Los list the names
of his sons and daughters in *The Four Zoas*, his language is more declarative than descriptive:

And these are the Sons of Los & Enitharmon. Rintrah Palamabron
Theotormon Bromion Antamon Ananton Ozoth Ohana
Sotha Mydon Ellayol Natho Gon Harhath Satan
Har Ochim Ijim Adam Reuben Simeon Levi Judah Dan Naphtali
Gad Asher Issachar Zebulun Joseph Benjamin David Solomon
Paul Constantine Charlemaine Luther Milton
These are our daughters Ocalythron Elynittria Oothoon Leutha
Elythiria Enanto Manathu Vorcyon Ethinthus Moab Midian
Adah Zillah Caina Naamah Tamar Rahab Tirzah Mary

(*FZ* 115.1–9; E 380)[8]

---

8 This passage has been discussed by both de Luca ('Proper Names' 7) and Essick (*William Blake* 211–12). De Luca cites the lines as an instance of 'the autonomy of the mythic name,' or Blake's habit of arbitrarily introducing unknown names which never appear again in his work, while Essick points to the 'onomastic glossolalia' of the catalogue, which makes the poet seem 'a name-crazy Adam with no animals before him.' I am in agreement with de Luca's conclusion that these names never have independently existing referents and with Essick's emphasis on non-referentiality, though both critics base these conclusions on the strangeness of the names themselves, while I would call attention to the declarative grammar of the lines.

The catalogue is anchored in the demonstrative 'these,' one of the class of deictics which, according to Wittgenstein, is only meaningful in the presence of a referent that can, at least figuratively, be pointed out ('The demonstrative "this" can never be without a bearer' [*Philosophical Investigations* §45]). But in Blake's lines the referential structure is collapsed, so that the referent of 'these' are sons and daughters who can only be identified by, and as, the names that follow, some of which never appear again in Blake's corpus. Signifiers which should refer to the object instead constitute the only object there is. The verb 'are' takes on performative force as the line brings forth, rather than referring to, the children of Los and Enitharmon. At the same time, in terms of Benveniste's distinction between 'is' as copula and 'is' as assertion of existence, 'are' seems to fulfil only the copula function of linking elements in the sentence with one another, and to lack the added force of asserting existence in the real world.[9] The primary function of the catalogue is to forge relations, to allow the connotations of the name 'Satan' to impose themselves on the names 'Solomon' or 'Milton' and vice versa, and to let all these names colour 'Palamabron' or 'Ohana,' almost as if a weakened copula function persisted between the elements of the catalogue (if not 'Satan is Solomon,' to choose two names linked by their line-end position, then at least 'Satan is like Solomon'). By altering the function of the third-person present indicative of 'to be,' Blake disrupts the linguistic structure that Western thought regards as its most reliable indicator of constation or predication. When we read 'there is' or 'there are' in his poetry, we are compelled to think twice about the sense in which things 'are,' about the conditions or conditionality of Being itself. Like so many other aspects of his linguistic practice, Blake's use of names exposes the dependence of constation on context and perspective.

Inspiration: A Revision

Another spot where the importance of context makes itself felt is in the performative language of Blake's invocations. In presenting the poet as first-person subject, and recording the spiritual inception of the work to which they also form the material beginning, invocations depend heavily

9 'Within the assertive utterance, the verbal function is twofold: there is the cohesive function, which is to organize the elements of the utterance into a complete structure; and there is the assertive function, which consists in endowing the utterance with a predicate of reality ... Added implicitly to the grammatical relationship that unites the members of the utterance is a "this *is!*" that links the linguistic arrangement to the system of reality' (Benveniste 133–4).

on deictics, the parts of speech which, according to Roman Jakobson, cause the code of an utterance to overlap with the message ('Shifters' 131). Being context-dependent, deictics, like performatives, evade objective standards of proof; depending on one's definition, they may evade the condition of truth altogether. Jean-François Lyotard, in an examination into the way social discourses achieve legitimation, reflects on the simultaneous arbitrariness and instability of deictics:

Deictics relate the instances of the universe presented by the phrase in which they are placed back to a 'current' spatio-temporal origin so named 'I-here-now.' These deictics are designators of reality. They designate their object as an extra-linguistic permanence, as a 'given.' Far from constituting a permanence in itself, however, this 'origin' is presented or co-presented with the universe of the phrase in which they are marked. It appears and disappears with this universe, and thus with this phrase. (*Differend* 33)

Considering the shifting nature of the legitimation that arises from deictics (and it is worth recalling that Jakobson's habitual term for deictics is 'shifters'), an invocation which relies on the terms 'I,' 'now,' and 'this song' may be inherently more suited to Blake's notion of truth as progressive and perspectival than to Milton's concept of Truth as universal. A primary effect of Blake's invocations is to emphasize, to the point of hyperbole, the contemporaneity of the first-person subject. The invocation with which *Milton* begins imitates the opening invocation in *Paradise Lost* in appealing to the aid of muse-figures, summarizing the action of the poem, enjoining the muse to 'Say first!' and concluding with a specific question, the answer to which sets the poem in motion. But where Milton was content with an allusion to 'th'upright heart and pure' as the temple of the Spirit, Blake invites the Daughters of Beulah to travel straight through his physical body:

> Come into my hand
> By your mild power; descending down the Nerves of my right arm
> From out the Portals of my Brain, where by your ministry
> The Eternal Great Humanity Divine. planted his Paradise,
> And in it caus'd the Spectres of the Dead to take sweet forms
> In likeness of himself.   (*M* 2:5–10, E 96)

Radical both in its intensely physical conception of the process of inspiration, and in the claims it makes for the compass of the individual mind, this passage is matched by the opening of chapter 1 of *Jerusalem*. Deliberate echoes of *Paradise Lost* can be heard in the phrasing of the first line and in the theme of nightly visitation:

> Of the Sleep of Ulro! and of the passage through
> Eternal Death! and of the awaking to Eternal Life.
>
> This theme calls me in sleep night after night, & ev'ry morn
> Awakes me at sun-rise, then I see the Saviour over me
> Spreading his beams of love, & dictating the words of this mild song.
>
> Awake! awake O sleeper of the land of shadows, wake! expand!
> I am in you and you in me, mutual in love divine
>
> (*J* 4.1–7, E 146)

In place of an invocation, *Jerusalem* begins with a personal experience of inspiration, one that makes greater claims than Milton does when he affirms that Urania visits him 'Nightly, or when Morn / Purples the East' (*PL* 7.29–30), since this poet claims to be visited by the Saviour himself. The opening lines direct the theme of the poem ('Of the Sleep of Ulro') toward the poet himself ('This theme calls *me*'), placing him at the centre of an act that is paradigmatic for the poem, the act of calling a sleeper to awaken. The poet is the object of this action during the process of inspiration, but the instigator of it in the rest of the poem, since he also addresses a call to the reader to 'wake! expand!' In both its conception and its execution, the communicative act which is the poem shapes, and is shaped by, the identity and role of the poet. The centrality of deictics in this process, and their shifty nature, is evident in the opening words of the 'mild song': 'I am in you and you in me,' which are equally the words of the Saviour to the poet or to Albion, and of the poet to Albion or to the reader.

In the process of reading, a deictic interrupts a constative statement by introducing a moment of ambiguity in which the reader must decide on the appropriate frame or frames of reference. Blake exploits the context-dependency and the disruptiveness of deictics to revise the concept of inspiration, not only in his poetry but also in his personal letters. In 1800 he writes to William Hayley, following the death of Hayley's son:

Thirteen years ago. I lost a brother & with his spirit I converse daily & hourly in the Spirit. & See him in my remembrance in the regions of my Imagination. I hear his advice and even now write from his Dictate. (E 705)

The passage begins as a narrative about inspiration but becomes an act of inspiration, in which the spirit of Blake's brother Robert dictates even the letter Blake is writing at that moment. Blake conflates literal and figurative representations of experience by setting his radical claim to converse 'with his [Robert's] spirit' alongside the more familiar Christian image of conversing 'in the Spirit,' thus acting on his affirmation in the annotations to Lavater that 'all who converse in the spirit, converse with spirits' (E 600).[10] The meetings with Robert take place 'in my remembrance' and 'in ... my Imagination,' yet the report is framed by the definite temporal markers 'thirteen years ago' and 'even now,' the final deictic leaving us with a sense of the actuality and immediacy of the experience. Here, as in Blake's poetry, Benveniste's contention that deictics have meaning only when they are actualized in particular acts of discourse is crucial to interpretation: 'When the individual appropriates it, language is turned into instances of discourse, characterized by this system of internal references of which *I* is the key, and defining the individual by the particular linguistic construction he makes use of when he announces himself as the speaker' (200). The introduction of deictics into key points in his representation of moments of inspiration reinforces Blake's focus on the individual as the defining term of vision – and on imaginative vision as that which defines the individual.

The invocatory passages in *Jerusalem* characterize the poem as a revision of the Bible, by which the events of biblical history themselves become images for the process of inspiration. Whereas Milton, in book 1 of *Paradise Lost*, asks to be inspired by the same agent and in the same manner as Moses on Horeb or Sinai, Blake's inspiration will redeem the experience of Moses. For Blake, the giving of the Tables of the Law on Mount Sinai represents a moment of imposition and tyranny. In the introduction to Chapter 1 of *Jerusalem*, he envisions a second Sinai in spiritual form:

> Reader! [*lover*] of books! [*lover*] of heaven,
> And of that God from whom [*all books are given,*]
> Who in mysterious Sinais awful cave
> To Man the wond'rous art of writing gave,
> Again he speaks in thunder and in fire!
> Thunder of Thought, & flames of fierce desire:
> Even from the depths of Hell his voice I hear,

10 Cf. Ian Balfour's discussion of the problem of locating the 'in' of Blakean '*in*spiration': 'Blake's rhetoric walks a consistent line between ascribing inspiration to the "outside" influence characteristic of the Hebrew prophet on the one hand and to the "inner light" of the radical Protestant tradition on the other' ('Future of Citation' 122).

Within the unfathomd caverns of my Ear.
Therefore I print; nor vain my types shall be:
Heaven, Earth & Hell, henceforth shall live in harmony

(J 3, E 145)

God is still the giver of books, only the significance of the gift lies not in the objectified volume and its fixed content, but in the potential of the 'wond'rous art of writing.' 'Mysterious Sinais awful cave,' an image of restriction and incomprehension which owes more to Plato than to Genesis, gives way to 'the unfathomd caverns of my Ear,' an image which asserts the limitless potential of human perception. Later in *Jerusalem* Blake revises other aspects of Moses' experience, figuring inspiration as an antitype of the Israelites' release from captivity. 'O Lord my Saviour open thou the Gates / And I will lead forth thy Words,' the poet prays (J 74.40–1, E 230), identifying his senses or 'gates of perception' with checks on human liberty, himself (as Milton did) with a second Moses, and (anticipating the image of words in human forms) the people of God with the words of visionary poetry.

Similarly, the four Living Creatures that heralded the call of the prophet Ezekiel become the four senses or four perspectives in every human being:

These are the four Faces towards the Four Worlds of Humanity
In every Man. Ezekiel saw them by Chebars flood.

(J 12.57–8, E 156)

Blake's program, more radical still than that of Milton when he claimed for himself the same sort of inspired voice as the biblical prophets and patriarchs, involves literalizing the concept of vision, or at least blurring the boundary between literal and figurative to the point where it is indistinguishable. When Joshua Reynolds deemed it 'absurd' to believe that a winged genius 'did really inform [the poet] in a whisper what he was to write,' Blake accused Reynolds of attempting to 'Disprove & Contemn Spiritual Perception' (Ann. Reynolds, E 658). Throughout Blake's epics, inspired vision does not require giving up sight in favour of insight, but rather expanding the limits of sensory perception beyond the bounds of the sensory world.

It is worth keeping the literal dimension of vision in mind in the face of criticism which focuses on the more mystical sources of Blake's concept of vision. Harold Bloom's brief but powerful essay on the relation of *Jerusalem* to biblical prophecy and eighteenth-century poetry of the sublime negotiates between a poetics of visionary experience and a poetics of textual experience, and centres on Ezekiel's vision of the Merkabah or divine chariot as a paradigm for Blake's poem.[11] Bloom recognizes, on the one hand, the performative force of prophetic language in *Jerusalem*; the 'visionary orator' of *Jerusalem* is superior to the Bard of Sensibility because 'his words are also acts,' and because he imitates the writing prophets of the Old Testament in making 'a declaration that is also a performance' (*Ringers* 72). But Bloom's persistent attraction to the Merkabah may obscure the immediacy of visionary experience in Blake. The vision of the divine chariot in Ezekiel 1 is curiously distanced from the seer by the use of simile, both as the vision is being described ('As for the likeness of the living creatures, their appearance was like burning coals of fire' [Ezekiel 1:13]) and when its interpretation is summed up at the end of the chapter ('This was the appearance of the likeness of the glory of the LORD' [Ezekiel 1:28]). Ezekiel's language of dream and metaphor contrasts with the language of actual and immediate experience which characterizes another possible analogue for Blake's visionary language: Moses' vision of the burning bush in Exodus 3. Like Ezekiel's 'visions of God,' this episode involves an unconsuming fire and a divine voice that issues a call, yet Moses sees an actual angel in a real flame of fire and hears the voice of God directly. Moses the shepherd, who decides to 'turn aside, and see' when his attention is attracted by the burning bush (Exodus 3:3), might almost be a prototype for Blake as he stops to converse with 'a Thistle across my way' (E 721). God does not address Moses until he has perceived Moses' decision to turn aside; as in Blake's poem, the individual must first demonstrate an openness to visionary experience.

The vision of the burning bush culminates in God's identification of himself as YHWH, an act of naming that partakes more of performance than it does of reference. God refers to himself by means of an ungrammatical term, a non-word, which may be a verbal form without a temporal marker, or a nominal form without an identifiable referent. The Revised Standard Version offers 'I am what I am,' ' I will be what I will be,' and 'He causes to be' as possible translations, demonstrating that the divine name is self-referential and context-dependent, and thus shares the major characteristics of performative utterance. God would seem, on one level, to be stonewalling, since he refuses to properly answer Moses' question ('they

---

11 In 'Blake's *Jerusalem*: The Bard of Sensibility and the Form of Prophecy' (*Ringers* 65–79), Bloom distinguishes Blake as prophet from his precursor Ezekiel in that Ezekiel has seen the vision of the Merkabah before he begins to prophesy, whereas Blake has only read about the vision in Ezekiel's text.

shall say to me, What is his name? what shall I say unto them?' [Exodus 3:13]) by giving himself a proper name. Yet on another level God's response is a performance which reveals precisely that essence of the signified which the name should point to, since it demonstrates that God is not to be contained by conventional names but is defined by his acts in history. The name and no name, YHWH, like Blake's neologistic signifiers, relates language to action and sign to being in a way that is either meaningless or overfull of meaning, depending on the imagination of the hearer or interpreter.

The words of Yahweh on Mount Horeb are central to a text as concerned as *Jerusalem* is with the relationship of representation to being. When Blake's characters cry, 'I am inspired!' or, 'I ... am that Satan,' their utterances seem to contain some of the performative force of the divine 'I am.' Like Yahweh, these characters are defining themselves by their action, assigning themselves a dynamic name or state which is subject to alter as their (and our) perspective alters. The hero Milton's declaration 'I in my Selfhood am that Satan' (*M* 14.30, E 108) implies that names in this poem are relative and subject to revision; Milton is Satan for as long as he perceives and declares himself to be, and for as long as he allows his selfhood to dominate his vision. The 'I am' formulation that is so frequently met with in Blake's epics represents another aspect of the modified value of the verb 'to be' in his visionary language.

The voice of Los as he contends with his Spectre in chapter 1 of *Jerusalem* contains one of the clearest echoes of biblical voices:

I am inspired: I act not for myself: for Albions sake
I now am what I am ... 　　　　　　　　　　　　　　　(*J* 8:17–18, E 151)

Los's cry first repeats the declaration made by the Bard of *Milton* ('I am Inspired! I know it is Truth!' [*M* 13.51, E 107]), then sounds like Jesus in the Gospels, who acts for the sake of others, and finally echoes the divine name the Lord gives himself: 'I ... am what I am.' The added deictic 'now' underlines the dynamism of Los's state, making his identity a function of the present moment; Blake recuperates the connotations of the Hebrew original in which the verb actually means not 'am,' but 'become.' At the same time, the dynamism of Los's self-presentation exposes the difference between his declaration and Yahweh's: while the Old Testament God is past change, Blake's characters are constantly becoming what they behold and declaring what they become.

The speech-act quality of Los's declaration emerges when we realize that these lines represent the climactic moment in a war of words between Los and his Spectre, where the one will prevail who can compel the world to conform to his words. As Los builds up to his declaration 'I am inspired,' he stresses the perlocutionary force of his language more and more explicitly, through threats and commands to obey: 'Listen! / Be attentive! be obedient!' (*J* 8.8-9, E 151); 'I will cast thee into forms of abhorrence & torment if thou / Desist not from thine own will, & obey not my stern command!' (*J* 8.11–12, E 151). As he expresses his recognition of his own divided self, Los's words function as an utterance/outerance which causes the Spectre to be ex-pressed and reified as a slave of Los. When Los suspends his speech, the Spectre sees 'now from the ou[t]side what he before saw & felt from within' (*J* 8.25, E 151), and when Los resumes speaking his words reveal a new externalized perspective: 'Thou art my Pride & Self-righteousness: I have found thee *out*. / Thou art reveald *before me* in all thy magnitude & power' (*J*8.30–1, E 151; my italics). To the extent that Los creates his Spectre by the process of expressing and addressing it, the episode offers a powerful and self-conscious way of conceptualizing psychic division. In the dialogue between Los and his Spectre, language represents a principle of separation and externalization; but language is also an irreducible material component of the text, and we are left wondering about the divisive nature of language in the poem as a whole.

Creation: A Division

Los's address to his Spectre has important implications for the role of language in creation throughout Blake's major epics. Not only does Los create the Spectre by externalizing it, but he threatens, if the Spectre does not obey his words, to 'create an eternal Hell for thee' (*J* 8.8, 38, E 151). The threat contains, but glosses over, the paradox that was so burdensome to theologians of Milton's time and emerges in the invocation in book 3 of *Paradise Lost*: in what sense is it possible to create something eternal? If the problem of addressing Light as the first-born of heaven or as co-eternal with the eternal causes Milton some, and his commentators a great deal more, uneasiness, Blake and his characters seem to have little difficulty creating an eternal hell or other eternal states. The difference lies in Blake's increasingly self-conscious awareness of creation as, essentially, a speech act.

The texts in which Blake works through the biblical and Miltonic representations of creation by the word most thoroughly are *The Book of Urizen* and *The Four Zoas*, while *Jerusalem* recapitulates the results of the analysis more concisely and in the context of a more fully developed philosophic system. As the previous chapter has shown, the demonic parody of creation in *The Book of Urizen* focuses on the inevitable limitations brought about by physical or poetic creation and on the divisive effects of creation by naming, while exposing the societal or institutional nature of the authority which imposes names. *The Four Zoas* continues to represent creation as division, by recapitulating the petrification of Urizen's body in six ages but also by probing further into the paradigm of creation by the word. As in *The Book of Urizen*, world-creation is an enterprise undertaken by Urizen, the would-be Yahweh Elohim of a fallen universe, who declares his intention to issue speech acts which will be institutional constraints: 'my Word shall be their law' (*FZ* 21.35, E 311). In Night the Second, Urizen attempts to play the role of the Elohim, confronting the 'indefinite space' and sending forth his voice:

> Terrific Urizen strode above, in fear & pale dismay
> He saw the indefinite space beneath & his soul shrunk with horror
> His feet upon the verge of Non Existence; his voice went forth
>
> Luvah & Vala trembling & shrinking, beheld the great Work master
> And heard his Word! Divide ye bands influence by influence
> Build we a Bower for heavens darling in the grizly deep
> Build we the Mundane Shell around the Rock of Albion
>
> (*FZ* 24.2–8, E 314)

Yet Urizen's voice lacks the intrinsic performative power of God's voice in Genesis 1. Whereas the Elohim could immediately cause the universe to conform to his words, Urizen can only issue commands in the manner of a construction supervisor. In response to the perlocutionary force of his utterance, the creation of the Mundane Shell is carried out by Urizen's subordinates, the 'Bands of Heaven' (where the terms 'Bands,' as in the earlier prophecies, signifies both armies and restraints). Here and in the recapitulation of this episode (*FZ* 28.21–30.22, E 318–19), the imagery of creation in *Paradise Lost* is conflated with images of slave labour, God's golden compasses with the forming of pyramids and the treading of the mortar by female slaves. At the end of Night the Fifth, when Urizen recognizes his errors and laments them in a lyric that recalls the idyllic state from which he fell, he recalls also the prototype of his 'creative' utterance:

> O Fool could I forget the light that filled my bright spheres
> Was a reflection of his face who calld me from the deep

I well remember for I heard the mild & holy voice
Saying O light spring up & shine & I sprang up from the deep

                                                        (*FZ* 64.19–22, E 344)

If this recollection still represents a slanted perspective on the original creative act, inasmuch as Urizen would like to see himself as the first-born offspring of Heaven, it nevertheless presents a paradigm for performative
utterance of which Urizen's own commands are a demonic parody. In the
absence of a divinely creative voice, *The Four Zoas* demonstrates how the
phenomenological performative can degenerate into an oppressive exercise of the power of command.

In *Jerusalem*, the potential tyranny of creation by the word is part of a
system which recognizes negative and divisive models of creation as well
as positive, regenerative ones. The goal of the poem, one could say, is to
replace a misguided method of creation with truly productive creativity.
Jerusalem reveals that the creation of a physical universe is the beginning
of the limited and limiting creative process known as Generation, which
encompasses both human sexuality and birth, and the delusive and seductive natural world. Creation is also an analogy for the separation brought
about by perception and language, since we interpret sensory data so as to
objectify the world and distance it from us, just as we externalize and reify
it by means of verbal expression. The climax of *Jerusalem*, however, suggests that a new, visionary interpretation of the creative word makes possible the realization of a new covenant and a new Jerusalem. This is what
Jerusalem portrays as divine activity, as well as what the poem, in its performative aspect, strives to accomplish.

'The Religion of Generation which was meant for the destruction / Of
Jerusalem' has 'become her covering,' Los cries (*J* 7.63–4, E 150), setting up
early in the poem a dichotomy between the visionary city and that false religion which sanctifies female chastity and the family romance. As in Blake's
other epics, the looms of Enitharmon and the Daughters of Albion are a
recurrent image of physical generation, or the weaving of fibres into human
bodies. All spirits who approach the seductive Daughters of Albion must 'be
Vegetated beneath / Their Looms, in a Generation of death & resurrection to
forgetfulness' (*J* 17.8–9, E 161). This holds true in the present world of nature
or Generation, but it is also a characteristic of the hellish universe of Ulro:

Such is the nature of the Ulro: that whatever enters:
Becomes Sexual, & is Created, and Vegetated, and Born.

                                                        (*J* 39.21–2, E 186)

The natural world, then, is only a slightly ameliorated perception of a demonic creation. 'There is the Cave; the Rock; the Tree; the Lake of Udan Adan; / The Forest, and the Marsh, and the Pits of bitumen deadly' (*J* 13.38–9, E 157), we are told in one of several catalogues of isolated and rather sinister natural objects which seem the poem's closest approximation to the description of a created world. But creation from chaos is (literally and figuratively) only a stop-gap measure: 'whatever is visible to the Generated Man, / Is a Creation of mercy & love, from the Satanic Void' (*J* 13.44–5, E 157). According to the first words on the frontispiece to *Jerusalem*, the 'Void, outside of Existence' becomes a womb to whoever enters it (*J* 1.1, E 144). The world we perceive is nothing but voidness revealing its negativity by turning into its opposite, limitation or constriction, as if in pessimistic before-and-after snapshots of an Elohistic creation of order from the boundless deep.

Sexual procreation is interwoven with the genesis of the physical world, and of a false religion. Sexual love initiates a chain of events which, in its emphasis on division, looks something like a Miltonic myth of creation in abbreviated form. After Los has separated from his Spectre, he condemns the 'false / And Generating Love' (*J* 17.25–6, E 161), which its adherents call 'Holy Love,' as

> Envy Revenge & Cruelty
> Which separated the stars from the mountains: the mountains from Man
> And left Man, a little grovelling Root, outside of Himself.
>
> (*J* 17.30–2, E 162)

The divisive emotions entwined with sexual generation are also the principle which separated the elements of the physical world, including the firmament and the heavenly bodies of Genesis 1, though this separation is at the same time a product of the false perception by which a human being separates himself or herself from the environment. Near the end of chapter 1, Albion articulates his view of cosmic division, albeit in a Job-like lament which allows him to disclaim responsibility for this division. He complains that his sons and daughters, his cattle and his dog, and even his physical surroundings have fled from him because of his 'disease,' though he fails to understand that his banishment of the world to a state of objectivity is the disease itself:

> the Forests fled
> The Corn-fields, & the breathing Gardens outside separated
> The Sea; the Stars: the Sun: the Moon: drivn forth by my disease
>
> (*J* 21.8–10, E 166)

Grammatically, the increasingly severe division is reflected by increasingly emphatic punctuation, from no mark at all between 'Forests' and 'Corn-fields' to comma, semicolon, and finally rigid colons.

Divisive punctuation is also a feature of the poem's most extended allusion to biblical creation. As the Sons of Los labour to build the city of Golgonooza, their project is falsely perceived as a Genesis-like cosmogony in reverse order, with the emphasis on hardening and contraction:

> Perusing Albions Tomb in the starry characters of Og & Anak:
> To Create the lion & wolf the bear: the tyger & ounce:
> To Create the wooly lamb & downy fowl & scaly serpent
> The summer & winter: day & night: the sun & moon & stars
> The tree: the plant: the flower: the rock: the stone: the metal:
> Of Vegetative Nature: by their hard restricting condensations.
>
> Where Luvahs World of Opakeness grew to a period: It
> Became a Limit, a Rocky hardness without form & void
> Accumulating without end: here Los. who is of the Elohim
> Opens the Furnaces of affliction in the Emanation
> Fixing The Sexual into an ever-prolific Generation
> Naming the Limit of Opakeness Satan & the Limit of Contraction
> Adam ...   (*J* 73.16–28, E 228)

The echo of phrases from Genesis ('without form & void,' 'Elohim') identifies the passage as a radical rereading of biblical creation. At the same time, the creative enterprise is literally enclosed within linguistic practice, beginning with a scene of reading ('Perusing Albions Tomb') and ending with an act of naming. The passage makes explicit the Bible's implicit association between textuality and world-creation, but also emphasizes the restrictive nature of creation as it grammatically separates the elements of the created world from one another and culminates in the establishment of sexual generation and the limited states of Satan and Adam.

Throughout *Jerusalem*, an understanding of 'utterance' as 'outerance,' or divisive externalization, is perpetuated by the frequent appearance of the words 'out' and 'outside,' along with the repeated formula 'uttering [or 'utterd'] thus his voice.'[12] In a text which reveals the way sensory percep-

---

12 For example: 'Albion again utterd his voice' (*J* 22.16, E 167); 'Los saw & was comforted at his Furnaces uttering thus his voice' (*J* 82.80, E 241). The phrase echoes *Paradise Lost*, at the moment when God first responds to the fall of humankind, 'the most High / Eternal Father from his secret Cloud, / Amidst in Thunder utter'd thus his voice' (*PL* 10.31–3). The image of thunder, which appears often in *Jerusalem* as a metaphor for the voice of Los, is

tion, like language, externalizes and objectifies, 'hearing-oneself-speak' is no longer a condition of ideal presence, nor does it offer a transcendence of the division between interior and exterior. Rather, hearing one's own utterance and the utterance of others both acknowledges and creates the division between self and other, subject and object, individual and environment.

Moral Law and Divine Voice

Even if utterance has become problematic as a medium of creation, the ideal of a divinely performative voice is still meaningful in Blake's epics. *Jerusalem* recognizes the potential for utterances to have an immediate and correspondent effect, and acknowledges that words can be equivalent to action because of the innate will and authority of the speaker. To varying degrees, however, this awareness enters into a compromise with socially constructed authority. In fact, the divisive effects of language in *Jerusalem* may be interpreted as what happens when the phenomenological performative is understood in terms of fallen communication and societal speech acts.

The fundamentally dialogic character of *Jerusalem* is evident to any reader of the poem. As in Blake's other epics, especially *The Four Zoas*, the vast majority of lines are spoken by a character other than the poet-narrator; significantly for speech-act analysis, most of them have, or are at least directed toward, a specific effect (to the extent that this is possible within the poem's unorthodox causality). Albion pleads, laments, exhorts, curses, and complains; he is rebuked, persuaded, comforted. He, of all the actants in *Jerusalem*, is most obviously aware of the power of words; ironically so, since his words, more obviously than those of others, derive their efficacy from convention. Chapter 1 comes to a climax with 'dying Albions Curse':

also present here, as is, tantalizingly, a possible model for the 'secret seat' from which Albion speaks in *Jerusalem* 28.5 (E 174), which is in Blake an image of insidious secular authority.

In Blake's later poetry, the word 'utter' often appears with a direct object other than 'voice' or 'words,' so as to emphasize the externalization of emotional response: 'Uttering this darkness' (*FZ* 10.19, E 306); 'utterd his fierce pangs of heart' (*FZ* 49.26, E 333); 'uttering such woes such bursts such thunderings' (*FZ* 73.36, E 350); 'Uttering not his jealousy' (*J* 34.4, E 179); 'their sorrow cannot be utterd' (*J* 59.28, E 209); 'utterd her Deceit' (*J* 82.21, E 239); 'began to utter his love' (*J* 87.2, E 246). Interestingly, virtually all uses of 'utter' in Blake's *prose* have to do with his trial for sedition; that is to say, in the prose 'utter' always carries connotations of public statement, especially statements that go on record in a court of law.

May God who dwells in this dark Ulro & voidness, vengeance take,
And draw thee down into this Abyss of sorrow and torture,
Like me thy Victim. O that Death & Annihilation were the same!

(J 23.38–40, E 169)

Having pronounced his call for vengeance, Albion immediately repents of his speech act: 'What have I said? What have I done? O all-powerful Human Words!' (*J* 24.1, E 169). As in reading all of Albion's utterances, it is necessary here to identify his delusions and the limits of his perspective. *Human words*, ironically, are not 'all-powerful' in this poem but have power only within the limits of a certain conceptual frame. Albion conceives of a curse, and more especially a dying curse, as a privileged utterance, immediately effective and recalled in vain. But a curse is so defined only within the same mental space that recognizes 'God who dwells in … voidness' as a figure of vengeance, acknowledges a hellish 'Abyss of sorrow and torture' as the archetypal place of punishment, and accords the subjunctive expression ('May God … vengeance take') a special invocatory effect.

Albion's curse is a prelude to chapter 2 of *Jerusalem*, the chapter in which the tyranny of speech acts grounded in convention becomes most explicit. The chapter is addressed to the Jews, who are criticized as a race and a state of consciousness which is overly influenced by legalism, or by the ability of institutionalized language to determine and valorize human behaviour. Albion appears in this chapter as a maker of laws, and the opening lines recount his construction of a world of moral virtue, in which 'every Act' has become 'a Crime' and 'Albion the punisher & judge' (*J* 28.4, E 174). His first speech exposes the linguistic basis of his authority:

And Albion spoke from his secret seat and said

All these ornaments are crimes, they are made by the labours
Of loves: of unnatural consanguinities and friendships
Horrid to think of when enquired deeply into; and all
These hills & valleys are accursed witnesses of Sin
I therefore condense them into solid rocks, stedfast!
A foundation and certainty and demonstrative truth:
That Man be separate from Man, & here I plant my seat.

(J 28.5–12, E 174)

Albion's utterance imitates the grammatical structure of a political pronouncement, which gives verbs in the first-person present a distinctive performative force ('I therefore condense them'), and relies on the illocutionary force of the subjunctive ('That Man be separate from Man') and of conventional verbal formulas such as the curse. Albion assumes the authority to define what is a crime and what is unnatural, and to institute a permanent state. By specifying that Albion speaks 'from his secret seat,' Blake exposes the way Albion's authority derives directly from his sociopolitical position: this is Albion speaking in his official capacity as punisher and judge. Like the Priest in 'A Little Boy Lost,' Albion assumes an insidious form of authority; the 'secrecy' of its terms is underlined by the fact that Albion's speech climaxes in the planting of the seat by which he is invested with authority in the first place. Albion, as lawmaker, directs his utterance toward the establishment and legitimation of his own seat of authority, the conditions of which are only articulated within his self-referential speech. Yet that authority endows Albion's speech with the power to bring about the state of moral virtue that predominates in the rest of the chapter.

Blake's summary comment on the end-leaf of Lavater's *Aphorisms* offers a much earlier recognition of the power that institutional speech acts can have over the beliefs even of good individuals. His one 'strong objection' to Lavater is that he has too readily accepted 'what the laws of Kings & Priests have calld Vice.' Blake demonstrates the significance of what human actions are called or named by proclaiming his own definition of vice as the negation of action:

Murder is Hindering Another
Theft is Hindering Another
Backbiting. Undermining C[i]rcumventing & whatever is Negative is Vice
(Ann. Lavater, E 601)

This early example of a speech act which attempts to counter or supplant the pronouncements of 'Kings & Priests' foreshadows the process which lies behind many of the speech acts of *Jerusalem*, particularly in chapter 2, where acts of naming are more frequent and prominent than in the rest of the poem. A tree sprouts from underneath Albion's secret seat, and he immediately names it 'Moral Virtue, and the Law / Of God who dwells in Chaos hidden from the human sight' (*J* 28.15–16, E 174). He erects altars and names them 'Justice, and Truth' (*J* 28.23, E 174); emphasizing the arbitrary and destructive nature of such naming, the poet reminds us that those who will be sacrificed on the altars are Albion's '(miscall'd) Enemies' (*J* 28.20, E 174).

If Albion's speech acts are governed by the rhetoric of societal institutions, Los typically uses a type of performative language which is more directly relevant to Blake's own role. Los's utterances in *Jerusalem* are often characterized by a deliberate stress on the perlocutionary effect the words should have on an audience, as if his hearers could never quite be trusted to recognize the authority of his language but must always be reminded of their proper response. To his Spectre Los cries, 'Obey my voice & never deviate from my will / And I will be merciful to thee'; he continues with a series of commands to the Spectre to know his place and keep it (*J* 10.29–36, E 153). If this call to unquestioning obedience seems sinister in a Blakean context, the suspicion is heightened by Los's stress on his own will, considering how Blake unilaterally condemns the will in his annotations to Swedenborg: 'There can be no Good-Will. Will is always Evil' (E 602). As the annotation comes early in Blake's career, it is tempting to conclude that by the time he writes *Jerusalem* he has entered into a compromise with will and authoritative rhetoric, recognizing that any language which aims to have an effect on a contemporary audience must utilize the formulas of verbal authority acknowledged by that audience. Thus Los needs to insist on obedience in the manner of an orator: 'Bristol & Bath, listen to my words, & ye Seventeen: give ear!' (*J* 38.55, E 185); 'You must my dictate obey from your gold-beam'd Looms' (*J* 56.31, E 206). The oratorical rhetoric recalls Blake's claim in the preface to chapter 1 to speak as 'a true Orator' (*J* 3, E 146), and in this context Los's exhortations may reflect Blake's own realization that his words are not having the effect on his contemporaries that texts such as *America, Europe,* and *The Marriage of Heaven and Hell* so urgently desire.

Just as Los compromises with necessity in building the universe of Generation, his language comes to terms with the exhortational rhetoric that a fallen audience requires. Blake, for his part, addresses this poem to four distinct audiences; in doing so, he imitates a rhetorical device popular with writers of tractate literature in his time. But if the fourfold address represents an attempt to exploit a rhetorical convention that his readers might recognize, and thus to adapt his words to an audience, the corollary is that Blake is also adapting an audience to his words. 'The Jews' and 'the Deists' in *Jerusalem* are not those who would call themselves Jews or Deists, but rather those people, or those aspects of the psyche, that Blake defines as Jews and Deists in his prefaces to chapters 2 and 3. Like neologistic names which create the characters to which they refer, Blake's prefaces are performative utterances which bring an appropriate audience into being in the ' process of addressing it.

A more positive view of Los's language emerges toward the end of the poem, where his words begin to have the sort of effect on other characters and the physical environment that one might associate with a creating deity. 'The river Severn stayd his course at my command,' Jerusalem recalls, lamenting that her power over the nations has declined (*J* 79.33, E 235); but Los increasingly demonstrates such power as the poem builds toward its conciliatory climax:

> And thus Los replies upon his Watch: the Valleys listen silent:
> The Stars stand still to hear: Jerusalem & Vala cease to mourn:
> His voice is heard from Albion: the Alps & Appenines
> Listen: Hermon & Lebanon bow their crowned heads
> Babel & Shinar look toward the Western Gate, they sit down
> Silent at his voice ...   (*J* 85.14–19, E 244)

These lines come tantalizingly close to echoing the effects of heavenly voices in *Paradise Lost*: 'Confusion heard his voice, and wild uproar / Stood rul'd' (*PL* 3.710–11); 'For *Chaos* heard his voice' (*PL* 7.221); 'suspense in Heav'n / Held by thy voice, thy potent voice he hears' (*PL* 7.99–100). On the following plate, 'the thick hail stones stand ready to obey / [Los's] voice' (*J* 86.36–7, E 245): as a prelude to the poem's final epiphany of living words, the humanized natural world demonstrates readiness to acknowledge supernaturally performative utterance.

The most resonant example of the phenomenological performative in *Jerusalem* is not the speech of Los, but rather that of the Divine Voice, which also appears as the Divine Vision, the Divine Family, and One Man Jesus the Saviour. The names 'Divine Voice' and 'Divine Vision' intimate a connection with Blake's concept of inspiration as expanded sensory perception, or perception redeemed from the divisive effect it normally has on our experience of the world. Voice and vision cannot be classed as either internal or external, but exist as potentialities of the individual which are actualized in utterance or in the seeing of a particular object. The terms 'Divine Voice' and 'Divine Vision' combine subjectivity and objectivity, as they refer to attributes of a deity (i.e., Jesus' vision) but also to the form in which the deity is revealed to human beings (i.e., a vision of Jesus). Finally, the name 'Divine Voice' focuses attention on verbal performance. Though it plays a crucial role in the poem, a Voice – not unlike the poet/orator himself – can only act through effective utterance.

On plate 43 of *Jerusalem* (E 191–2), the Divine Voice addresses Albion as the Lord addressed Job, gathering together past, present, and future perspectives, recalling Albion's former glory, lamenting his fallen condition, and predicting his future resurrection. The efficacy of the speech is borne out by the text itself, since what the Divine Voice prophesies – the sleep of Albion until his misguided system and his repentant aspect are revealed, at which time the Divine Man will come and Albion will arise again – actually happens in the rest of the poem. In contrast to the speeches of other characters, including Albion, the Spectre of Los, Jerusalem, and Vala, the utterance of the Divine Voice occupies a privileged position in that the world, as it is represented by the events of the poem, comes to correspond to its words. The Divine Voice, that is to say, is the most truly prophetic voice in the poem, but prophetic in the way that the poet himself might be called prophetic, in that he 'foresees' the outcome of the poem and uses his words to bring it about. The parallel between Divine Voice and narrative voice, intensified by Blake's well-known claim that the true authors of the poem are in fact divine voices ('I dare not pretend to be any other than the Secretary the Authors are in Eternity' [E 730]), suggests that the model of divine creation by the word may yet influence Blake's construction of a fictional world.

Creating States

If *Jerusalem* redefines physical creation so as to bring out its affinities with pity, sexual love, generation, limitation, and death, the most sublime kind of creative action must be that which does not produce a physical object, but a state of being. 'I go forth to Create / States: to deliver Individuals evermore!' the Divine Voice repeats, vowing to save Albion from eternal death (*J* 31.15–16, E 178). In *Jerusalem*, salvation involves separating human beings from their destructive perceptions and behaviour by defining these errors as states rather than permanent attributes. The redefinition of permanences into states takes place through the utterance of the Divine Voice, which counters the restrictive, institutionalized speech acts of Albion. This occurs most clearly in chapter 2, where the poem's recurrent image of furnaces in which the universe is forged metamorphoses into the punitive furnaces of Babylon in the Old Testament:

> And the Divine voice came from the Furnaces, as multitudes without
> Number! the voices of the innumerable multitudes of Eternity.
> And the appearance of a Man was seen in the Furnaces;
> Saving those who have sinned from the punishment of the Law,
> (In pity of the punisher whose state is eternal death,)
> And keeping them from Sin by the mild counsels of his love.
> ...
> Albion hath enterd the State Satan! Be permanent O State!

And be thou for ever accursed! that Albion may arise again:
And be thou created into a State! I go forth to Create
States: to deliver Individuals evermore! Amen.
So spoke the voice from the Furnaces ...

(J 31.3–8, 13–17; E 177–8)

The allusion to the third chapter of the Book of Daniel highlights the significance of this act as a salvation from the decrees of state authority, since the biblical story hinges on the arbitrary and (in secular terms) all-powerful decrees of King Nebuchadnezzar. The king commands that three civil servants, who have disobeyed his decrees concerning state religion, be brought before him and that they be cast into a fiery furnace heated to seven times its normal temperature; when they miraculously survive, he countermands his previous order to proclaim that their God shall be honoured in his state. The entire chapter may be read in speech-act terms as the story of a political decree – Nebuchadnezzar's official dedication of a golden idol and the declaration that all his subjects must fall down and worship it at prescribed times – which is overturned by a second decree prescribing honour to Yahweh. In the biblical story, the reversal comes about through the miraculous preservation of the lawbreakers and the appearance in the furnaces of a fourth Man, who remains, significantly, silent. In Blake's version, it is precisely the speech act of the divine Man in the furnaces which supersedes and invalidates Albion's legalistic decrees. The Divine Voice, in other words, issues decrees with a more powerful authority but in complicity with the type of speech act recognized by Albion; the voice, one is tempted to say, fights fire with fire.

The speech act of the Divine Voice invalidates Albion's proclamations by redefining what Albion calls 'Eternal Death' as the 'State Satan.' Creating a condition 'into a State' involves the setting of limits, so that what was thought permanent is no longer so. 'States abolish Systems,' Blake adds in a line that he later gouged out but used elsewhere. The countervailing effect of the Divine Voice on Albion's institution of moral virtue reveals that 'Eternal Death,' as Albion knows it, is precisely not eternal; its eternality is a delusion Albion is under because he has decreed it to be so.

One of the difficulties posed by Blake's doctrine of states is that he seems to contradict himself on the question of their permanence or non-permanence. How are we to reconcile the words of the Seven Angels of the Presence in *Milton*, 'States Change: but Individual Identities never change nor cease' (*M* 32.23, E 132), with Blake's epigraph to chapter 3 of *Jerusalem*: 'The Spiritual States of the Soul are all Eternal' (*J* 52, E 200)? To a certain extent these two statements reflect a shift in emphasis from the temporality of states and permanence of individual identity in *Milton* to the opposite in *Jerusalem*. Yet Blake also reveals how both statements can be true at once, by alluding repeatedly to an analogy between psychological states and political ones. From a political point of view, it indeed appears that states may change; they adopt new names, new borders, new constitutions and systems of government, while the people living in them retain their individual identity. As with the disintegration of the Soviet Union and the redefinition of Eastern Europe in recent times, Blake witnessed bewildering changes in political boundaries throughout Europe during the Napoleonic era. Conversely, when regarded from a synchronic point of view and from the perspective of the individual, it seems that states continue to exist while individuals travel in and out of them:

As the Pilgrim passes while the Country permanent remains
So Men pass on: but States remain permanent for ever

(J 73.44–5, E 229)

These lines recapitulate a more extensive explanation of the relation between individuals and states in *A Vision of The Last Judgment*:

These States Exist now Man Passes on but States remain for Ever he passes thro them like a traveller who may as well suppose that the places he has passed thro exist no more as a Man may suppose that the States he has passd thro exist no more Every Thing is Eternal (E 556)

Throughout Blake's work, the term 'state' seems more strongly influenced than has been realized by the notion of state as a political entity and, secondly, the state(ment) as a linguistic entity.[13] An expanded sociopolitical context can reveal profound connections among Blake's states, political

---

13 In 'Blake's Metaphorical States,' the most extensive study of this topic, Edward J. Rose characterizes the state as a metaphor which represents not only a certain object (a world, a psychological or emotional condition, a biblical character, etc.) but also the metaphorical process itself, since states determine perspective. Rose makes a strong case for the centrality of states to Blake's symbolic process but dismisses any political interpretation of 'state' as an 'obvious' reading. The obviousness results, though, from Rose's assumption that if 'state' is interpreted to mean 'nation,' then Blake must be talking about good citizenship. My discussion of states is intended, in part, to counterbalance the dominant tendency to regard Blake's states solely in the context of his aesthetic and poetic practice; despite the active study of sociopolitical contexts for Blake's work in recent years, this perspective has not been brought to bear sufficiently on his concept of states.

states, and the speech acts on which both depend. 'State' is the word self-consciously chosen by Saussure to refer to the object of study in the field of synchronic linguistics, and he defends the term 'linguistic state' as the most appropriate designation for a period during which a language undergoes little change, so that the linguist's attention can be focused on relations between elements of the language (*Course* 100). In Blake's myth, too, states are the static conditions (although their stasis is more an effect of perspective than actual duration in time) during which relationships can be recognized. Blake's states, like political states, are instituted and constituted by statements, which may in turn be understood as the reified form of the act of stating, analogously to the way Blake's 'lineaments' are the external, recognizable characteristics formed by the dynamic, creating 'line' ('the Lineaments of the Countenances ... are all descriptive of Character & not a line is drawn without intention' [*VLJ*, E 560]).

The semantic and grammatical inflections of the term 'state' in Blake's corpus fall into four categories, which are, in order of frequency:

(a) a psychological condition or spiritual disposition (mainly in *The Book of Urizen*, *The Four Zoas*, and *Milton*)
(b) a political entity, usually with negative connotations in constructions such as 'State Government' and 'State Religion' (mainly in the annotations, 'Auguries of Innocence,' and later prose)
(c) a condition of inanimate objects or of health (mainly in the letters when Blake is describing the state of completion of commissioned pieces)
(d) a verb meaning 'to affirm,' used a single time in echo of Bacon, whom Blake is annotating

The works which are not mentioned in this approximate list, but in which 'state' frequently appears (primarily *A Vision of The Last Judgment* and *Jerusalem*), are those in which the definition of the word compromises, in interesting and significant ways, between definitions (a) and (b).

A Vision of The Last Judgment, which is concerned, among other things, with the representation of states in visual art, invests the term with more obvious spatial connotations than it has in Blake's earlier writing, where it can generally be understood in a psychological context. In his picture of the Last Judgment, Blake uses biblical figures to represent states, but he explains in the accompanying prose that the individuals are to be taken as representing a collectivity: 'when distant they appear as One Man but as you approach they appear Multitudes of Nations' (*VLJ*, E 556–7). Blake's iconographical practice is authorized by the language of the Old Testament, where 'Israel' or 'Judah' is both an individual and a nation, but he extends the same interpretation to historical figures in the New Testament who are not otherwise identified with nations: 'these are Caiphas & Pilate Two States where all those reside who Calumniate & Murder <under Pretence of Holiness & Justice>' (*VLJ*, E 558). The mode of representation introduced here as a visual iconography culminates in later statements of Blake's which no longer make significant distinctions between the names of political entities and psychological, social, or economic conditions. In the *Laocoön*, for instance, both are combined into one aphorism under the term 'state': 'There are States in which all Visionary Men are accounted Mad Men   such are Greece & Rome   Such is Empire or Tax' (E 274).

In *Jerusalem*, a similar conflation of spiritual dispositions, individuals, and political or geographic divisions is at work in the description of 'Albions Land.' 'These States we now explore,' Blake declares, going on to list 'the Names of Albions Twelve Sons, & of his Twelve Daughters / With their Districts' (*J* 71.9–11, E 225). With the exception of this passage, virtually all uses of the term 'state(s)' are clustered in chapter 2, and in the closing lines of chapter 1 and the epigraph to chapter 3. Chapter 2, 'To the Jews,' is the only chapter addressed to a culturally and politically defined nation (a 'state,' though Blake does not use the term here). The Jews' defining characteristic is, for Blake, a misplaced faith in the letter of the law, and the adherence to written codes or verbal decrees contributes to the prevalence of states in this chapter. In speech-act terms, the primary theme of chapter 2 is Albion's misguided, though successful, creation of states such as Moral Virtue and Eternal Death through authoritative speech acts, and the attempt of the Divine Voice to counter these proclamations in the only way it can: by pronouncing its own performatives, which are guaranteed by the innate authority of the Divine Family yet participate in the rhetoric of political proclamation, the only rhetoric that fallen characters in the poem understand.

When Albion goes to Eternal Death, he does so because he himself has decreed that Eternal Death shall be the punishment for breaking his laws – laws which, according to the Divine Voice, 'No individual can keep ... for *they* are death / To every energy of man' (*J* 31.11–12, E 177; my italics). The laws and their punishment are products of language, and Albion's delusion reveals itself in his conversation with Los on plate 35. When he proclaims, 'I die! I go to Eternal Death!' (*J* 35.16, E 181), Albion *believes* he goes to Eternal Death because he has named and thus created such a state. Other aspects of his speech reveal his self-delusion, for he has bound on the 'black shoes of death' and 'death's iron gloves' (*J* 35.21, E 181), he believes

God has forsaken him, and Los recognizes that he has 'turn'd his back against the Divine Vision' (J 35.14, E 181). His predicament is described and universalized by 'those in Great Eternity who contemplate on Death':

> What seems to Be: Is: To those to whom
> It seems to Be, & is productive of the most dreadful
> Consequences to those to whom it seems to Be: even of
> Torments, Despair, Eternal Death; but the Divine Mercy
> Steps beyond and Redeems Man in the Body of Jesus Amen
> And Length Bredth Highth again Obey the Divine Vision Hallelujah
>
> (J 32.50–6, E 179)

The Eternal Ones acknowledge the performative power of the copula, which is emphasized and made self-sufficient by being separated off visually and aurally: 'Is.' Beyond affirming the conditions under which Eternal Death 'is,' the speakers imply that the overcoming of verbal delusion occurs through a contrary affirmation. Their claim that the Divine Mercy redeems man is completed by an 'Amen' – 'so be it' – which lends performative force to the assertion they have just made.[14]

What the Eternal Ones imply about the performative power of 'is' is relevant to Blake's use of the copula, perhaps the main vehicle for his creation of reality through language. When Blake claims that 'The Male *is* a Furnace of beryll; the Female *is* a golden Loom' (J 5.34, E 148; my italics), or 'Ulro *is* the space of the terrible starry wheels of Albions sons' (J 12.51, E 156; my italics), he defeats our assumptions about the way constative statements should be read, by equating literal and figurative, abstract and concrete, and by employing referents of which we have no experience outside of his poetry – even, at times, outside of the passage at hand. Blakean grammar relies on constative statements but invests such statements with performative effect. 'There is a place where Contrarieties are equally True / This place is called Beulah' (M 30.1–2, E 129) shares the basic propositional form of 'There is a cat on the mat.' Yet, as Austin has shown, the most stereotypical of propositions can be made to display the characteristics of explicit performatives. Both constatives and performatives convey the assumption that the speaker believes what he or she is saying; in both cases, their felicity depends on context and on the expectations of speaker and audience. The performativity of the prop-

---

14 Significantly, four of the five uses of 'Amen' in *Jerusalem* are clustered in the final lines of chapter 1 and the opening plates of chapter 2, and accompany the poem's most explicit passages on the creation of states.

osition can be recognized by expanding it to include an implicit preamble: '[I claim that] there is a cat on the mat,' or '[I state that] this place is called Beulah.'

It seems difficult to escape the implication that creating a state involves making a statement – and vice versa. One could say that the aim of Blake's art, like that of *How to Do Things with Words*, is to demonstrate the illocutionary force of constative statements, or to emphasize that all speech *acts*. The Divine Voice has no way of creating states except by uttering them into existence. So also with Los's creation of a system, and with Blake's creation of, for instance, Beulah. By making a statement about the 'place where Contrarieties are equally True,' Blake simultaneously creates the state and gives it a name.

Derrida, following Heidegger, habitually places the verb 'is' *sous rature*, while Blake relies extraordinarily heavily on the same verb. The difference may be less indicative of irreconcilable differences between the two philosophies[15] than of different solutions to the problem of taking responsibility for ontological statements. Where Derrida, by crossing out 'is,' tries to evade the hierarchies constructed by the preoccupation of Western philosophy with Being, Blake shifts the word 'is' into a different ontology. 'Is' and 'are' function in his epics not as indicators of being but as indicators of what Thomas Pavel has called an 'analogy of being.' The examples Pavel gives of realms in which special ontologies may function are theology and fiction. Blake's poetry participates in both and thus invokes an ontology 'in which *being* and *existence* are only analogically similar to the same notions in plain ontologies' (Pavel 176). The alternative ontology is homologous with that of societally authorized speakers, for whom 'This session *is* now open' is a performative rather than a descriptive utterance, matching the world to the words, as well as of fiction writers, for whom 'Wuthering Heights *is* the name of Mr. Heathcliff's dwelling' (Bronte 2; my italics) is performative in a different sense, matching *a* world to the words. Both uses of language expose the way reality (including the commonly accepted one) is constructed by acts of speech. It is worth recalling, though, that Albion's judicial pronouncement has the same declarative structure: 'All these ornaments *are* crimes, they *are* made by the labours / Of loves' (*J* 28.6–7, E 174; my italics). The process which creates a fictional world looks the same as that which creates a restrictive social order; therein lies the self-consciousness of Blake's performative language.

15 For instance, Blake and Derrida both recognize the plenitude of the *written* word and the importance of play, and they subject structures of tyranny and hierarchy to rigorous analysis. See David Simpson, 'Reading Blake and Derrida.'

Living Words

There is hardly a passage in Blake's major prophecies that has attracted
more critical commentary than the final text plates of *Jerusalem*, not only
because they form the finale of Blake's epic project, but because they are
an obvious focal point for discussions of language and representation. In
describing the apocalyptic moment of Albion's awakening, plates 94 to 99
commit themselves to representing a state in which 'Time was Finished!' (*J*
94.18, E 254) and the duality of subject and object overcome – that is, a
state in which the fundamental elements of linguistic structure no longer
exist. The consequence would seem to be a passage which offers scope for
the post-structuralist project of demonstrating the disjunction between sign
and referent and the way representation is ultimately conscious of itself as
representation. On the other hand, these final plates strike many readers as
a resolution to the problems of linguistic representation raised earlier in
Jerusalem, and are cited by these readers as a caution to post-structuralists
that Blake's view of language is not their own.

One of the many precursor texts relevant to the end of *Jerusalem* is
book 7 of *Paradise Lost*. The awakening of Albion is preceded by a kind of
chaos: the revelation of the Covering Cherub as 'Disorganizd' (*J* 89.18, E
248), 'A terrible indefinite Hermaphroditic form' (*J* 89.3, E 248), and 'a
reflexion / Of Eden all perverted' (*J* 89.14–15, E 248), accompanied by the
thunders of Los at his anvil 'in the horrible darkness weeping' (*J* 91.31, E
251). The poet's declaration 'Time was Finished!' echoes Christ's 'It is finished,' another utterance which marks a critical point in history, but in
structural terms it also parallels the Son's command for silence among the
troubled waves. All these utterances inaugurate a new order by effecting
what they announce. The act of awakening and inspiration which follows
this utterance in *Jerusalem* may be read as a revision of the account of creation in *Paradise Lost*, which radically extends Milton's implications about
creation as arbitrary beginning and about the organization of nature
according to the nature of language.

While Miltonic creation, in the invocations as in book 7 of *Paradise Lost*,
begins with the first appearance of light amidst chaos, Albion's awakening
is experienced as a sunrise. The visionary nature of the divine *fiat* has been
transformed into a type of enlightenment which is available to sensory
perception and reoccurs each day:

> Thou seest the Sun in heavy clouds
> Struggling to rise above the Mountains. in his burning hand

He takes his Bow, then chooses out his arrows of flaming gold
Murmuring the Bowstring breathes with ardor!

(*J* 95.11–14, E 255)

The second-person address to the reader, 'thou seest,' conspicuous because it is the first time such an address has appeared in the poem outside of the prefaces, identifies this passage as not only the poet's vision, but the reader's. Blake's 'thou' contrasts with the deictics in Milton's creation narrative (e.g., 'thou thir Natures know'st, and gav'st them Names' [*PL* 7.493]). Whereas the line from *Paradise Lost* ironically distances the reader by foregrounding the original scene of discourse between Raphael and Adam, Blake's line emphasizes the reader's immediacy by unexpectedly referring us to our everyday experience of the natural world.

Yet what Blake does with this experience is extraordinary. Having suggested that the familiar sight of the sunrise is an appropriate way of visualizing the apocalyptic scene of Albion's awakening, he at once informs us that what we see when the sun struggles to rise is not what we think we see; rather, the sunrise is a vision of a hero shooting flaming arrows from a breathing bowstring. In other words, while seeming to make a visionary experience easier to grasp, Blake is actually defamiliarizing ordinary vision. Sunrise is both a visionary experience and a re-creation, since it is the moment when the world once again becomes available to human eyes.

This is significant for Blake's theory of inspiration, but also for linguistic representation. In the final plates of *Jerusalem*, as in some of his prose, the sun and moon come naturally to Blake as touchstones of visionary experience. The language with which he refers to sun and moon refuses to commit itself to either analogy or identification. In a passage which he repeats twice, Blake relies on the ambiguity of 'as' to make the sun and moon represent the reconciliation of Albion and Brittannia:

As the Sun & Moon lead forward the Visions of Heaven & Earth
England who is Brittannia entered Albions bosom rejoicing

(*J* 95.21–2, 96.1–2; E 255)

Despite the familiar names and natural images, referentiality almost needs to be dispensed with here. Is 'as' a temporal adverb ('*While* the Sun & Moon lead forward') or a conjunctive adverb which introduces a simile ('*Just as* the Sun & Moon lead forward')? In an annotation to the works of Bishop Watson, Blake claims that 'Inspiration needs no one to prove it   it is Evident as the Sun & Moon' (E 614). How evident *are* the sun and the moon when Blake is constantly undermining our ordinary perception of them? 'As' acts as a fulcrum on which the apparent simile, in which sun and moon are simply examples of phenomena evident to the senses, can become a testimony to expanded perception, in which Sun and Moon are themselves vehicles of imaginative vision. Not only is it as clear that inspiration exists as that the sun and the moon exist, but anyone capable of really seeing Sun and Moon can be confident of being inspired. What a true vision of nature is like may be gathered from Blake's description of the sunrise as 'an Innumerable company of the Heavenly host crying Holy Holy Holy is the Lord God Almighty' (*VLJ*, E 566). If imaginative vision can be an expanded form of sensory perception, there can be no reliable demarcation between literal and figurative language. The reader must negotiate between the adverbial and conjunctive meanings of 'as,' between the constative and declarative uses of 'is,' and between the defamiliarization of familiar referents and the habitual use of unfamiliar ones ('Sun,' 'Moon,' 'Albion,' 'Brittannia').

This flexibility may begin to explain what Blake means by the 'Words of Eternity in Human Forms' (*J* 95.9, E 255), which appear at the end of *Jerusalem*. Words in human form are as literal an image as one could imagine of speech acts, an image which renders the term 'speech acts' still more dynamic by representing speech which has the ability to act independently of a speaker:

> And they conversed together in Visionary forms dramatic which bright
> Redounded from their Tongues in thunderous majesty, in Visions
> In new Expanses, creating exemplars of Memory and of Intellect
> Creating Space, Creating Time according to the wonders Divine
> Of Human Imagination, throughout all the Three Regions immense
> Of Childhood, Manhood & Old Age[;] & the all tremendous unfathomable
>   Non Ens
> Of Death was seen in regenerations terrific or complacent varying
> According to the subject of discourse & every Word & Every Character
> Was Human according to the Expansion or Contraction, the Translucence or
> Opakeness of Nervous fibres ...   (*J* 98.28–37, E 257–8)

This is a vision of language as an ideal phenomenological performative, and behind the passage lies the first chapter of Genesis, with its divine words that create space and time. By analogy with the image of sunrise, Blake's image of creative language in one sense draws it into everyday experience. Words on a page, particularly an illuminated page, 'create space'; they 'create time,' as Saint Augustine discovers in his analysis of Psalm-reading in the *Confessions*, when they are read aloud. Yet, as with the sunrise, the image also goes in the opposite direction, to defamiliarize the experience of using words by revealing the extent to which words create their referents. Words instantiate, create types or 'exemplars' (a word Blake uses only this one time) of memory and intellect; they open up new expanses of and to vision; they make even infinite non-being available to vision by expressing it as 'the all tremendous unfathomable Non Ens / Of Death.'

Language, perception, and experience become interdependent at the end of *Jerusalem*, so that utterance affects perception ('varying / According to the subject of discourse'), experience affects utterance ('every Word & Every Character / Was Human according to the Expansion or Contraction ... of Nervous fibres'), and perception affects experience ('such was the variation of Time & Space / Which vary according as the Organs of Perception vary'). The echo of Blake's prefatory remark about his style, 'Every word and every letter is studied and put into its fit place' (*J* 3, E 146), in 'every Word & Every Character / Was Human' is intensified by the attendant allusion to 'regenerations terrific or complacent,' which recalls Blake's distinction between terrific, mild and gentle, and prosaic parts of his text in the preface to chapter 1. No longer elements to be put passively into place by the author, words are now endowed with power and agency and released to assume their own place in a human order. 'Creating Space, Creating Time,' the word-visions redeem the activity of characters earlier in the poem who created *a* time or *a* space, temporary and comforting limits for fallen imagination. Now that the 'Body of Death,' the old earth and the old body of physical creation, is 'into Vacuum evaporating' (*J* 98.19–20, E 257), words are free to create a visionary city and a visionary human body. Words supersede limited and limiting episodes of creation to achieve the 'Eternal Creation flowing from the Divine Humanity' that Blake describes in *The Design of The Last Judgment* (E 554).

Conflating the experiential narrative of Revelation with the divine voice of Genesis, Blake presents himself as a witness of the act of regeneration:

> And I heard Jehovah speak
> Terrific from his Holy Place & saw the Words of the Mutual Covenant Divine
> On Chariots of gold & jewels with Living Creatures starry & flaming
> With every Colour, Lion, Tyger, Horse, Elephant, Eagle Dove, Fly, Worm,
> And the all wondrous Serpent clothed in gems & rich array Humanize

In the Forgiveness of Sins according to the Covenant of Jehovah.

(J 98.40–5, E 258)

In this passage, the biblical and Miltonic paradigm of creation by the word is redeemed. What might otherwise be a tenuous allusion to God's creation of the multitude of living creatures on the sixth day is supported by the culminating and extended evocation of the serpent, which parallels Milton's description of the serpent at the end of his catalogue of animals (*PL* 7.494–8). Blake's syntax tempts the reader to think that (as in *Paradise Lost*) the appearance of the catalogue of animals is itself the subject of the passage ('And I ... saw the ... Living Creatures'). Only at the end of the sentence do we realize that the source of wonder is their humanization ('And I ... saw [them] *Humanize*'), a process which comes about through forgiveness of sins according to the terms of a new covenant.

The final utterance by characters in the poem, a series of rhetorical questions posed by the Living Creatures, is a speech act about speech acts:

Where is the Covenant of Priam, the Moral Virtues of the Heathen
Where is the Tree of Good & Evil that rooted beneath the cruel heel
Of Albions Spectre the Patriarch Druid! where are all his Human Sacrifices
For Sin in War & in the Druid Temples of the Accuser of Sin: beneath
The Oak Groves of Albion that coverd the whole Earth beneath his Spectre
Where are the Kingdoms of the World & all their glory that grew on Desolation
The Fruit of Albions Poverty Tree when the Triple Headed Gog-Magog Giant
Of Albion Taxed the Nations into Desolation & then gave the Spectrous Oath

(J 98.46–53, E 258)

The utterance itself seems at least to symbolize, but more likely to constitute, the Creatures' humanization: its illocutionary effect is to reject the law and its attendant sacrifice, to reject warfare and false religion. If plate 98 contains a subtle but significant extended allusion to the biblical account of creation, the Living Creatures rewrite the end of the story by denying its central symbol, the 'Tree of Good & Evil,' along with the tree's consequences: the accusation of sin, the legalism and patriarchy of the Old Testament, the 'Moral Virtues of the Heathen' and the 'Kingdoms of the World,' the poverty brought about in these kingdoms through ruinous taxation, and especially the 'Druid Temples' and 'Oak Groves of Albion.' The machinery of destruction the Living Creatures denounce is that which is kept running by legalistic and officially sanctioned speech acts, by the 'Accuser of Sin' and the 'Spectrous Oath' of Albion's devouring giant.

But how is the new order proclaimed by the Living Creatures different from the old order? And how different is it? The cry that goes out from the earth announces the end of the 'Covenant of Priam,' but also institutes the 'Covenant of Jehovah.' The terms of the latter covenant are spelled out in chapter 3 of *Jerusalem*:

> And this is the Covenant
> Of Jehovah: If you Forgive one-another, so shall Jehovah Forgive You:
> That He Himself may Dwell among You.   (*J* 61.24–6, E 212)

In other words, the new covenant comprehends two of the central pronouncements of Jesus in the New Testament: the institution of the Lord's Prayer ('forgive us our debts, as we forgive our debtors' [Matthew 6:12]) and the new commandment ('This is my commandment, That ye love one another, as I have loved you' [John 15:12]). Like these phrases, which Jesus offers in place of the 'vain repetitions' of the heathen and the commandments of the Old Testament, and like the declaration at the end of *The Marriage of Heaven and Hell*, the new covenant proclaims freedom from restrictive verbal formulas. The Living Creatures maintain this freedom by framing their cry, not as an assertion or declaration, but as a series of rhetorical questions ('where is ... where are ... where are'), so as to mark the end of the old order without circumscribing the new. The Creatures' utterance represents an act of forgiveness performed '*according to* the Covenant of Jehovah' (*J* 98.45, E 258), rather than a declaration of the terms of that covenant; the covenant, that is to say, is demonstrated rather than being prescribed. Yet a new covenant *is* being substituted for an old one, just as Jesus substitutes a new commandment and pronounces a prayer which has become part of the official liturgy. While it is possible for new speech acts to supersede the old, there seems to be an ultimate awareness that our language cannot supersede the forms of sociopolitical discourse altogether; that performative utterance, as we know it, derives its power from convention and consensus; that a new vision must come to terms with the old language.

The final text plate of *Jerusalem* conveys a similar intuition inasmuch as it revises the act of naming, bringing together the second chapter of Genesis, the end of Ezekiel, and the end of Revelation:

> All Human Forms identified even Tree Metal Earth & Stone. all
> Human Forms identified, living going forth & returning wearied
> Into the Planetary lives of Years Months Days & Hours reposing

And then Awaking into his Bosom in the Life of Immortality.
And I heard the Name of their Emanations they are named Jerusalem

(J 99.1–5, E 258–9)

The debate over whether or not *Jerusalem* reaches a resolution centres on this final text plate. Despite the variety of readings these lines have received, the majority of critics have found in them a sense of fulfilment and an ultimate correspondence between Blake's language and his vision.[16] Among the few critics who feel that the end of *Jerusalem* problematizes Blake's visionary ideal is Dan Miller, who feels that this conclusion, which has generally been taken as a promise of ultimate clarity and unity, rests on oppositions and interpretive difficulties. Blake does not manage to integrate speech and sight, or freedom and order, 'concepts that, though not antithetical, coexist only with some tension' ('Blake and the Deconstructive Interlude' 165); his figure of words on chariots is 'a complex and spatially involuted image' (167) which sends the reader who would grasp its full meaning on an intertextual search after the Merkabah and related images. In sum, Blake's revelation reveals 'the intransigence of

---

16 Robert Essick points to the lines as a caution to post-structuralist readers that Blake's view of language is not their own, since Blake relies on the medieval tradition that stresses the 'individual positivity of words' ('Blake Today and Tomorrow' 399). V.A. de Luca also underlines the disjunction between our contemporary understanding of the signifier and Blake's concept of language ('A Wall of Words' 237). For de Luca, the final word, 'Jerusalem,' is a unifying and familiar 'name to bring us home' ('Proper Names' 22), while Daniel Stempel describes the final vision of *Jerusalem*, more generally, as one in which 'the relation between words and things is immediately visible as language and representation become one' (398).

Even critics who find the language of the final plates disruptive and troubling recognize its disruptiveness as appropriate to Blake's vision of liberty and non-subordination. Peter Middleton stresses the ambiguities made possible by the 'lack of good grammar,' and especially by the lack of grammatical subordination: 'The series of states is allowed to remain a series, without subordination or sublation into a final state or subject, because the subordination of conventional written syntax is not employed. The possible syntactic constructions form a dynamic set which is the actual grammar of the lines' ('Revolutionary Poetics, Part I' 36). Edward Rose also argues that the passage eludes a definitive reading, noting that participles such as 'identified' are simultaneously transitive and intransitive, passive and active ('Visionary Forms Dramatic' 119). Nelson Hilton understands the names bestowed here as 'the occasion and intersection both of difference (each form is individually "identified") and identity (all are "identified" together)' ('Becoming Prolific Being Devoured' 422). For him, as in a different way for de Luca, the primary effect of the passage is to show forth language itself, and not something that language might represent, as the ultimate subject/object of Blake's vision, or to determine 'the "literal" meaning of writing as metaphoricity itself' (*Literal Imagination* 261).

allegorical representation and the interminable analysis that allegory pro-
vokes' (167).

Leaving aside the question of what constitutes 'clarity' in the eyes of the
poet who claims that 'That which can be made Explicit to the Idiot is not
worth my care' (E 702), I would argue that the 'interminable analysis'
encouraged by the end of *Jerusalem* is of a different kind. Like the cry of
the Living Creatures on plate 98, the act of naming in the final lines of the
poem may be read both as a liberating speech act and as a potentially self-
referential or self-legitimating utterance which replaces one kind of political pronouncement with another. The first four lines of plate 99 seem to
promise a liberation from conventional rhetoric and a demonstration of the
way visionary language can create meaning. Omitting almost all punctuation, and obliterating distinctions between past and present, active and
passive, subject and object, these lines rely on participles: 'identified,' 'living going forth & returning,' 'reposing,' 'Awaking.' Because they lack a
main verb, nothing is 'stated' the way we would expect from a constative
utterance. Meaningfulness is achieved less by declaration than by ordering
and repetition – that is, by the creation of space and time. When 'All
Human Forms identified' is modified slightly to 'all / Human Forms identified,' the emphasis on plurality gives way to an emphasis on unity through
the line-end stress on 'all.' The parallelism between 'Tree Metal Earth &
Stone' and 'Years Months Days & Hours' implies the identity between the
categories of physical-spatial elements and temporal units (all of them
being identified, of course, as 'human forms') in place of a statement to that
effect.

Only in the final line do a subject and a main verb reappear, with the
performative force that Blake's active verbs often receive against a background of participles: 'And *I heard* the Name of their Emanations they are
named Jerusalem' (*J* 99.5, E 259; my italics). The ring-composition effect
achieved by this final reference back to the title renders the speech act, on
one level, meaningful and fulfilling, since the intervening poem has provided many kinds of motivation for pronouncing the name 'Jerusalem.' The
utterance names the awakened Emanation of Albion, who becomes a symbolic unification of the Emanations of all human forms in the moment
when everything takes on human form. It also names the present text; and,
since the text is made up of words which are human forms, this act is virtually equivalent to naming a people.

Ring-composition creates an attractive symmetry, but perhaps also a
fearful one. By sending us back to the beginning, the final word of the text
closes a circle and compels us to recognize that Blake's *Jerusalem* is mani-

festly, and merely, defining *Blake's* Jerusalem. The encompassing nature of the definition is also its narrowness and idiosyncrasy. This is not to accuse Blake of writing a text that has no connection with a real world, so much as to argue that Blake's text ultimately reveals the fate of rhetoric in real-world politics, where the legitimation of a speech act inevitably depends on another speech act. It may be impossible to decide which utterance is logically prior, the final declaration 'they are named Jerusalem' or the 'original' title/poem 'Jerusalem.'

The final line of the poem relates authoritative declaration to subjective perception, but the lack of punctuation between the two halves of the line makes it difficult to determine the extent to which one depends on the other. On the one hand, the first-person construction brings the genesis of the poem, and its apocalypse, back to the experience of the individual human subject, recalling Benveniste's claim that the structure of language is radically open to the exercise of subjectivity: 'Language is so organized that it permits each speaker to *appropriate to himself* an entire language by designating himself as *I*' (226). It is possible that the act of naming is effective *because* it has been experienced by the poet as a sensory phenomenon. 'And I heard the Name of their Emanations [therefore] they are named Jerusalem,' we might read, as a final confirmation of the visionary power contained in expanded sensory perception. Of course, this is also to identify the act of naming as one term in an infinitely regressive series of speech acts, an utterance which can be repeated here only because a similar utterance has been heard before. On the other hand, there is not necessarily a causal link between hearing the name and pronouncing it, and the final line may be read as two separate phrases, wherein constative narrative ('And I heard the Name of their Emanations') gives way to arbitrary declaration ('they are named Jerusalem'). By virtue of his visionary experience, the poet assumes the right to make the kind of declaration that would normally be made by someone with political authority. This is the text's ultimate example of the creation of a state: Jerusalem, as a social and spiritual entity, is brought into existence by the verbal pronouncement of the visionary poet.

The Community of Phrases

'Where does Blake get his authority from?' Geoffrey Hartman asks ('Envoi' 244), calling attention to the discrepancy between Blake's assumption of an inspired voice, on the one hand, and his lack of respect for conventional authoritative stances, on the other. By rewriting and parodying Milton's invocations in *Paradise Lost*, and by flaunting or sensationalizing visionary experience as he does in his correspondence and conversation, is Blake not disrupting the very tradition on which he should be drawing for credibility as an inspired speaker? The readings I have elaborated suggest that Blake replaces the conventions of inspired poetry with a belief in the sensory experience of the individual, and with a mode of writing that highlights the performative nature of language.

Speech-act theory is a theory of language in society, and the class of utterances it identifies most explicitly as performatives are those which require socially or institutionally conferred authority on the part of the speaker in order to be successful. 'I pronounce you husband and wife,' 'I declare this session open,' and 'these united Colonies are ... free and independent states' are all examples of this class. If we apply Hartman's question – 'Where do they get their authority from?' – to the speakers of these sentences, we find ourselves embarking on the interminable analysis of a world of words. Stanley Fish describes declarative speech acts as infinitely regressive and infinitely self-perpetuating:

... if declarative utterances, when they have their intended force, alter states of affairs, what brings about the state of affairs in which a declarative utterance is endowed with its intended force? The answer is, another declarative utterance, and it is an answer one would have to give no matter how far back the inquiry was pushed. The conclusion is inescapable: declarative (and other) utterances do not merely mirror or reflect the state; they *are* the state, which increases and wanes as they are or are not taken seriously. (*Is There a Text* 216)

Fish, in accordance with his interest in interpretive communities, is using 'state' as a sociopolitical term, with connotations that we may now also hear behind Blake's use of 'state.' Blake's authority rests on his ability to create a state by making a statement – one which supersedes a previous state brought about by a previous statement, his own or someone else's. If he participates in a tradition, it is not by claiming authority based on his status as a bard or prophet, but by practising a mode of speaking and writing that comes to him through the Bible and Milton, repressed as that mode might be in the earlier texts in favour of a theologically and poetically more attractive model of performative speech issuing from divine will.

Writing on the American Declaration of Independence, Derrida has described a situation in which identity and agency depend on a self-reflexive structure of performative language. The scandal, or what Derrida calls the 'fabulous retroactivity,' of the Declaration lies in the fact that it guaran-

tees the freedom of 'the people,' while 'the people' simultaneously guarantees the Declaration by signing it as a free agent. The Declaration
retroactively creates its own signatory by designating certain individuals as
representatives who have the authority to sign a constitution: 'There was
no signer, by right, before the text of the Declaration which itself remains
the producer and guarantor of its own signature' ('Declarations' 10). This
unheard-of everyday occurrence repeats itself each time the state changes
its constitution: the signing of the Declaration effaces a previous 'state signature' in ' "dissolving" the links of colonial paternity or maternity' ('Declarations' 11). Jean-François Lyotard refers the same argument to a text from
Blake's era, analysing the self-referentiality and the self-authorization of the
French Declaration of 1789:

If the nation is authorized in the Preamble to prescribe the Articles, and Article 3 in
particular, it is because in that article the nation is declared to be authorized to prescribe in general. The Article names the sovereign, and the sovereign states the
source that names him. But the sovereign had to begin his declaration before being
authorized to do so by the Article he is going to declare, thus before being the
authorized sovereign. (*Differend* 146)

But for Lyotard this particular paradox is 'a trivial one in the legitimation of
authority' (*Differend* 146), and he concentrates on a more profound and
influential paradox in the Declaration of 1789. There is a tension between
the Declaration's philosophical or speculative appeal to the Idea of Man,
and its historical-political appeal to the French people, or to a name which
grounds the referent in historical reality. Lyotard exposes the way the Declaration attempts to legitimate itself by appealing equivocally to a sociopolitical entity and to individual will:

The splitting of the addressor of the Declaration into two entities, French nation and
human being, corresponds to the equivocation of the declarative phrase: it presents
a philosophical universe and copresents a historical-political universe. The revolution in politics that is the French Revolution comes from this impossible passage
from one universe to another. (*Differend* 146–7)

Like Lyotard, I have been arguing that the distinction between phrases
which create sociopolitical states and the Logos which creates spiritual or
imaginative worlds comes to (self-)consciousness in the wake of the
French Revolution, in the period we have called Romantic. Lyotard's two
universes, the historical-political and the philosophical, correspond to my

two types of performativity, the sociopolitical and the phenomenological. The disjunction between them is evident in the texts of both Milton and Blake, revolutionaries who are also visionaries, speakers of a politicized language who need to preserve their commitment to an ideally performative language. Blake's *Jerusalem* demonstrates how much the composition of a text resembles the constitution of a state, and how a distinctive vision, when committed to language, can turn into a distinct society. If, in the beginning, performative power was lodged in the words of God, the product of those words is a societal system that forms and reforms itself through speech acts, committed to being, as Wallace Stevens says, a world of words to the end of it.

Bibliography

Aarsleff, Hans. *From Locke to Saussure: Essays on the Study of Language and Intellectual History.* Minneapolis: U of Minnesota P, 1982.

Abrams, M.H. *Doing Things with Texts: Essays in Criticism and Critical Theory.* Ed. Michael Fischer. New York: Norton, 1989.

– *The Mirror and the Lamp: Romantic Theory and the Critical Tradition.* Oxford: Oxford UP, 1953.

– *Natural Supernaturalism: Tradition and Revolution in Romantic Literature.* New York: Norton, 1971.

Ackland, Michael. 'Blake's Problematic Touchstones to Experience: "Introduction," "Earth's Answer," and the Lyca Poems.' *Studies in Romanticism* 19 (1980): 3–17.

Adams, Hazard. 'Blake and the Philosophy of Literary Symbolism.' In Hilton, ed., *Essential Articles* 1–14.

– *Philosophy of the Literary Symbolic.* Tallahassee: UP of Florida, 1983.

– *William Blake: A Reading of the Shorter Poems.* Seattle: U of Washington P, 1963.

Adamson, J.H. 'The Creation.' In *Bright Essence: Studies in Milton's Theology.* Ed. W.B. Hunter, C.A. Patrides, and J.H. Adamson. Salt Lake City: U of Utah P, 1971. 81–102.

– 'Milton and the Creation.' *Journal of English and Germanic Philology* 61 (1962): 756–78.

Anderson, Bernhard W. *Creation versus Chaos: The Reinterpretation of Mythical Symbolism in the Bible.* New York: Association P, 1967.

– 'A Stylistic Study of the Priestly Creation Story.' In *Canon and Authority: Essays in Old Testament Religion and Theology.* Ed. George W. Coats and Burke O. Long. Philadelphia: Fortress P, 1977. 148–62.

Ault, Donald [D.]. 'Incommensurability and Interconnection in Blake's Anti-Newtonian Text.' *Studies in Romanticism* 16 (1977): 277–303.

- 'Re-Visioning *The Four Zoas.*' In Hilton and Vogler, eds., *Unnam'd Forms* 105–39.
- *Visionary Physics: Blake's Response to Newton.* Chicago: U of Chicago P, 1974.
Austen, Jane. *Sense and Sensibility.* Harmondsworth: Penguin, 1969.
Austin, J.L. *How to Do Things with Words.* 1962. Ed. J. O. Urmson and Marina Sbisà. 2d ed. Cambridge: Harvard UP, 1975.
- *Philosophical Papers.* Ed. J.O. Urmson and G.J. Warnock. 3rd ed. Oxford: Oxford UP, 1979.
Balfour, Ian [Grant]. 'The Future of Citation: Blake, Wordsworth, and the Rhetoric of Romantic Prophecy.' In *Writing the Future.* Ed. David Wood. London: Routledge, 1990. 115–28.
- 'The Rhetoric of Romantic Prophecy.' Diss. Yale U, 1986.
Barthes, Roland. *The Rustle of Language.* Trans. Richard Howard. New York: Hill & Wang, 1986.
Beer, John. *Blake's Humanism.* Manchester: Manchester UP, 1968.
Benjamin, Walter. 'Über Sprache überhaupt und über die Sprache des Menschen.' In *Gesammelte Schriften.* Ed. Rolf Tiedemann and Hermann Schweppenhäuser. Vol. 2. Frankfurt a.M.: Suhrkamp, 1980. 140–57.
Bentley, G.E., Jr. *Blake Records.* Oxford: Clarendon P, 1969.
- *Blake Records Supplement.* Oxford: Clarendon P, 1988.
- 'Blake's Works as Performances.' *Text* 4 (1988): 319–41.
Benveniste, Emile. *Problems in General Linguistics.* Trans. Mary Elizabeth Meek. Coral Gables FL: U of Miami P, 1971.
Berry, Boyd M. *Process of Speech: Puritan Religious Writing and Paradise Lost.* Baltimore: Johns Hopkins UP, 1976.
Billigheimer, Rachel V. 'The Eighth Eye: Prophetic Vision in Blake's Poetry and Design.' *Colby Library Quarterly* 22 (1986): 93–110.
Blake, William. *The Complete Poetry and Prose of William Blake.* Ed. David V. Erdman. Rev. ed. Berkeley: U of California P, 1982.
- *Jerusalem: The Emanation of the Giant Albion.* Ed. Morton D. Paley. Princeton: Princeton UP, 1991. Vol. 1 of *Blake's Illuminated Books.* Gen. ed. David Bindman. 2 vols. to date. 1991–.
- *The Marriage of Heaven and Hell.* Ed. Geoffrey Keynes. Oxford: Oxford UP, 1975.
- *The Notebook of William Blake: A Photographic and Typographic Facsimile.* Ed. David V. Erdman and Donald K. Moore. Rev. ed. [n.p.]: Readex, 1977.
- *Songs of Innocence and of Experience.* Ed. Andrew Lincoln. Princeton: Princeton UP, 1991. Vol. 2 of *Blake's Illuminated Books.* Gen. ed. David Bindman. 2 vols. to date. 1991–.
Blakemore, Steven. *Burke and the Fall of Language: The French Revolution as Linguistic Event.* Hanover: UP of New England, 1988.

– 'Language and Logos in *Paradise Lost.*' *Southern Humanities Review* 20 (1986): 325–40.

Bloom, Harold. *The Anxiety of Influence: A Theory of Poetry.* London: Oxford UP, 1973.

– *Blake's Apocalypse: A Study in Poetic Argument.* Garden City NY: Doubleday, 1963.

– 'Criticism, Canon-Formation, and Prophecy: The Sorrows of Facticity.' *Raritan* 3 (1984): 1–20.

– *The Ringers in the Tower: Studies in Romantic Tradition.* Chicago: U of Chicago P, 1971.

–, ed. *William Blake.* New York: Chelsea, 1985.

Bracher, Mark. 'Rouzing the Faculties: Lacanian Psychoanalysis and the Marriage of Heaven and Hell in the Reader.' In Miller et al., eds., *Critical Paths* 168–203.

Brisman, Leslie. ' "The Four Zoas": First Things.' In Bloom, ed., *William Blake* 145–57.

– *Milton's Poetry of Choice and Its Romantic Heirs.* Ithaca: Cornell UP, 1973.

Broch, Hermann. *The Death of Virgil.* Trans. Jean Starr Untermeyer. New York: Pantheon Books, 1945.

– *Kommentierte Werkausgabe.* Ed. Paul Michael Lützeler. 13 vols. Frankfurt a.M.: Suhrkamp, 1975.

Bronte, Emily. *Wuthering Heights.* Ed. Ian Jack. Oxford: Oxford UP, 1976.

Buber, Martin. *I and Thou.* Trans. Ronald Gregor Smith. 2d ed. New York: Scribner's, 1958.

Budick, Sanford. *The Dividing Muse: Images of Sacred Disjunction in Milton's Poetry.* New Haven: Yale UP, 1985.

Burke, Kenneth. *A Grammar of Motives.* Berkeley: U of California P, 1945.

– *Language as Symbolic Action: Essays on Life, Literature, and Method.* Berkeley: U of California P, 1966.

– *The Rhetoric of Religion: Studies in Logology.* Berkeley: U of California P, 1961.

Burkhardt, Arnim, ed. *Speech Acts, Meaning and Intentions: Critical Approaches to the Philosophy of John R. Searle.* Berlin: de Gruyter, 1990.

Campbell, Gordon. 'ברא, κτιζειν, and *Creare* Again.' *Notes and Queries* 226 (1981): 42–3.

– 'Milton's Theological and Literary Treatments of the Creation.' *Journal of Theological Studies* 30 (1979): 128–37.

Carr, Stephen Leo. 'Visionary Syntax: Nontyrannical Coherence in Blake's Visual Art.' *The Eighteenth Century: Theory and Interpretation* 22 (1981): 222–48.

Cassuto, U. *A Commentary on the Book of Genesis.* Trans. Israel Abrahams. Part 1. Jerusalem: Magnes P, 1961.

The Censure of the Rota upon Mr Miltons Book, Entituled, The Ready and

Easie Way to Establish a Free Common-wealth. 1660. Rpt. in *Milton's Contemporary Reputation.* Ed. William Riley Parker. Columbus: Ohio State UP, 1940. 229–44.

Certeau, Michel de. 'What We Do When We Believe.' In *On Signs.* Ed. Marshall Blonsky. Oxford: Blackwell, 1985. 192–202.

Chase, Cynthia. *Decomposing Figures: Rhetorical Readings in the Romantic Tradition.* Baltimore: Johns Hopkins UP, 1986.

Christopher, Georgia B. *Milton and the Science of the Saints.* Princeton: Princeton UP, 1982.

Clark, David L. ' "The Innocence of Becoming Restored": Blake, Nietzsche, and the Disclosure of Difference.' *Studies in Romanticism* 29 (1990): 91–113.

Clark, Matthew C., and Eric Csapo. 'Deconstruction, Ideology, and Goldhill's *Oresteia.*' *Phoenix* 45 (1991): 95–125.

Coleridge, Samuel Taylor. *Biographia Literaria.* Ed. James Engell and W. Jackson Bate. Princeton: Princeton UP, 1983. Vol. 7 of *The Collected Works of Samuel Taylor Coleridge.* Gen. ed. Kathleen Coburn. Bollingen Series 75. 10 vols. to date. 1969-.

– *The Complete Poetical Works of Samuel Taylor Coleridge.* Ed. Ernest Hartley Coleridge. 2 vols. Oxford: Clarendon P, 1912.

Constitutions and Canons Ecclesiastical 1604, Latin and English. Ed. J.V. Bullard. London: Faith P, 1934.

Corns, Thomas N. 'New Light on the Left Hand: Contemporary Views of Milton's Prose Style.' *Durham University Journal* 72 (1980): 177–81.

Cox, Stephen. *Love and Logic: The Evolution of Blake's Thought.* Ann Arbor: U of Michigan P, 1992.

Culler, Jonathan. *On Deconstruction: Theory and Criticism after Structuralism.* Ithaca: Cornell UP, 1982.

Cumberland, George. *Thoughts on Outline, Sculpture, and the System That Guided the Ancient Artists in Composing Their Figures and Groups.* London: Wilson, 1796.

Daiches, David. 'The Opening of *Paradise Lost.*' In *The Living Milton: Essays by Various Hands.* Ed. Frank Kermode. London: Routledge, 1960. 55–69.

Damon, S. Foster. *A Blake Dictionary: The Ideas and Symbols of William Blake.* Providence: Brown UP, 1965.

Damrosch, Leopold, Jr. *Symbol and Truth in Blake's Myth.* Princeton: Princeton UP, 1980.

Dasenbrock, Reed Way, ed. *Redrawing the Lines: Analytic Philosophy, Deconstruction, and Literary Theory.* Minneapolis: U of Minnesota P, 1989.

Davies, Stevie, and William B. Hunter. 'Milton's Urania: "The Meaning, Not the Name I Call." ' *Studies in English Literature* 28 (1988): 95–111.

de Luca, V.A. 'Proper Names in the Structural Design of Blake's Myth-making.'
    Blake Studies 8 (1978): 5–22.

– 'A Wall of Words: The Sublime as Text.' In Hilton and Vogler, eds., *Unnam'd
    Forms* 218–41.

– *Words of Eternity: Blake and the Poetics of the Sublime.* Princeton: Princeton UP,
    1991.

de Man, Paul. *Allegories of Reading: Figural Language in Rousseau, Nietzsche,
    Rilke, and Proust.* New Haven: Yale UP, 1979.

– *The Rhetoric of Romanticism.* New York: Columbia UP, 1984.

Deen, Leonard W. *Conversing in Paradise: Poetic Genius and Identity-as-
    Community in Blake's Los.* Columbia: U of Missouri P, 1983.

Derrida, Jacques. 'Declarations of Independence.' Trans. Tom Keenan and Tom
    Pepper. *New Political Science* 15 (1986): 7–15.

– *Dissemination.* Trans. Barbara Johnson. Chicago: U of Chicago P, 1981.

– *Limited Inc.* Trans. Samuel Weber and Jeffrey Mehlman. Ed. Gerald Graff.
    Evanston: Northwestern UP, 1990.

– *Margins of Philosophy.* Trans. Alan Bass. Chicago: U of Chicago P, 1982.

– *Of Grammatology.* Trans. Gayatri Chakravorty Spivak. Baltimore: Johns Hopkins
    UP, 1974.

– *Otobiographies: L'enseignement de Nietzsche et la politique du nom propre.*
    Paris: Galilée, 1984.

– *Speech and Phenomena, and Other Essays on Husserl's Theory of Signs.* Trans.
    David B. Allison. Evanston: Northwestern UP, 1973.

DiSalvo, Jackie. *War of Titans: Blake's Critique of Milton and the Politics of Reli-
    gion.* Pittsburgh: U of Pittsburgh P, 1983.

Doskow, Minna. *William Blake's 'Jerusalem': Structure and Meaning in Poetry and
    Picture.* London: Associated UP, 1982.

Du Bartas, Guillaume de Saluste. *The Divine Weeks and Works of Guillaume de
    Saluste Sieur du Bartas.* Trans. Josuah Sylvester. Ed. Susan Snyder. 2 vols.
    Oxford: Clarendon P, 1979. Vol. 1.

Eaves, Morris. 'Romantic Expressive Theory and Blake's Idea of the Audience.'
    PMLA 95 (1980): 784–801.

– *William Blake's Theory of Art.* Princeton: Princeton UP, 1982.

Eaves, Morris, and Michael Fischer, eds. *Romanticism and Contemporary Criti-
    cism.* Ithaca: Cornell UP, 1986.

Edwards, Gavin. 'Mind-Forg'd Manacles: A Contribution to the Discussion of
    Blake's "London." ' *Literature and History* 5 (1979): 87–105.

– 'Repeating the Same Dull Round.' In Hilton and Vogler, eds., *Unnam'd Forms*
    26–48.

Eichrodt, Walther. 'In the Beginning: A Contribution to the Interpretation of the

First Word of the Bible.' In *Creation in the Old Testament*. Ed. Bernhard W. Anderson. Philadelphia: Fortress P, 1984. 65–73.

Entzminger, Robert L. *Divine Word: Milton and the Redemption of Language*. Pittsburgh: Duquesne UP, 1985.

Epstein, E.L. 'Blake's "Infant Sorrow" – an Essay in Discourse Analysis.' In *Current Trends in Stylistics*. Ed. Braj B. Kachru and Herbert F.W. Stahlke. Edmonton: Linguistic Research, 1972. 231–41.

Erdman, David V. *Blake, Prophet against Empire: A Poet's Interpretation of the History of His Own Times*. 3rd ed. Princeton: Princeton UP, 1977.

–, ed. *The Illuminated Blake*. Garden City NY: Doubleday, 1974.

Erdman, David V., Tom Dargan, and Marlene Deverell-Van Meter. 'Reading the Illuminations of Blake's *The Marriage of Heaven and Hell*.' In *William Blake: Essays in Honour of Sir Geoffrey Keynes*. Ed. Morton D. Paley and Michael Phillips. Oxford: Clarendon P, 1973. 162–207.

Essick, Robert N. 'Blake Today and Tomorrow.' *Studies in Romanticism* 21 (1982): 395–9.

– *William Blake and the Language of Adam*. Oxford: Clarendon P, 1989.

The European Fame of Isaac Newton. Catalogue of an exhibition at the Fitzwilliam Museum. Cambridge, 1973.

Evans, John Martin. *'Paradise Lost' and the Genesis Tradition*. Oxford: Clarendon P, 1968.

Fanto, James A. 'Speech Act Theory and Its Applications to the Study of Literature.' In *The Sign: Semiotics around the World*. Ed. R.W. Bailey, L. Matejka, and P. Steiner. Ann Arbor: Michigan Slavic, 1978. 280–304.

Felman, Shoshana. *The Literary Speech Act: Don Juan with J.L. Austin, or Seduction in Two Languages*. Trans. Catherine Porter. Ithaca: Cornell UP, 1983.

Fisch, Harold. 'Creation in Reverse: The Book of Job and *Paradise Lost*.' In *Milton and Scriptural Tradition: The Bible into Poetry*. Ed. James H. Sims and Leland Ryken. Columbia: U of Missouri P, 1984. 104–16.

Fischer, Michael. 'William Blake's Quarrel with Indeterminacy.' *New Orleans Review* 10 (1983): 43–9.

Fish, Stanley. *Is There a Text in This Class? The Authority of Interpretive Communities*. Cambridge: Harvard UP, 1980.

– *Self-Consuming Artifacts: The Experience of Seventeenth-Century Literature*. Berkeley: U of California P, 1972.

– *Surprised by Sin: The Reader in 'Paradise Lost.'* Berkeley: U of California P, 1971.

– 'With the Compliments of the Author: Reflections on Austin and Derrida.' *Critical Inquiry* 8 (1982): 693–721.

Fletcher, Harris F. *The Intellectual Development of John Milton*. 2 vols. Urbana: U of Illinois P, 1956–61.

– *Milton's Rabbinical Readings*. Urbana: U of Illinois P, 1930.

Fogel, Aaron. 'Pictures of Speech: On Blake's Poetic.' *Studies in Romanticism* 21 (1982): 217–42.

Fox, Susan. *Poetic Form in Blake's 'Milton.'* Princeton: Princeton UP, 1976.

French, J. Milton. *Milton in Chancery: New Chapters in the Lives of the Poet and His Father*. New York: MLA, 1939.

Fry, Paul H. *The Poet's Calling in the English Ode*. New Haven: Yale UP, 1980.

Frye, Northrop. 'Blake's Introduction to Experience.' *Huntington Library Quarterly* 21 (1957): 57–67. Rpt. in *Blake: A Collection of Critical Essays*. Ed. Northrop Frye. Englewood Cliffs NJ: Prentice-Hall, 1966. 23–31.

– *Creation and Recreation*. Toronto: U of Toronto P, 1980.

– *Fearful Symmetry: A Study of William Blake*. Princeton: Princeton UP, 1947.

– *The Great Code: The Bible and Literature*. Toronto: Academic P, 1981.

– *Words with Power: Being a Second Study of 'The Bible and Literature.'* Markham: Viking, 1990.

Gallagher, Philip J. 'Creation in Genesis and in *Paradise Lost.'* *Milton Studies* 20 (1984): 163–204.

– 'The Word Made Flesh: Blake's "A Poison Tree" and the Book of Genesis.' *Studies in Romanticism* 16 (1977): 237–49.

Gallant, Christine. *Blake and the Assimilation of Chaos*. Princeton: Princeton UP, 1978.

Gillham, D.G. *Blake's Contrary States: The 'Songs of Innocence and of Experience' as Dramatic Poems*. Cambridge: Cambridge UP, 1966.

– *William Blake*. Cambridge: Cambridge UP, 1973.

Glannon, Walter. 'What Literary Theory Misses in Wittgenstein.' *Philosophy and Literature* 10 (1986): 263–72.

Gleckner, Robert F. 'Blake's Verbal Technique.' In *William Blake: Essays for S. Foster Damon*. Ed. Alvin H. Rosenfeld. Providence: Brown UP, 1969. 321–32.

– 'Most Holy Forms of Thought.' In Hilton, ed., *Essential Articles* 91–117.

– *The Piper and the Bard: A Study of William Blake*. Detroit: Wayne State UP, 1959.

– 'Point of View and Context in Blake's Songs.' *Bulletin of the New York Public Library* 61 (1957): 531–8.

Glen, Heather. *Vision and Disenchantment: Blake's 'Songs' and Wordsworth's 'Lyrical Ballads.'* Cambridge: Cambridge UP, 1983.

Goethe, Johann Wolfgang von. *Goethe's Faust*. Trans. Walter Kaufmann. Garden City NY: Doubleday, 1961.

Greenstein, Edward L. 'Deconstruction and Biblical Narrative.' *Prooftexts* 9 (1989): 43–71.

Gregory, E.R. *Milton and the Muses*. Tuscaloosa: U of Alabama P, 1989.

Grice, H. Paul. 'Logic and Conversation.' In *Speech Acts.* Ed. Peter Cole and Jerry Morgan. Syntax and Semantics 3. New York: Academic P, 1972. 41–58.

Guetti, James. 'Wittgenstein and Literary Theory.' *Raritan* 4.2 (1984): 67–84; 4.3 (1985): 66–84.

Guillory, John. *Poetic Authority: Spenser, Milton, and Literary History.* New York: Columbia UP, 1983.

Hale, Matthew. *History of the Common Law of England.* Ed. Charles M. Gray. Chicago: U of Chicago P, 1971.

Hancher, Michael. 'Beyond a Speech-Act Theory of Literary Discourse.' *Modern Language Notes* 92 (1977): 1081–98.

– 'Understanding Poetic Speech Acts.' *College English* 36.6 (1975): 632–9.

Handelman, Susan A. *The Slayers of Moses: The Emergence of Rabbinic Interpretation in Modern Literary Theory.* Albany: State U of New York P, 1982.

Hanford, James Holly. 'That Shepherd, Who First Taught the Chosen Seed: A Note on Milton's Mosaic Inspiration.' *University of Toronto Quarterly* 8 (1939): 403–19.

Harding, D.W. 'William Blake.' In *From Blake to Byron.* Ed. Boris Ford. Rev. ed. Vol. 5 of *A Guide to English Literature.* London: Cassell, 1962. 67–84.

Hartman, Geoffrey H. 'Envoi: "So Many Things." ' In Hilton and Vogler, eds., *Unnam'd Forms* 242–8.

– *The Fate of Reading and Other Essays.* Chicago: U of Chicago P, 1975.

– 'The Poetics of Prophecy.' In *High Romantic Argument: Essays for M.H. Abrams.* Ed. Lawrence Lipking. Ithaca: Cornell UP, 1981. 15–40.

Häublein, Ernst. 'Milton's Paraphrase of Genesis: A Stylistic Reading of *Paradise Lost,* Book VII.' *Milton Studies* 7 (1975): 101–25.

Helms, Randel. 'Blake's Use of the Bible in "A Song of Liberty." ' *English Language Notes* 16 (1979): 287–91.

Herbert, George. 'Outlandish Proverbs.' In *The Works of George Herbert.* Ed. F.E. Hutchinson. Oxford: Clarendon P, 1941. 321–55.

Herder, Johann Gottfried. *The Spirit of Hebrew Poetry.* Trans. James Marsh. 2 vols. Burlington: Smith, 1833.

Hilton, Nelson. 'Becoming Prolific Being Devoured.' *Studies in Romanticism* 21 (1982): 417–24.

– 'Blake and the Mountains of the Mind.' *Blake / An Illustrated Quarterly* 14 (1981): 196–204.

– 'Blakean Zen.' *Studies in Romanticism* 24 (1985): 183–200.

–, ed. *Essential Articles for the Study of William Blake, 1970–1984.* Hamden CT: Archon, 1986.

– *Literal Imagination: Blake's Vision of Words.* Berkeley: U of California P, 1983.

Hilton, Nelson, and Thomas A. Vogler, eds. *Unnam'd Forms: Blake and Textuality.* Berkeley: U of California P, 1986.

Hirsch, E.D., Jr. *Innocence and Experience: An Introduction to Blake.* New Haven: Yale UP, 1964.

Hoagwood, Terence Allan. *Prophecy and the Philosophy of Mind: Traditions of Blake and Shelley.* University: U of Alabama P, 1985.

Hölderlin, Friedrich. *Poems and Fragments.* Trans. Michael Hamburger. Cambridge: Cambridge UP, 1980.

– *Sämtliche Werke.* Ed. Friedrich Beissner. 8 vols. Stuttgart: Kohlhammer, 1946–85.

Howard, John. 'An Audience for *The Marriage of Heaven and Hell.*' *Blake Studies* 3 (1970): 19–52.

– *Infernal Poetics: Poetic Structures in Blake's Lambeth Prophecies.* Toronto: Associated UP, 1984.

Hughes, Merritt Y. 'Milton and the Symbol of Light.' *Studies in English Literature* 4 (1964): 1–33. Rpt. in *Ten Perspectives on Milton.* New Haven: Yale UP, 1965. 63–103.

Hunter, William B., [Jr.] 'The Meaning of "Holy Light" in *Paradise Lost* III.' *Modern Language Notes* 74 (1959): 589–92.

– 'Milton's Urania.' *Studies in English Literature* 4 (1964): 35–42. Rpt. as 'Milton's Muse.' In *Bright Essence: Studies in Milton's Theology.* Ed. W.B. Hunter, C.A. Patrides, and J.H. Adamson. Salt Lake City: U of Utah P, 1971. 149–56.

– 'Prophetic Dreams and Visions in *Paradise Lost.*' *Modern Language Quarterly* 9 (1948): 277–85.

Huntley, John F. 'The Images of Poet and Poetry in Milton's *The Reason of Church-Government.*' In *Achievements of the Left Hand: Essays on the Prose of John Milton.* Ed. Michael Lieb and John T. Shawcross. Amherst: U of Massachusetts P, 1974. 83–120.

Husik, Isaac. *A History of Mediaeval Jewish Philosophy.* 1916. Philadelphia: Jewish Publication Society of America, 1940.

The Interpreter's Bible. Ed. George Arthur Buttrick et al. 12 vols. New York: Abingdon P, 1952.

Iser, Wolfgang. 'The Reality of Fiction: A Functionalist Approach to Literature.' *New Literary History* 7 (1975): 7–38.

Jackson, Mary V. 'Prolific and Devourer: From Nonmythic to Mythic Statement in *The Marriage of Heaven and Hell* and *A Song of Liberty.*' *Journal of English and Germanic Philology* 70 (1971): 207–19.

Jakobson, Roman. 'Linguistics and Poetics.' In *Poetry of Grammar and Grammar of Poetry.* Vol. 3 of *Selected Writings.* The Hague: Mouton, 1981. 18–51.

– 'Shifters, Verbal Categories, and the Russian Verb.' In *Word and Language.* Vol. 2 of *Selected Writings.* The Hague: Mouton, 1971. 130–47.

Jarrett-Kerr, M. 'Milton, Poet and Paraphrast.' *Essays in Criticism* 10 (1960): 373–89.

Johnson, Barbara. *The Critical Difference: Essays in the Contemporary Rhetoric of Reading.* Baltimore: Johns Hopkins UP, 1980.

Josipovici, Gabriel. *The Book of God: A Response to the Bible.* New Haven: Yale UP, 1988.

Kaufman, Andrew. 'Authority and Vision: William Blake's Use of the Gospels.' *University of Toronto Quarterly* 57 (1987–8): 389–403.

Keats, John. *The Poems of John Keats.* Ed. Jack Stillinger. Cambridge: Cambridge UP, 1978.

Kelley, Maurice. *This Great Argument: A Study of Milton's 'De Doctrina Christiana' as a Gloss upon 'Paradise Lost.'* Gloucester MA: Smith, 1962.

Kerrigan, William. *The Prophetic Milton.* Charlottesville: UP of Virginia, 1974.

– *The Sacred Complex: On the Psychogenesis of Paradise Lost.* Cambridge: Harvard UP, 1983.

Kranidas, Thomas. 'Milton's *Of Reformation*: The Politics of Vision.' *ELH* 49 (1982): 497–513.

Kroeber, Karl. 'Delivering *Jerusalem.*' In *Blake's Sublime Allegory: Essays on 'The Four Zoas', 'Milton', 'Jerusalem.'* Ed. Stuart Curran and J.A. Wittreich, Jr. Madison: U of Wisconsin P, 1973. 347–67.

Lacoue-Labarthe, Philippe. 'The Caesura of the Speculative.' Trans. Robert Eisenhauer. *Glyph* 4 (1978): 57–84.

Land, Stephen K. *From Signs to Propositions: The Concept of Form in Eighteenth-Century Semantic Theory.* London: Longman, 1974.

Lanigan, Richard L. *Speech Act Phenomenology.* The Hague: Martinus Nijhoff, 1977.

Larreya, Paul. 'Enoncés performatifs, cause, et référence.' *Degrés* 1 (1973): m–m25.

Larrissy, Edward. *William Blake.* Oxford: Blackwell, 1985.

Leader, Zachary. *Reading Blake's 'Songs.'* Boston: Routledge, 1981.

Leavis, F.R. 'A Reply.' In *The Importance of Scrutiny: Selections from Scrutiny: A Quarterly Review, 1932–1948.* Ed. Eric Bentley. New York: Stewart, 1948. 35–7.

– *Revaluation: Tradition and Development in English Poetry.* New York: Stewart, 1947.

Leonard, John. *Naming in Paradise: Milton and the Language of Adam and Eve.* Oxford: Clarendon P, 1990.

Levin, Samuel P. 'Concerning What Kind of Speech Act a Poem Is.' In *Pragmatics of Language and Literature.* Ed. Teun A. van Dijk. North-Holland Series in Theoretical Linguistics 2. Amsterdam: North-Holland, 1976. 141–60.

Lieb, Michael. *The Dialectics of Creation: Patterns of Birth and Regeneration in 'Paradise Lost.'* Amherst: U of Massachusetts P, 1970.

Linkin, Harriet Kramer. 'The Language of Speakers in *Songs of Innocence and of Experience.*' *Romanticism Past and Present* 10 (1986): 5–23.

Lundeen, Kathleen. 'Urizen's Quaking Word.' *Colby Library Quarterly* 25 (1989): 12–27.

Lyotard, Jean-François. *The Differend: Phrases in Dispute*. Trans. Georges Van Den Abbeele. Minneapolis: U of Minnesota P, 1988.

– *The Postmodern Condition: A Report on Knowledge*. Trans. Geoff Bennington and Brian Massumi. Minneapolis: U of Minnesota P, 1984.

McColley, Grant. 'Milton's Golden Compasses.' *Notes and Queries* 176 (1939): 97–8.

– 'Milton's Technique of Source Adaptation.' *Studies in Philology* 35 (1938): 61–110.

– *Paradise Lost: An Account of Its Growth and Major Origins*. Chicago: Packard, 1940.

McGann, Jerome. *Towards a Literature of Knowledge*. Chicago: U of Chicago P, 1989.

– 'William Blake Illuminates the Truth.' *Critical Studies* 1 (1989): 43–60.

Maclean, Ian. 'Un dialogue de sourds? Some Implications of the Austin-Searle-Derrida Debate.' *Paragraph* 5 (1985): 1–26.

MacLeish, Archibald. *Collected Poems 1917–1952*. Boston: Houghton Mifflin, 1952.

Madsen, William G. *From Shadowy Types to Truth: Studies in Milton's Symbolism*. New Haven: Yale UP, 1968.

Malinowski, Bronislaw. *The Language of Magic and Gardening*. 2d ed. Vol. 2 of *Coral Gardens and Their Magic*. London: Allen, 1966.

Mann, Paul. '*The Book of Urizen* and the Horizon of the Book.' In Hilton and Vogler, eds., *Unnam'd Forms* 49–68.

Margolis, Joseph. 'Literature and Speech Acts.' *Philosophy and Literature* 3 (1979): 39–52.

Martin, Andrew. *The Knowledge of Ignorance: From Genesis to Jules Verne*. Cambridge: Cambridge UP, 1985.

Martin, Richard P. *The Language of Heroes: Speech and Performance in the 'Iliad.'* Ithaca: Cornell UP, 1989.

Merrill, Thomas F. *Epic God-Talk: 'Paradise Lost' and the Grammar of Religious Language*. Jefferson NC: McFarland, 1986.

– 'Miltonic God-Talk: The Creation in *Paradise Lost.*' *Language and Style* 16 (1983): 296–312.

Middleton, Peter. 'The Revolutionary Poetics of William Blake, Part I: The Critical Tradition.' In *1789: Reading Writing Revolution*. Ed. Francis Barker et al. Colchester: U of Essex, 1982. 110–18.

– 'The Revolutionary Poetics of William Blake: Part II – Silence, Syntax, and Spectres.' *Oxford Literary Review* 6 (1983): 35–51.

Miles, Josephine. *Eras and Modes in English Poetry*. Berkeley: U of California P, 1957.

Miller, Dan. 'Blake and the Deconstructive Interlude.' In Miller et al., eds., *Critical Paths* 139–67.

– 'Contrary Revelation: *The Marriage of Heaven and Hell.' Studies in Romanticism* 24 (1985): 491–509.

Miller, Dan, Mark Bracher, and Donald Ault, eds. *Critical Paths: Blake and the Argument of Method.* Durham: Duke UP, 1987.

Milton, John. *Complete Poems and Major Prose.* Ed. Merritt Y. Hughes. New York: Macmillan, 1957.

– *Complete Prose Works of John Milton.* Gen. ed. Don M. Wolfe. 8 vols. New Haven: Yale UP, 1953–82.

Mitchell, W.J.T. *Blake's Composite Art: A Study of the Illuminated Poetry.* Princeton: Princeton UP, 1978.

– 'Dangerous Blake.' *Studies in Romanticism* 21 (1982): 410–16.

– 'Visible Language: Blake's Wondrous Art of Writing.' In Eaves and Fischer, eds., *Romanticism* 46–95.

– 'Wittgenstein's Imagery and What It Tells Us.' *New Literary History* 19 (1988): 361–70.

Morris, Joseph E. 'Milton's Golden Compasses.' *Notes and Queries* 176 (1941): 176–7.

Nietzsche, Friedrich. *Friedrich Nietzsche on Rhetoric and Language.* Trans. Sander L. Gilman, Carole Blair, and David J. Parent. New York: Oxford UP, 1989.

– *Das Philosophenbuch: Theoretische Studien.* Paris: Aubier-Flammarion, 1969.

– *Werke: Kritische Gesamtausgabe.* Ed. Giorgio Colli and Mazzino Montinari. 8 vols. to date. Berlin: Walter de Gruyter, 1967–.

Norris, Christopher. 'Home Thoughts from Abroad: Derrida, Austin, and the Oxford Connection.' *Philosophy and Literature* 10 (1986): 1–25.

– 'Suspended Sentences: Textual Theory and the Law.' *Southern Review: Literary and Interdisciplinary Essays* 18 (1985): 123–41.

Northrup, Mark D. 'Milton's Hesiodic Cosmology.' *Comparative Literature* 33 (1981): 305–20.

Nurmi, Martin K. *Blake's 'The Marriage of Heaven and Hell': A Critical Study.* Kent OH: Kent State U, 1957.

Nyquist, Mary. 'The Genesis of Gendered Subjectivity in the Divorce Tracts and in *Paradise Lost.'* In Nyquist and Ferguson, eds., *Re-membering Milton* 99–127.

Nyquist, Mary, and Margaret W. Ferguson, eds. *Re-membering Milton: Essays on the Texts and Traditions.* London: Methuen, 1987.

Ohmann, Richard. 'Literature as Act.' In *Approaches to Poetics.* Ed. Seymour Chatman. New York: Columbia UP, 1973. 81–107.

– 'Speech, Action, and Style.' *Literary Style: A Symposium.* Ed. Seymour Chatman. London: Oxford UP, 1971. 241–59.

– 'Speech Acts and the Definition of Literature.' *Philosophy and Rhetoric* 4 (1971): 1–19.

- 'Speech, Literature, and the Space Between.' *New Literary History* 5 (1974): 37–63.

Ostriker, Alicia. *Vision and Verse in William Blake*. Madison: U of Wisconsin P, 1965.

Otto, Peter. *Constructive Vision and Visionary Deconstruction: Los, Eternity, and the Productions of Time in the Later Poetry of William Blake*. Oxford: Clarendon P, 1991.

Pagliaro, Harold. *Selfhood and Redemption in Blake's 'Songs.'* University Park: Pennsylvania State UP, 1987.

Paley, Morton D. *The Continuing City: William Blake's 'Jerusalem.'* Oxford: Clarendon P, 1983.

Parker, William Riley. *Milton: A Biography*. 2 vols. Oxford: Clarendon P, 1968.

Pavel, Thomas G. 'Ontological Issues in Poetics: Speech Acts and Fictional Worlds.' *Journal of Aesthetics and Art Criticism* 40 (1981): 167–78.

Pechey, Graham. '*The Marriage of Heaven and Hell*: A Text and Its Conjuncture.' *Oxford Literary Review* 3 (1979): 52–76.

Petrey, Sandy. 'Castration, Speech Acts, and the Realist Difference: *S/Z* versus *Sarrasine.*' *PMLA* 102 (1987): 153–65.

- 'The Realist Speech Act: Mimesis, Performance and the Facts in Fiction.' *Neohelicon* 15 (1988): 9–29.

- 'The Reality of Representation: Between Marx and Balzac.' *Critical Inquiry* 14 (1988): 448–68.

- *Speech Acts and Literary Theory*. New York: Routledge, 1990.

- 'Speech Acts in Society: Fish, Felman, Austin and God.' *Texte* 3 (1984): 43–61.

Pocock, J.G.A. 'Verbalizing a Political Act: Towards a Politics of Speech.' *Political Theory* 1 (1973): 27–45.

Prado, C.G. *Making Believe: Philosophical Reflections on Fiction*. Westport CT: Greenwood P, 1984.

Pratt, Mary Louise. 'Ideology and Speech-Act Theory.' *Poetics Today* 7 (1986): 59–72.

- *Toward a Speech Act Theory of Literary Discourse*. Bloomington: Indiana UP, 1977.

Preminger, Alex, and Edward L. Greenstein, eds. *The Hebrew Bible in Literary Criticism*. New York: Unger, 1986.

Quigley, Austin E. 'Wittgenstein's Philosophizing and Literary Theorizing.' *New Literary History* 19 (1988): 209–37.

Rajan, Tilottama. 'Displacing Post-Structuralism: Romantic Studies after Paul De Man.' *Studies in Romanticism* 24 (1985): 451–74.

- *The Supplement of Reading: Figures of Understanding in Romantic Theory and Practice*. Ithaca: Cornell UP, 1990.

Riede, David. 'Blake's *Milton*: On Membership in the Church Paul.' In Nyquist and Ferguson, eds., *Re-membering Milton* 257–77.

Rivers, Elias L., ed. *Things Done with Words: Speech Acts in Hispanic Drama.* Newark DE: Juan de la Cuesta, 1986.

Rose, Edward J. 'Blake's *Jerusalem*, St. Paul, and Biblical Prophecy.' *English Studies in Canada* 11 (1985): 396–412.

– 'Blake's Metaphorical States.' *Blake Studies* 4 (1971): 9–31.

– '"Mental Forms Creating": "Fourfold Vision" and the Poet as Prophet in Blake's Designs and Verse.' *Journal of Aesthetics and Art Criticism* 23 (1964): 173–83.

– 'The Spirit of the Bounding Line: Blake's Los.' *Criticism* 13 (1971): 54–76.

– 'Visionary Forms Dramatic: Grammatical and Iconographical Movement in Blake's Verse and Designs.' *Criticism* 8 (1966): 111–25.

Rosenberg, Marc. 'Style and Meaning in *The Book of Urizen*.' *Style* 4 (1970): 197–212.

Rosenblatt, Jason P. 'Angelic Tact: Raphael on Creation.' In *Milton and the Middle Ages.* Ed. John Mulryan. London: Associated UP, 1982. 21–31.

Roston, Murray. *Prophet and Poet: The Bible and the Growth of Romanticism.* Evanston: Northwestern UP, 1965.

Ryan, Marie-Laure. 'When "Je" is "un autre": Fiction, Quotation, and the Performative Analysis.' *Poetics Today* 2 (1981): 127–55.

Said, Edward. *Beginnings: Intention and Method.* 2d ed. New York: Columbia UP, 1985.

Samek, Robert. 'Performative Utterances and the Concept of Contract.' *Australasian Journal of Philosophy* 43 (1965): 196–210.

Sandler, Florence. 'The Iconoclastic Enterprise: Blake's Critique of "Milton's Religion."' *Blake Studies* 5 (1972–3): 1–57.

Saussure, Ferdinand de. *Cours de linguistique générale.* Ed. Charles Bally and Albert Sechehaye. 3rd ed. Paris: Payot, 1972.

– *Course in General Linguistics.* Ed. Charles Bally and Albert Sechehaye. Trans. Roy Harris. La Salle IL: Open Court, 1986.

Schindler, Walter. *Voice and Crisis: Invocation in Milton's Poetry.* Hamden CT: Archon, 1984.

Schmidt, Werner H. *Die Schöpfungsgeschichte der Priesterschrift: Zur Überlieferungsgeschichte von Genesis 1.1–2.4a und 2.4b–3.24.* 2d ed. Neukirchen-Vluyn: Neukirchner Verlag, 1967.

Schwartz, Regina M. *Remembering and Repeating: Biblical Creation in 'Paradise Lost.'* Cambridge: Cambridge UP, 1988. Rpt. as *Remembering and Repeating: On Milton's Theology and Poetics.* Chicago: Chicago UP, 1993.

Scriabine, Marina. 'La Genèse comme mythe du langage.' In *Au Carrefour de Thèbes.* Gallimard, 1977. 39–64.

Scrivener, Michael. 'A Swedenborgian Visionary and *The Marriage of Heaven and Hell.' Blake / An Illustrated Quarterly* 21 (1987–8): 102–4.

Searle, John R. *Expression and Meaning: Studies in the Theory of Speech Acts.* Cambridge: Cambridge UP, 1979.

– 'Proper Names.' In *Philosophy and Ordinary Language.* Ed. Charles E. Caton. Urbana: U of Illinois P, 1963. 154–61.

– 'Reiterating the Differences: A Reply to Derrida.' *Glyph* 2 (1977): 198–208.

– *Speech Acts: An Essay in the Philosophy of Language.* Cambridge: Cambridge UP, 1969.

Shaffer, E.S. *'Kubla Khan' and 'The Fall of Jerusalem': The Mythological School in Biblical Criticism and Secular Literature 1770–1880.* Cambridge: Cambridge UP, 1975.

Shaheen, Naseeb. 'Milton's Muse and *De Doctrina.' Milton Quarterly* 8 (1974): 72–6.

Shakespeare, William. *The Complete Works of Shakespeare.* Ed. David Bevington. 3rd ed. Glenview IL: Scott, Foresman, 1980.

Shaviro, Steven. ' "Striving with Systems": Blake and the Politics of Difference.' *boundary 2* 10 (1982): 229–50.

Shawcross, John T. 'The Metaphor of Inspiration in *Paradise Lost.'* In *Th'Upright Heart and Pure.* Ed. Amadeus P. Fiore. Pittsburgh: Duquesne UP, 1967. 75–85.

– *With Mortal Voice: The Creation of 'Paradise Lost.'* Lexington: UP of Kentucky, 1982.

Sheppard, William. *The Touchstone of Common Assurances, Being a Plain and Familiar Treatise on Conveyancing.* Ed. Edmund Gibson Atherley. 8th ed. 2 vols. London: Samuel Brooke, 1826.

Sherry, Peggy Meyer. 'The "Predicament" of the Autograph: "William Blake." '*Glyph* 4 (1978): 130–55.

Shoaf, R.A. *Milton, Poet of Duality: A Study of Semiosis in the Poetry and the Prose.* New Haven: Yale UP, 1985.

Shullenberger, William. 'Linguistic and Poetic Theory in Milton's *De Doctrina Christiana.' English Language Notes* 19 (1982): 262–78.

Simpson, A.W.B. *A History of the Common Law of Contract: The Rise of the Action of Assumpsit.* Oxford: Clarendon P, 1975.

Simpson, David. 'Reading Blake and Derrida – Our Caesars Neither Praised nor Buried.' In Hilton and Vogler, eds., *Unnam'd Forms* 11–25.

Sims, James H. *The Bible in Milton's Epics.* Gainesville: U of Florida P, 1962.

Smith, Barbara Herrnstein. 'Poetry as Fiction.' *New Literary History* 2 (1971): 259–81.

Souza Filho, Danilo Marcondes de. *Language and Action: A Reassessment of Speech Act Theory.* Amsterdam: Benjamins, 1984.

Spacks, Patricia Meyer. *The Poetry of Vision: Five Eighteenth-Century Poets.* Cambridge: Harvard UP, 1967.

Staten, Henry. 'The Secret Name of Cats: Deconstruction, Intentional Meaning, and the New Theory of Reference.' In Dasenbrock, ed., *Redrawing the Lines* 27–48.

Stein, Arnold. *The Art of Presence: The Poet and 'Paradise Lost.'* Berkeley: U of California P, 1977.

Stempel, Daniel. 'Blake, Foucault, and the Classical Episteme.' *PMLA* 96 (1981): 388–407.

Stevens, Paul. 'Discontinuities in Milton's Early Public Self-Representation.' *Huntington Library Quarterly* 51 (1988): 260–80.

Stevenson, Warren. *Divine Analogy: A Study of the Creation Motif in Blake and Coleridge.* Salzburg: Institut für englische Sprache und Literatur, U Salzburg, 1972.

Stocker, Margarita. 'God in Theory: Milton, Literature and Theodicy.' *Literature and Theology* 1 (1987): 70–88.

Swaim, Kathleen M. *Before and after the Fall: Contrasting Modes in 'Paradise Lost.'* Amherst: U of Massachusetts P, 1986.

Tannenbaum, Leslie. *Biblical Tradition in Blake's Early Prophecies: The Great Code of Art.* Princeton: Princeton UP, 1982.

– 'Blake's Art of Crypsis: *The Book of Urizen* and Genesis.' *Blake Studies* 5 (1972): 141–64.

Taylor, Anya. 'Blake's Moving Words and the Dread of Embodiment.' *Cithara* 15 (1976): 75–85.

Taylor, George Coffin. *Milton's Use of Du Bartas.* Cambridge: Harvard UP, 1934.

Taylor, Ronald Clayton. 'Semantic Structures and the Temporal Modes of Blake's Prophetic Verse.' *Language and Style* 12 (1979): 26–49.

Valdés, Mario J. *World-making: The Literary Truth-Claim and the Interpretation of Texts.* Toronto: U of Toronto P, 1992.

Vogler, Thomas A. 'Intertextual Signifiers and the Blake of That Already.' *Romanticism Past and Present* 9 (1985): 1–33.

– *Preludes to Vision: The Epic Venture in Blake, Wordsworth, Keats, and Hart Crane.* Berkeley: U of California P, 1971.

Warminski, Andrzej. 'Facing Language: Wordsworth's First Poetic Spirits.' In *Romantic Revolutions: Criticism and Theory.* Ed. Kenneth R. Johnston, Gilbert Chaitin, Karen Hanson, and Herbert Marks. Bloomington: Indiana UP, 1990. 26–49.

Weber, Samuel. 'It.' *Glyph* 4 (1978): 1–31.

Weiskel, Thomas. *The Romantic Sublime: Studies in the Structure and Psychology of Transcendence.* Baltimore: Johns Hopkins UP, 1976.

Welburn, Andrew J. *The Truth of Imagination: An Introduction to Visionary Poetry.* New York: St. Martin's P, 1989.

Wellek, René. 'A Letter.' In *The Importance of Scrutiny: Selections from Scrutiny: A Quarterly Review, 1932–1948.* Ed. Eric Bentley. New York: Stewart, 1948. 23–30.

Westermann, Claus. *Creation.* Trans. John J. Scullion. Philadelphia: Fortress P, 1974.

– *Genesis I-II: A Commentary.* Trans. John J. Scullion. Minneapolis: Augsburg Publishing House, 1984.

White, Hugh C. *Narration and Discourse in the Book of Genesis.* Cambridge: Cambridge UP, 1991.

Whiting, George W. 'The Golden Compasses in *Paradise Lost.*' *Notes and Queries* 172 (1937): 294–5.

– *Milton and This Pendant World.* Austin: U of Texas P, 1958.

Williams, Arnold. 'Commentaries on Genesis as a Basis for Hexaemeral Material in the Literature of the Late Renaissance.' *Studies in Philology* 34 (1937): 191–208.

– 'Renaissance Commentaries on "Genesis" and Some Elements of the Theology of *Paradise Lost.*' *PMLA* 56 (1941): 151–64.

Williams, Meg Harris. *Inspiration in Milton and Keats.* London: Macmillan, 1982.

Williams, William Carlos. 'This Is Just to Say.' In *The Collected Poems of William Carlos Williams.* Ed. A Walton Litz and Christopher MacGowan. 2 vols. New York: New Directions, 1986–8. Vol. 1.

Winspur, Steven. 'Text Acts: Recasting Performatives with Wittgenstein and Derrida.' In Dasenbrock, ed., *Redrawing the Lines* 169–88.

Wittgenstein, Ludwig. *Philosophical Investigations.* Trans. G. E. Anscombe. 2d ed. Oxford: Blackwell, 1958.

Wittreich, Joseph Anthony, Jr. *Angel of Apocalypse: Blake's Idea of Milton.* Madison: U of Wisconsin P, 1975.

– 'Blake's Milton: "To Immortals ... a Mighty Angel." ' *Milton Studies* 11 (1978): 51–82.

–, ed. *Milton and the Line of Vision.* Madison: U of Wisconsin P, 1975.

– *Visionary Poetics: Milton's Tradition and His Legacy.* San Marino: Huntington Library, 1979.

Woodhouse, A.S.P. 'Notes on Milton's Views on the Creation: The Initial Phases.' *Philological Quarterly* 28 (1949): 211–36.

Woodman, Ross G. 'Milton's Urania and Her Romantic Descendants.' *University of Toronto Quarterly* 48 (1979): 189–208.

Wordsworth, William. *Selected Poems and Prefaces.* Ed. Jack Stillinger. Boston: Houghton Mifflin, 1965.

Yeats, William Butler. *The Variorum Edition of the Poems of W.B. Yeats.* Ed. Peter Allt and Russell K. Alspach. New York: Macmillan, 1957.

York, R.A. *The Poem as Utterance.* London: Methuen, 1986.

Youngquist, Paul. *Madness and Blake's Myth.* University Park: Pennsylvania State UP, 1989.

Index